Problem Questions for Law Students

Law students rarely have experience answering problem questions before university, and lecturers concentrate on teaching content rather than the exam skills needed. This book bridges the gap on how to transpose knowledge and research into structured and coherent answers to problem questions while earning a law degree.

Aimed at undergraduates, international students, and foundation and SQE candidates, the book gives a step-by-step study guide on how to navigate what a problem question is asking you to do. It deconstructs the process using examples from a range of different fields of law, providing essential guidance from research and critical thinking to style and tone.

Including a range of examples to test yourself against, this is an indispensable resource for any law student who wants to tackle problem questions with confidence.

Geraint Brown is the Coordinator of English for Specific Purposes and a tutor of English for Academic Purposes at Swansea University. Since 2008, he has taught UK and international students who are about to start their LLMs at Southampton University, as well as master's and undergraduate law students at Swansea University where he is the Coordinator of the Law Pre-sessional course. He specialises in developing, teaching and delivering medical English, English for Sports, English for Academics, English for International Lecturers in UK universities and, of course, legal English. He is Chair and a panel member of the Academic Integrity Committee deciding on cases where students have been suspected of committing academic misconduct and unfair practice, and a Fellow of the Higher Education Academy (FHEA).

Problem Questions for Law Students

A Study Guide

Geraint Brown

Routledge
Taylor & Francis Group

LONDON AND NEW YORK

First published 2022
by Routledge
2 Park Square, Milton Park, Abingdon, Oxon OX14 4RN

and by Routledge
605 Third Avenue, New York, NY 10158

Routledge is an imprint of the Taylor & Francis Group, an informa business

British Library Cataloguing-in-Publication Data
A catalogue record for this book is available from the British Library

Library of Congress Cataloging-in-Publication Data
A catalog record for this book has been requested

ISBN: 978-0-367-64671-4 (hbk)
ISBN: 978-0-367-64670-7 (pbk)
ISBN: 978-1-003-12574-7 (ebk)

DOI: 10.4324/9781003125747

Typeset in Galliard
by Apex CoVantage, LLC

Contents

Part C
Good academic practice   **102**

Part D
Resources   **163**

Part E
Answers   **195**

Preface

This book is written specifically to help untangle the single biggest problem that law students face when they enter university – how to answer legal writing tasks, specifically the problem question.

Most of my time at university is spent with students who are unsure of how to answer their legal writing tasks. It's not normally the content (that is, the cases and legal background to support the argument) that is the problem, nor is it the style and academic legal register which makes students lose marks in their assignments. More often than not, it's the identification of and application of the law to the situation in the writing task that is the problem.

And it's because of this misunderstanding that I hear many 17- and 18-year-olds dismiss a career in law because the subject is seen as *too hard*. You are probably committed to a university undergraduate or postgraduate degree in law (an **LLB** or **LLM**), but I think it's important to reassure you that it's only hard from the point of view there is not one correct answer, such as in mathematics. A lot of law can be open to interpretation, especially in problem questions where the situation can be deliberately vague or unclear. This is purposely done to allow the student to explore the gap in the given facts.

This book is suitable for home (UK) students as well as international students who are about to study a **Foundation Year, LLB** or **LLM** at a UK university, and also UK students who are completing a **CPE** (Common Professional Examination), **GDL** (Graduate Diploma in Law) or **LPC** (Legal Practice Course), as well as the **SQE** (Solicitors Qualifying Exam) which will be replacing the preceding three entry pathways. Also, professional law exams, such as **ICS** (Institute of Chartered Shipbrokers) and **CILEx** (Chartered Institute of Legal Executives), use problem questions as a form of assessment. This workbook provides important information, guidance and practice for home students because:

- Following **GCSEs, iGCSEs, A-levels, AS-levels** or the **International Baccalaureate**, UK students may not have had exposure to this type of question.

- The structure of your answer may be significantly different to your previous experience, especially if you have not come across problem questions before.

- The format of the question will be significantly different to what you have previously experienced.

- Students' research skills may not be sufficiently honed for university, especially the jump from A-Levels to LLB.

- Universities may not have the support mechanisms in place to explicitly help students with their legal writing skills.

- Legal grammar can also be challenging to read, understand and apply in your answers.

- International students will have the added complexity of language difficulties – and this can *prima facie* be challenging enough for UK students!

- International students may have a different legal system (ie codified law) and therefore different processes.

- Practice makes perfect, or at least, better and more confident!

With basic legal knowledge and good critical thinking, this book will show you the type of questions you will face, how to break down the question, how to conduct research, how to identify the key points from the findings and relate these back to the question, and how to provide a plan from which you can answer the question. There are sample answers to the problem questions set, ongoing self-check questions, notifications of academic skills in practice, end of chapter questions and answers to check your understanding, all presented in various teaching methodologies to suit different learning styles and teaching approaches, and finally a bank of resources containing useful tools to use in your studies.

The scenarios given are about potential legal situations in English law in the most commonly studied areas of law, namely:

Commerce
Company
Contract
Criminal
Human Rights
Intellectual Property
Maritime
Tort
Trade

The writing structures outlined in this book can be used for all fields of law. However, given the complexities of each field, the purpose of this book is to give a flavour of the type of writing tasks you will be given at university while earning your LLB or LLM degree, as it would be impractical to write a detailed book outlining the writing structures for each of these separate yet sometimes overlapping fields of law for a student entering university level.

To help, there is one fully worked through basic and non-legal problem question, one fully worked through legal problem question, and 16 new and authentic problem questions in the question bank section of the book.

Again, the purpose of this book is to improve your legal writing skills, not to teach you law. Therefore, there is a caveat that some legal arguments may be omitted for the sake of clarity, conciseness or space constraints. The language used has been adapted to be clear and comprehensible to meet the requirements of the target readers of the book, and the end of chapter test will make sure you understand the skills of writing, researching and developing the structural content.

Additionally, law is a field which is forever adapting to the current social, economic and political climate, therefore there may be aspects of arguments put forward that may become outdated. This is particularly true at the moment regarding EU, UK and devolved law since at the time of writing, Britain's withdrawal agreements from the EU are uncertain.

This book has colour coordinated sections which have been organised to help the reader identify specific elements which can help to understand, learn and practise.

How to use this book

I hear, and I forget
I see, and I remember
I do, and I understand

Chinese proverb

You have picked up this book because it is less of a 'text' on how to answer problem questions, and more of a guided walk-through on the stages and steps involved in becoming a more proficient writer and university-skilled student. There are, of course, tasks and exercises to ensure what you have seen and read is done correctly and the reasons and rationale understood. This is the key difference with this book. It shows you the ropes, gives you the tools and allows you to put into practice what you've learnt with a bank of material to try.

This book could be used to dip in and out of topics of interest, such as following the correct format for referencing and citation, as a course to follow by a self-studying student, or for an EAP/ESP tutor looking for learning and practice material for their students.

The five parts are written in order to build up the reader with the knowledge needed to understand what the task demands, the main part addressing how to research and write an answer, the academic skills to be aware of and referencing skills needed, a collection of self-learning materials across all academic legal skills discussed and finally, suggested answers.

Self-check questions are brief questions to prompt the reader into questioning their understanding, while chapter **Tasks** on the other hand put into practice the skills discussed and explained. **Tests** at the end of each writing chapter consolidate that learning to ensure the reader has accomplished the skill before moving on to further develop their legal academic skills.

Throughout the book you will see helpful hints and tips which are accumulated; examples and insights from genuine law courses; as well as both explicit and implicit learning of legal vocabulary, grammatical sentence structures, verb usage, collocations and colligations.

Part A introduces problem questions and allows the reader to understand what they look like, how they are broken down into constituent parts and the information that is required for each stage. Readers are introduced to problem questions through an everyday example, learn the persuasive value of different authorities and identify the different organisational patterns that an answer can employ. A key part to answering a question fully is understanding what is required of you, and Part A will be useful to pre-university students and those from overseas venturing into law for the first time.

If you are already familiar with problem questions, you may like to start at **Part B** which deals with the researching, planning and writing stages. Academic skills such as building research, note-taking and evaluating cases are presented and drilled with tasks and exercises. Remember that legal knowledge isn't necessary at this stage, and exercises are differentiated for readers with legal experience, and for those who are venturing into university expectations for the first time. Once research is gathered, planning examines the different organisational patterns before moving onto the writing stages to answer the identified stages within a problem question.

Tests, tasks and exercises to check understanding intersect and end each section. Part B provides you with the tools and knowledge needed to take on any problem question you will face during your law course or professional exam.

Part C deals with academic skills that are unknown to international students, let alone most UK students entering university. It then progresses to deal with discrete legal skills by examining the legal authorities you will be using as research, where to find the key information within legal sources, understanding the idiosyncrasies of the citation and referencing system which includes a guide to compiling citations to the most frequently used legal sources, and of course exercises to notice, create and correct footnote and bibliography entries.

Throughout your academic legal career, is it likely that Part C will be revisited the most because it contains instruction and guidance on the content and formatting of the sources you'll actually need in easy-to-follow stages. As you'd expect, exercises and tasks accompany the content to make sure you are learning as well as doing.

Part D contains the bank of resources which are relevant study skills material for educational and professional tasks which use the problem question style. Here you'll find worked examples of higher and lower scoring answers complete with lecturer annotated comments and overall feedback, a bank of 16 new problem questions across all fields of law and problem questions where reference to primary law sources are needed.

Additionally, blank copies of the learning tools used throughout are provided or are modelled for your use to continue your learning on your course. By learning good academic skills early on, you are teaching yourself how to be a good learner, and will enter your institution aware and prepared of the exciting academic world that awaits you.

Part E simply contains the answers to the questions, tasks and tests set throughout the previous four parts of the book. Remember that this book isn't telling you how to do something, it's not just showing you, but it's guiding you, making you realise, reflect and remedy your practice. After all, a learnt skill such as answering a legal problem question needs a practical solution.

Acknowledgements

I'd like to acknowledge the help of all my current and former law students who have opened up to me. Their feedback following my classes, seminars and individual tutorial sessions has given me an insight into the mindset of how new international university students best acculturise to UK universities and learn academic skills, and whose progress first encouraged me to start putting pen to paper. To my colleagues at the Hillary Rodham Clinton School of Law for the work they do following my students' matriculation onto LLBs and LLMs, especially Dr Tabetha Kurtz-Shefford and other lecturers who regularly give up their time to present guest lectures on my pre-sessional course.

To my former law colleague, a lawyer and member of the New York Bar Danielle Capretti who gave up her time so generously to look over and give invaluable feedback on early draft versions of this book.

Finally, to Professor Baris Soyer for giving me the confidence to try to get my ideas published in the first place, and to Russell George at Routledge for orchestrating all these moving parts and making this work appear in print.

November 2020

A About problem questions

Part A aims

In this chapter you will discover:

- The style in which to write an answer to a problem question
- The different type of PQs that examiners set as writing tasks in law
- What exactly CLEO is, and what it stands for
- What each stage of CLEO means for a writer
- The information that's required for each CLEO stage
- What a basic (non-legal) CLEO essay looks like
    - The persuasive power of different legal authorities
    - An exemplar structure of a basic problem question
    - How to identify the organisational pattern
- How to recognise and learn strong legal vocabulary
- Your understanding of the preceding

Understanding CLEO questions

The CLEO structure is a method of organisation in order to answer a legal problem, also known as a problem question (herein PQ).

The organisation of law essays will be useful for you throughout your pre-sessional, undergraduate and postgraduate studies, so it is essential that you understand how to structure and answer PQs in order to get the marks you deserve.

DOI: 10.4324/9781003125747-1

CLEO structures have four constituent parts:

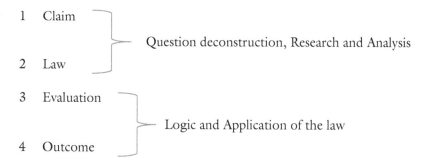

1   Claim

2   Law

> Question deconstruction, Research and Analysis

3   Evaluation

4   Outcome

> Logic and Application of the law

It can also be known as BaRAC (bold assertion, rule, application, conclusion), CREXAC (conclusion, rule, explanation, application, conclusion), IGPAC (issue, general rule, precedent, application, conclusion), IRAC (issue, rule, application, conclusion), IDEA (identify, define, explain, apply), IPAC (issue, principle, apply, conclusion), ILAC (issue, law, application, conclusion), IDAR (issue, doctrine, application, result), MIRAC (material facts, issues, rules, arguments, conclusion), RAFADC (rule, authorities, facts, analogising and distinguishing, conclusion), TREACC (topic, rule, explanation, analysis, counter-arguments, conclusion) and many more variations.

No matter which you may have come across so far in your career, what you will notice is that all of them essentially have the same pattern, and the longer acronym-ed structures simply break up some section into subsections.

For the sake of simplicity and consistency, CLEO will be used throughout. Each stage is further described later.

Understanding problem questions

There are three broad styles of PQ: one question with one event, a multiple-event question and multiple but separate sub-questions on the same area(s) of law with different circumstances.

Examples of each type of PQ are provided in the problem question bank on page 177.

Needless to say, reading the PQ carefully is an essential first step. Reread it as many times as is needed. PQs will outline a scenario replicating real life, and will usually close the scenario with a question prompt. Legal questions generally appear in one of six question prompts:

1   To advise person A (the claimant or defendant)

2   To advise person A and person B (the claimant and the defendant)

3   To not specify who to advise, but to discuss the scenario

4   To determine if the act constitutes an offence under a particular crime

5   To identify what offences, if any, have been committed by all parties in the scenario

6   To explore what defences are available to the defendant

Naturally, you can expect to receive a lower score if you answer the incorrect question, and with a PQ, giving advice to the claimant when the question requires advice to the defendant will result in not having answered the question. Getting the parties right, and your role in the situation is a basic academic skill.

Key points in brief to answering PQs

*   PQs will rarely, if ever, tell you who the defendant or claimant is, therefore it is up to you to identify this early on.

*   Identify the key points within the PQ. This will help you diagnose the problems and identify the correct areas of law.

*   Once you have the right facts of the case, you can set about finding statutes and cases that support your client's position in the PQ.

*   In contract law, for example, the timings can be crucial to the scenario and the outcome, so in these instances, it is worth making a timeline (writing the events in chronological order) to help make the order of events clearer.

*   PQs require you to give specific advice about a situation, not to write all you know about that area of law.

These broad points will be discussed and explained in the next chapter.

■ Self-check A1

1   The four stages of CLEO are:

   a)   C_____

   b)   L_____

   c)   E_____

   d)   O_____

2   PQ means _____

3   Put these stages of reading the PQ into the correct order

   a)   __ Identify the key facts

   b)   __ Identify the legal problem

   c)   __ Identify the party or parties, and the role of your client in the PQ

   d)   __ Identify who you are advising and what you are advising them about

   e)   __ Make a timeline of events

f) __ Read the question

g) __ Read the scenario

4   Match a typical question prompt of the question (1–6) to the description (a-f)

a)   Does not specify who to advise, but to discuss the scenario(s)

b)   Does the act constitute an offence under a particular crime

c)   To advise person A (the claimant or defendant)

d)   To advise person A and person B (the claimant and the defendant)

e)   To idenitfy what offences have been committed by all parties in the scenario(s)

f)   To identify which elements of a specific Act are relevant to the situation

1)   Advise X and Y.

2)   Advise X.

3)   Consider if there has been any misrepresentation under the Sale of Goods Act 1979.

4)   Consider what offences, if any, have been committed in each of the given circumstances.

5)   Consider what offences, if any, have been committed.

6)   Upon which sections provided by the Defamation Act 2013 could Alex rely as a defence?

The CLEO stages

To use a mathematical comparison or analogy, CLEO is a bit like working out an equation:

Task – We need to work out the area of a circle

The rule to work out the area of a circle = πr^2

The length of r in our PQ is 3cm, therefore the area = $\pi \times 3 \times 3$ (or $3.14159 \times 3 \times 3$)

The area of our PQ circle = 28.27cm^2

But what has that got to do with law you may ask.

Identifying the **Claim** is needed in the first instance as you need to correctly identify what the question is asking of you.

The rule (or **Law**) for working out the area is given in its raw form without any interpretation.

The workings out are clearly shown by expressing the **Evaluation** in the context of the Claim (3cm length which is specific to this PQ).

Finally, the **Outcome** states your final answer.

While simplified, this is the basic formula for answering a PQ. In a bit more detail:

Claim: The first step is to identify the Claims, or problems, within the question. Essentially, this answers what area(s) of law does this situation need addressed. As we will discover, it is not enough to say just *criminal law*, or even *if the defendant intended to kill or not.*

Better Claims will briefly identify the area, the principle and the elements needed for that particular act to be unlawful, and state in a sentence what the actual issue is in the PQ. You are basically answering "what is the problem in this situation?" In the final sentence of the Claim section, the answer will be along the lines of *The issue is whether X's termination of the contract is valid.*

Some universities like their students to give a neutral Claim sentence, building the argument and law as facts are presented, while other tutors prefer students' positions to be clear from the outset, and then supported. Compare the objectivity of these two statements:

> *Therefore, X will be under an obligation to pay Y the money owed under the contract signed*

> *The issue is whether X's termination of the contract is valid.*

Both are perfectly acceptable final sentences of the Claim section, but have been framed very differently, and yet both flow seamlessly into the following Law section. The first example sentence would argue why an obligation exists, while the second would be of a more discursive nature, and then lead to the same conclusion (that X must pay Y).

The first clearly states a position, and a strong, cohesive answer would follow on with the reasons why X is obligated to pay. The Claim is firmly stated and would need to be supported in later sections with relevant law, evaluation and justification of why X cannot lawfully renege on the contract.

The second sentence allows more scope for discussion, and arguably is more of a skilled style of writing, as the writer needs to guide and weave the reader through the legal cases, positions, justifications and arguments of both sides, before concluding on the strength of argument of either party. Even though the L and E sections may suggest being in favour of one way or another, it is only in the Outcome that the reader will discover the writer's decisions.

Law: Any act committed by a party, as identified in the PQ, needs to have its legal principle identified. Put simply, how do you know the act is unlawful?

It may be sourced from statutes, so a law is passed by parliament to prohibit a certain act (ie murder is unlawful as per the Offences Against the Person Act (1861), or there may be cases that have had similar circumstances, and the outcomes of that case are so closely related to the given case, judges have used the prior judgment as guidance (called precedent), or key terms may be defined more clearly in a treatise (a legally authoritative book, eg *Chitty on Contract*) with guidance on its use and application than in the legislation.

This stage allows you to identify the correct authority to start addressing the Claims in the PQ. Essentially, this paragraph is used to show that during a contract law PQ where the Claim is the supplier's skill and care for example, you are able to identify the correct law is the Supply of Goods and Services Act (1982) rather than the Sale of Goods Act (1979).

As you progress through your law course, you will discover that the issues you spot in the PQ become less clear cut, more contentious, and open to argument and interpretation of the law. It would be highly unlikely that you are given a murder or contract question where there is a clear situation that one party met all the conditions of murder or breach of contract.

For example, imagine a Maritime law PQ on piracy. You are unlikely (at this stage) to know there are four elements that must be met before an act can be called piratical. One element is that of "Private Ends", which essentially means it is a private person or persons rather than a government state committing the act. But UNCLOS, which governs the law regarding piracy doesn't give its own definition of "Private Ends". Neither does the definition come from English law. The closest thing we have to a definition actually comes from a Belgian court's ruling in the case of the ship *Castle John*.

This definition may not even be acceptable in English courts, but for the purposes of PQs, it is the closest one can use to an authoritative definition and shows good research on the part of the student. This legal point would be argued for and against in the Evaluation section.

As your knowledge and skills develop, so will the complexity of the PQs, and it will be more likely that the legal authority will be less clear (as the piracy example), or more conflicted, where two authorities (ie court rulings) do not agree on the same point of law.

When you're writing your Law section, prioritise the most persuasive arguments from binding authorities first, therefore the most authoritative sources of law will hold the most weight in your arguments. The main types of legal authorities and their importance are ranked as follows:

1   Statutes

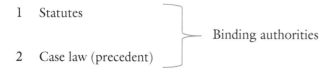 Binding authorities

2   Case law (precedent)

3   Treatises, legal journals, textbooks

4   Legislative papers   ── Persuasive authorities

5   Statutes/case law from other countries

Evaluation: This will be the lengthiest and most complex section of the whole answer. Here, you will link the legal principles (Law section) with the issues identified in the PQ (Claim section). It is the evaluation section that differentiates the PQ from a standard essay-style question. The trick is to think of it as a logic puzzle.

Students tend to find it unsettling to apply their workings out to an issue that is not based on certain facts, such as when there is no accepted definition, or if the act in the PQ does not fully meet the criteria of the crime by not explicitly mentioning an element. This is the whole purpose of a PQ – to throw you a red herring (a distraction), to see if you can explain your thoughts in multiple scenarios: eg one where the final element is not strictly met (as per PQ), and the alternative *if* the final element is met, but not mentioned in the PQ.

Outcome: After such a long, expanded and detailed Evaluation section, the Outcome is usually surprisingly short in comparison. Here, you summarise what you have been working through in the previous stages of the answer, and it's your opportunity to succinctly say what your judgement is. In more complex questions, you may find that you are using lots of conditional, or *if*-clauses. For example:

> *If the goods had passed over the ship's rail, then the buyer would be liable. However, if the goods hadn't been placed "on board the vessel", the seller can select the point that best suits their purposes, and thus would be the seller's liability.*

This Outcome paragraph may seem a little lost without the context of the PQ and the previous stages of the writing to inform the conclusion, but this stands to show how there must be flow, cohesion and coherence between one section of the writing and the next.

■ Self-check A2

1   In which CLEO section would you most likely:

Discuss legal principles?

Give advice to the person(s) in the situation?

Identify any problem areas from the text describing the situation?

State the course of action or liability of each party?

2   Match the CLEO section with its general purpose

    a)   Claim   Here's my answer

    b)   Law   These are the tools I need to answer

    c)   Evaluation   This is how I worked out the answer

    d)   Outcome   This is what the questions asks

3   In which CLEO section would you most likely find the following ten sentences:

    a)   "The question at issue is whether a contract has been formed."

    b)   "In the case at hand, Bob telephones Amy at 10am to terminate the contract."

    c)   "In *Carlill v Carbolic Smoke Ball Co Ltd*, an advert with clear terms and precise intentions was held to be an Invitation to Treat."

    d)   "Thus the note could be reasonably held to be an advert."

    e)   "Silence cannot be imposed upon another party as acceptance."

    f)   "The defendant's actions don't appear to be consistent with someone who has accepted the offer."

    g)   "It is unclear in which order Bob read the acceptance letters."

    h)   "According to the principles of contract law, there are four elements to a legally binding agreement."

    i)   "An offer is a promise from the offeror to enter into a contract with the intention of being bound by the offeree's terms."

    j)   "The notice states 'or nearest offer' suggesting that the price can be negotiated."

4   Put the following sources of law into order according to their strength of argument:

Case law (precedent)

Legislative papers

Statutes

Statutes/case law from other countries

Treatises, legal journals, textbooks

5   Match the following sources to the type listed in item 4:

Department for Media, Culture and Sport, *Online Harms White Paper* (CP 57, 2019)

Fitch v Snedaker (1868) 38 NY 248

Norrie, A., 'After Woollin' [1999] Crim LR 532

Copyright, Designs and Patents Act 1988

Donoghue v Stevenson [1932] AC 562

6   Which of the following outlines is the most representative of PQ answers?

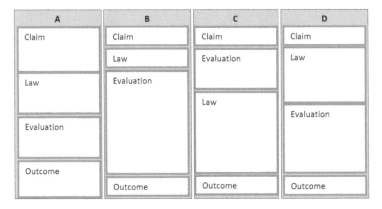

7   Look at the final sentences of two Claims sections from two different student answers and consider their neutrality.

a)   *Therefore, X will be under an obligation to pay Y the money owed under the contract signed.*

b)   *The issue is whether X's termination of the contract is valid.*

Tick the relevant box(es) to identify the characteristics of each final Claim sentence

Which sentence (1, 2 or both):	a	b
Gives the position		
Suggests a discussion of both sides will follow		
Identifies the Claim		
Suggests the focus will be on contract terms		
Will be more persuasive than expository/ explanatory		
Is neutral		

8   Following is a blank plan of a PQ on contract law given to a student. It contains the four CLEO sections and space for three Evaluation points. The lecturer has provided nine (a–i) jumbled up subheadings and first sentences (also known as topic sentences). You must identify which are subheadings, which are first sentences for those same subheadings and where they would logically fit in the plan. Use the spaces provided to write your answer.

Claim		
Law		
Evaluation option A	Evaluation option B	Evaluation option C
Outcome		

   a)   If it's an ITT

   b)   If it's an offer

   c)   Method of acceptance

   d)   *Offeror* v *Offeree A*

   e)   *Offeror* v *Offeree B*

   f)   The acceptance is valid only when . . . It would follow that the contract is immediately effective, preventing a revocation of contract.

   g)   The advert

   h)   The first question is whether the advert is an offer or an Invitation to Treat (ITT).

   i)   Under English law there are four elements needed for a contract to be formed . . . Therefore, X will be under an obligation to pay *Offeree A* the money owed under the contract signed.

9   Repeat the same exercise as in the previous question for another classmate's answer to the same PQ. Here the subheadings have been provided, and the topic sentences are mixed up. Think about which topic sentence best fits the purpose of the structure.

Claim		
Law		
[Evaluation option A] If it's an ITT	[Evaluation option B] The advert	[Evaluation option C] Offeree v Offeror A
If it's an offer	Method of revocation	Offeree v Offeror B
Outcome		

a) A bilateral contract has been entered into in this case as . . . had formed a binding contract.

b) By introducing a new term, *B* has . . . a contract had been concluded at that time.

c) Revocation must be communicated, but needn't be directly received . . . the offer had not been withdrawn at the time it was accepted.

d) Should the advert be an offer and subsequent counter-offer . . . a contract exists due to a lack of retraction.

e) The acceptance is valid only when . . . It would follow that the contract is immediately effective, preventing a revocation of contract.

f) The basic difference between and offer and ITT . . . the advert lacked the certainty to be an offer.

g) The case is related to the provision of IT services . . . The issue is whether A's revocation of the contract is valid.

h) The first question is whether the advert is an offer or an Invitation to Treat (ITT).

i) The general rule is that an offer cannot be accepted without knowledge of it . . . even if knowledge came from a third party.

Understanding the CLEO process

CLEO stages are interconnected and run logically. Without a Claim which sets the scene, the Law does not have context, just as the Evaluation has little meaning in answering your particular Claim without stating the relevant Law. This process must be followed through each CLEO stage to make a fully coherent and structurally sound answer.

The first step is to identify the Claims within the question and what information is not needed.

Looking at the question, highlight areas that you know or think may be contentious or worth exploration in your research. Explain any reasons for their inclusion, be they, at this stage, factually right or wrong.

Your legal knowledge should help you identify Claims within the PQ, and you will learn to develop your instinct about whether an issue is contentious or not as your knowledge grows.

Further research on these claims will answer if you can apply a principle to the given problem. Students often complain that the Evaluation stage is the most difficult. Students can identify the Claims and understand the Law, but it's stating how these laws apply to the PQ that is most challenging.

The final Outcome stage is to rephrase your findings and informed opinion in a short summary.

You will use the CLEO structure not only for your immediate intention, which may be to pass a particular course or exam, but you will also use it when writing letters to clients, and even if you progress to be a judge!

Critical thinking – Do a simple search for the full judgment in *Oscar Chess Ltd v Williams* [1957], and then search for Lord Denning's words "The crucial question is". Read this and see how clearly the Claims within his PQ (or case) are stated.

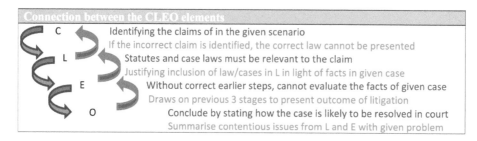

Figure 1.1 Connection between the CLEO elements

Task A1 – Using the same judgment, identify the start of the Law, Evaluation and Outcome sections.

Claim	The crucial question is: was it a binding promise or only an innocent misrepresentation?
Law	
Evaluation	
Outcome	

A non-legal work through

The best way to familiarise yourself with a PQ, with all its new and strange organisation and conventions, is to try a simple answer on a topic with which you are already familiar, and that you can relate to.

Task A2 – Without distracting yourself with the answer, read the non-legal problem **only** (upcoming box) and see if you can identify what information is relevant, what is essential and what information is not necessary. A PQ containing only the essential details for research is given in the Answers section.

Note: The words in square brackets, for example [Outcome], are not needed in your answer but are shown to guide you through the structure. The subheadings shown in italics are generally allowable in PQ answers and could be substituted for underlining.

Also, for the purposes of this book, footnotes and references are omitted, and the cases cited are for illustration purposes only.

A NON-LEGAL PROBLEM

Jack is a pre-sessional law student at Sometown University and wants to go on to study employment law. He was set his assignment on the 2nd, with the deadline on the 16th at 5pm. He works really hard: planning, researching in the library and writing several drafts of his work until he is happy.

Eventually, Jack submits his work at 5.10pm on the 16th and later discovers he received a score of zero due to his late submission.

Advise Jack

[Claim]The problem is that Jack handed in his essay ten minutes beyond the 5pm deadline.

[Law]

Lateness

Sometown University's regulations (s10.1) state that late submissions are awarded a zero.

Mitigation

University regulations state that minor illnesses are unlikely to be accepted. A previous student had a doctor's certificate supporting the claim that he had suffered from terrible headaches before an exam (*James v Sometown University 2018*).

In *Donald v Sometown University (2014)*, the defendant was unable to prove he had serious financial difficulties during the time of his submission. Donald claimed that his father, who gave him £1000 every month to cover costs, had been imprisoned and was no longer able to financially support his son. Evidence of imprisonment was provided, but none as to the student nor his father's financial position. The university rejected Donald's claim.

Timeliness

Regulation 23.4.1 states that any complaint for mitigation must be made to the university within five days of the deadline in order to be considered, or within three days if there is a problem with the university's computers during submission (s23.4.4).

[Evaluation]

Lateness

In the case at hand, it appears to be straightforward that Jack's submission was beyond the deadline.

Mitigation

In James (2018), the situation was in an exam setting rather than for assessed work. James was able to provide medical evidence to support his claim. Jack

cont.   would need to have medical evidence, such as an appointment card, doctor's note or pharmacy prescription to submit to the university.

Donald (2014) was unable to support his claim during a stressful time submitting coursework, but for financial rather than health mitigation.

Timeliness

The time that has passed since Jack's submission isn't given. If Jack is within the five-day limit, he has the opportunity to register a mitigation claim for his illness. It is also unclear if Jack had computer issues causing his late submission, and if the problems were his own personal computer or that of the university's. Furthermore, the university rules (s23.4.4) only provide for their own computers, not that of personal computers.

[Outcome]

Jack has submitted his work late and is therefore liable to be awarded a score of zero. However, if he has medical proof to provide to the university within five days of the submission date, therefore before the 21st of the month, the university will accept this evidence. If Jack had computer problems with the university's equipment, he must register his claim before the 19th. The rulings regarding the failure of a student's personal computer are unclear, but Jack would be advised to claim within the same timescale as mentioned earlier. If this time has passed, Jack will be unable to claim mitigation and must accept a score of zero.

Tip: Noticing new words and grammatical structures is a very good way to increase your awareness of how language is used in legal writing. Pay attention not just to the individual words but the words around them, too. These will form common phrases or *collocations* which you will use in your own writing.

■ **Self-check A3**

1   Look back at the provided non-legal answer. How has the author structured his or her answer?

2   The author has used subheadings (lateness, mitigation, timeliness). Why has the author used this approach?

3   What do you notice about the pattern of the subheadings?

4   Have a look at some of the vocabulary used. Highlight any words that are either new to you or are being used in a new (technical/legal) way.

5   There may be collocations (that is combinations of words frequently used together) that you have noticed (eg personal computer, time passed, late submission, as well as legal terms such as: liable to be awarded, mitigation claim). Look through the preceding answer to help identify these collocations (noun + noun/adjective/adverb combinations) and colligations (verb and noun).

   a)   Set *an assignment*

   b)   Regulations

   c)   Minor

   d)   Suffer

   e)   Certificate

   f)   Support *a Claim*

   g)   Financially

   h)   Financial

   i)   Reject

   j)   Submit

   k)   University

   l)   Rules

   m) Medical

   n)   Submission

   o)   Register

6   Identify which words or phrases from the preceding answer are used to:

   a) Introduce a section

   b) Introduce another point

   c) State a stronger point

   d) Introduce an opposing point   *Rather than*

7   Which word in the *Mitigation* section suggests a lack of certainty and caution in its assertions?

8   Which word in the *Timeliness* section is repeated several times in order to tell the reader that there is caution in the conclusions drawn?

PART

B Researching and writing

Part B aims

In this chapter you will learn how to:

- Identify the legal problem within the question
- Organise main and sub-Claims
- Begin researching and note-taking
- Recognise legal authority and the power of each source
- Understand case law citation and abbreviation
- Perform searches and understand the returns
- Turn your research into an outline answer
- Find some seminal (key) cases dealing with contract law
- Use cases in your answer
- Make notes on your selected cases
- Create a plan for your answer
- Evaluate the pros and cons of each type of CLEO structure
- Identify the three basic structures of a problem question
- Understand which structure is the most suitable for your PQ
  - And have an end of chapter test

Identifying Claims in a PQ

The situation that follows is based in criminal law, but think about the scenario as if it happened in <u>your country</u>. The following tasks are set to prepare your critical thinking and analysis of the question. Whether you answer them correctly or not is not important at this stage.

DOI: 10.4324/9781003125747-2

Task B1 – Identify any criminal acts that have been committed. Write notes on the right.

An example PQ in criminal law	
Lucy is upset following the break-up of her relationship with George, so she goes for a walk in the woods to make her less angry.	_____ _____ _____
She soon finds herself lost at the entrance of a very large house.	_____ _____
She ignores the 'private property' sign on the gate and walks around the beautiful gardens. Soon, an elderly man shouts at her and manages to grab her, but Lucy struggles free by pushing him away and hides in the house where the man follows her.	_____ _____ _____ _____ _____
She picks up a large boiling cup of coffee left on a table and throws the hot liquid at the man.	_____ _____
The coffee misses the man, landing on an old picture on the wall and the floor in front of the man, but he slips on the coffee and hits his head against the marble floor.	_____ _____ _____ _____
Lucy runs away, with the cup still in her hand.	_____
That evening, Lucy hears on the local news that the gardener at a nearby country estate had died from a head injury.	_____ _____ _____ _____

See Answer section for identification of potential offences.

Why do this for your own country and not UK law? Regardless of your home jurisdiction, the **processes** of identifying Claims are the same, and to start off, you are looking at offences which you are familiar with in your legal system rather than jumping head-first into UK law.

What you have just done in Task B1 is consider the **breadth** of claims in the PQ (ie what needs to be included).

Next, you will need to think about the **depth**, or how much detail is needed.

Task B2 – Using the **Task B1** criminal law PQ:

1   Put a tick (√) next to points that you think are the most important which need a lot of detail.

2   Which remaining points are minor (not as essential) but need less detail and exploration? Mark these with a plus (+).

3   The previous two points are likely to be agreed (ie given) by both sides and presented in the PQ, however there may be facts which are disputed in your own assessed PQs. Mark these with a (Y, N or ?) to show if the facts are agreed (yes), in disagreement (no), or if further research is required by yourself to discover this by using a question mark.

4   Are there any hidden issues not directly written? Tutors will place hidden (or *oblique*) issues in a PQ to test the critical thinking of the students. Be careful you are not identifying a red herring (*irrelevant claims*).

Task B3 – Look again at the example criminal law PQ. Read the line *Lucy runs away* . . . and consider these questions:

•   What can you infer (*guess/assume*) about what happened to the particular item mentioned in the PQ?

•   What are the consequences of doing this? Is this a separate offence?

•   How is this related to the question (who to advise)?

•   Is it a major or a minor point?

•   Therefore, should you write about this?

Revisit the earlier task on the non-legal PQ for another attempt at identifying the breadth and depth of claims.

Task B4 – Have a look at the following PQ, and try to identify claims that may be worth researching. Follow the same steps as in **Task B1**.

Important – The following PQ will be used as a basis for tasks for the rest of the book.

A basic PQ on contract

Jack, who is a private watch collector, is selling one of his watches for £3000 on a specialist pre-owned watches website.

Peter sees the advertisement and immediately emails Jack on May 10th to say he'd like to buy the watch for £2800.

The next day, Peter decides he'd like to revoke the offer, so he posts a letter to Jack's home address stating that he wishes to withdraw from the sale.

On May 12th, Jack reads Peter's email, and posts a letter to Peter stating that he'd like to accept his offer of £2800.

On the third day, Jack receives Peter's letter of withdrawal.

Advise Jack

Task B5 – Consider:

What is the overarching theme or argument of the points in the question?

What area of law is the problem raising?

Are any sub-Claims arising?

Task B6 – Number each potential Claim you see in the PQ, and write a short note detailing your thoughts, queries and possible points of contention. At this stage it doesn't matter if they are legally or factually right.

The student example below contains a reference number, source information and a note/query

1   "A private watch collector." Not selling as a professional

You'll need to consider:

- Which facts are not in dispute?
- Which facts are disputed?
- Which facts may be contentious, deliberately unclear or incomplete?
- Which absent facts are needed to make a judgment on the preceding?

> *Tip:* You are looking for all claims at this stage, not just the obvious ones that are in the PQ.
>
> Coming up are some of the issues that could be raised from this PQ. Avoid looking at them too early on as it will become a skill in itself to identify claims.

Fact in general English means a provable, actual or real statement, opinion or conclusion. However, in law and PQs, a fact is an impartial, non-judgemental, objective observation of what happened; for example, the previous PQ in **Task B4** stated that Peter emailed Jack on May 10th offering £2800 for the watch. Your PQ answer needn't question this or any other 'presented fact', whereas in legal practice, the timing may have an important bearing on the contract.

It is unlikely that any of the PQs you will be facing will include factual issues, for example, a delivery of sweet crude oil contained 0.6% sulfer where the general accepted sulfer content of the product is 0.5%, and by definition, the delivery is actually sour crude oil.

If a PQ states a delivery was of sweet crude oil (unless you're specialising in oil and gas law, and your lecturer is testing your knowledge of sulfer content as well as problem solving), it must be accepted that your delivery is sweet crude oil.

Normally, if your lecturer wanted to test your knowledge about this, the PQ would be phrased something like . . . *the delivery contained crude oil with a sulfer content of 0.6%* . . . thereby putting the onus on you to identify the type of oil by its sulfer concentration.

Legal claims are more common in PQs and can be answered by the question *what does the law mean?* Or *how does the law apply in this situation?*

> *Tip:* Lecturers often adapt a real case to make a PQ.

It could be a seminal case, a recent case or an obscure case from lectures has been used as a basis of the PQ, but the facts may have been altered and the names most definitely will have been changed. But you can identify the Claims of a PQ by:

• Reading the facts of the PQ and it reminding you of a case

• Reading the PQ and recognising the legal area(s) within

The following text shows some example claims identified in the given PQ, and each potential claim is given a number. Following are some student notes explaining why they think each point is worthy of research.

A BASIC PROBLEM QUESTION ON CONTRACT – ANNOTATED CLAIMS FOR FURTHER RESEARCH

Jack, who is a private watch collector[1], is selling one of his watches for £3000 on a specialist[2] pre-owned[3] watches website. Peter sees the post[4] online[5] and immediately[6] emails[7] Jack on May 10th to say he'd like to buy the watch for a slightly reduced price of £2800[8].

The next day, Peter decides he'd like to revoke[9] his earlier email, so he posts[10] a letter to Jack's home address[11] stating that he wishes to withdraw[12] from the sale.

On May 12th, Jack reads Peter's email[13], and posts a letter[14] to Peter stating that he'd like to accept[15] his offer of £2800.

On the third day, Jack receives Peter's letter of withdrawal[16].

Advise Jack[17].

STUDENT'S THOUGHTS, QUERIES AND POSSIBLE POINTS OF CONTENTION FOR EACH OF THE 17 IDENTIFIED CLAIMS IN THE PQ

1 "A private watch collector." Not selling as a professional

2 "Specialist . . . watches website." Check if this is still shown to 'the public'

3 "Pre-owned." Not new, so less buyer protection for Peter?

4 "Sees the post." Not stated if the advert is an offer. How can it therefore be accepted to form a contract?

5 "Online." Is this different to seeing it in a shop, magazine?

6 "Immediately emails/Next day, Peter revokes." Explore the timing

7 "Peter . . . emails Jack." Delivery of communication (email) versus letter

---

continued . . .

> **cont.**   8   A £200 reduction is requested by Peter. How does this impact if it's an offer and how it can be accepted (see point 4)?
>
> 9   "Revoke." Does the purpose impact any communication method?
>
> 10   Method of communication (again) of withdrawal to home address
>
> 11   Home v business address – which is the correct correspondence address?
>
> 12   How should a withdrawal be communicated? Same as first communication or is any method acceptable? This isn't a price renegotiation.
>
> 13   Jack doesn't read the email the same day/time as it's sent.
>
> 14   "Jack . . . posts." Jack doesn't accept by the same method as the email.
>
> 15   Jack hasn't yet received Peter's letter of withdrawal.
>
> 16   Withdrawal is sent by letter (again, method of delivery issue).
>
> 17   Advise only Jack (seller/offeree) not Peter (buyer/offeror)

These points can either be listed individually or grouped together with other Claims you've identified as follows. It's up to you which you try, although grouping will be beneficial as the complexity of PQs increases.

Task B7 – Try to group the Claims into similar points. Use the point numbers to help.

The points identified earlier can be broken down into six key *research questions*:

a)   What is Jack's role as a seller? (Point 1)

b)   _____ (Points 2, 4, 5)

c)   _____ (Point 3)

d)   Does the nature of the correspondence matter? (4, 6, 8, 9, 10, 12, 14, 15)

e)   _____ (6, 7, 8, 10, 11, 12, 13, 14, 16)

f)   _____ (7, 13, 15)

You will notice that point D has a lot of information regarding the communication, in which case it would be worth subdividing the point further.

Critical thinking – How would you subdivide D?

We can clearly see that most of the research focus is on:

*   The nature of the communication (ie how can an offer, an acceptance and a withdrawal be made?)

- The method of that communication (ie does a withdrawal have to be of the same communication type as the original offer method, and does an emailed acceptance need to be replied to via email, or will any method be suitable?), and

- The timing of those correspondences (ie does the time that the emails and letters are sent, or the time they are received or read have a bearing on this situation?)

That is not to say that the other issues in the PQ are not important; mainly this shows where the focus of our answer will be. Ask yourself if you think the direction of your answer will be correct, does this match your gut instinct about the Claims in the PQ, and are you answering the correct question.

Task B8 – Check the answers [**purple box**] with your own points. It may be that you haven't included an issue as you know it's irrelevant or not important. At this stage, the correctness of the Claims you've identified isn't important as you will be eliminating oblique or incorrect Claims at a later stage. Nevertheless, this exercise is to show you the process of how to include potential Claims before going on to dismiss them through research.

Task B9 – We will later be looking through the earlier points. Mark with a tick ($\sqrt{}$) each point you think is a key (major) Claim a plus sign (+) if it's a minor issue and leave blank if it is of no importance.

Suggested answers will follow in the *Turning research into Law* section.

Task B10 – Put the events into chronological (time) order (the furthest in the past to the most recent). Putting the information into chronological order as shown earlier may seem a simplistic exercise, but as PQs become longer and more complex (as you will see), making a timeline as shown earlier will be invaluable in breaking down each point and making it clearer in your mind, which will result in your answer also being better structured and clearer for the reader.

Put the events into chronological order	
Date	Event
10 May	
11 May	
12 May	
13 May	

Now that you have isolated the main events according to the order in which they happened, your mind should be more focussed on identifying the major and minor Claims in the PQ.

Researching skills

Having identified and isolated the Claims in the PQ, we can then go about researching each of our points. The purpose of this is to see if the suspicions we have about a Claim are legitimate issues, or if our initial suspicions and guesses were wrong. Eliminating non-contentious issues is an important stage as we will be left with only the important Claims.

It is quite normal to discover that some Claims need expanding as they are too big for a single section, or the Claim is much more complex than we first expected, or that there is more depth of comment or clarification needed than we initially expected. Sometimes, we find that there are more questions after initial research. This is normal, and don't feel overwhelmed by this. What you are doing is making your research more focused, and earning yourself better grades by getting right into the detail of the answer.

But a caveat now. There are whole books written about the process of researching for assignments, legal skills and conducting research in general. The focus of this book is on writing the answer to PQs, not conducting research for them, so this section includes the very basics.

If you require more information about researching your legal assignment, a good place to start for further information on this would be the Palgrave Macmillan series on study skills (Stella Cottrell's *The Study Skills Handbook,* and Askey and McLeod's *Studying Law*).

Before you invest a lot of time and effort in researching, you need to get an idea of where the broad area of interest will be. A good place to start identifying an area you believe is worth researching is with course textbooks.

There are several excellent books which are written in various knowledge depths, and the author will likely explain the legal outcome in different ways, concentrating on a different element of law, for example, if *Carlill v Carbolic Smoke Ball Co Ltd* discusses an intention to be bound by its terms, or, equally important, if this case is used to exemplify a unilateral contract. Spend time finding a book that appeals to your style of learning (ie does it use pictures, text only, flowcharts, quizzes or space to write your own notes?).

Personally, I like the Directions series from OUP as this is written for someone who is not fully versed in legal language, and the points are kept brief and give an overview of a ruling. It does not go into the depth other textbooks do, but it is what is needed at this stage of your work, and, most importantly for your purposes.

Using your university's law library for course books or textbooks, and databases such as Westlaw, LexisNexis and i-law, you should be able to search for key terms relevant to the Claim you have identified in the PQ. A lot of time could be dedicated to writing about researching for law, so only the basics are mentioned here.

Tip: Your university's law librarians will be able to demonstrate and explain to you how to make best use of the online databases which are relevant to your PQ.

Key terms need to be understood correctly in order to find relevant research and to make your point as persuasively as possible. Searching for "non-pecuniary losses" or Latin terms such as *quantum meruit* correctly will return you more specific results than, say, "offer and acceptance". However, since it is being more specific, you must ensure that your search term matches exactly what you are looking for. At the early stages of research, use a wider, more general word or term. As you identify the Claim more precisely, you can use additional or specific terms to filter and return better results.

The search results will include commentaries, case notes, legislation, books, journal articles and many more, so choosing the source that supports your point from the highest authority will strengthen your argument.

To recap, in terms of authority, the most to least persuasive sources are:

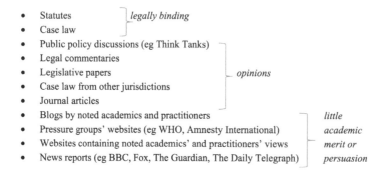

- Statutes   *legally binding*
- Case law
- Public policy discussions (eg Think Tanks)
- Legal commentaries
- Legislative papers   *opinions*
- Case law from other jurisdictions
- Journal articles
- Blogs by noted academics and practitioners   *little*
- Pressure groups' websites (eg WHO, Amnesty International)   *academic*
- Websites containing noted academics' and practitioners' views   *merit or*
- News reports (eg BBC, Fox, The Guardian, The Daily Telegraph)   *persuasion*

Hint: See www.theguardian.com/politics/2013/sep/30/list-thinktanks-uk for a list of British Think Tanks and a short description of their aim and political persuasions.

This does not mean that you need to include a source from a binding authority and an authoritative opinion, only to show you the weight of authority that each source type has. A typical PQ answer would have one or two statutes and multiple case laws. There may be one of two from the *Opinions* category if they are of exceptional relevance to the PQ (for example the *Castle John* case for the definition of piracy). In all PQs for different areas of law, there will be key statutes that you will need to mention based on correct identification of the Claim.

There will be key statutes that you will need to mention based on correct identification of the Claim.

Case law has a wider remit in what you can search for:

* Cases that add extra information, examples or explanations to the statutes
* Cases that have similar facts to the given problem (eg acceptance by email, or advert on the internet)
* Cases that are legally similar (eg cases that match your problem, such as the method of communication or revocation of contract)

> *Tip*: As you remember certain cases that may (or may not) be relevant, write them down. You can always discard them at a later stage. A model revision sheet is provided for you to copy in the Resources section.

Knowing what to research is a difficult step, especially if you're new to studying law. At this stage, let's imagine that this is your first attempt.

In the first of our Claims, we want to know if there's any purpose in researching the point about Jack being a "private watch collector" and "not selling as a professional". We need to eliminate this as a point of inclusion in our answer.

There is no suggestion that Jack doesn't own the watch he is selling, so mentioning this would be a waste of time. Only go down this route if it is made clear (eg Jack found a watch on the beach) or questionable (eg Jack is selling a watch on behalf of his friend).

Mentioning that Jack is selling the watch as a private person may give rise to some consumer law (for example, the Consumer Rights Act 2005, the Sales of Goods Act 1979, and the Supply of Goods and Services Act 1982), which after researching if you weren't aware, essentially covers the terms of the contract, respectively, by:

* Mis-selling of goods due to an inaccurate description
* Providing for the item's quality and fitness for purpose
* The sales by a business for a good or service

None of these would be relevant for our PQ so we can discount them for further inclusion.

Most of the sources you will be researching and citing will be case law, therefore it is worthwhile knowing which cases are seen as more trustworthy, and the reasons for this.

Across the UK, think of the number of cases that happen each year. Not all of these cases are written up for lawyers and professors to consider because there is not a new or significant change to the application of the law. Alternatively, if the way that previous statutes or cases have been understood and implemented has changed, they will be included in a law report.

So only a small percentage of those court cases actually make it to publication.

• All Supreme Court cases will be reported as this is the highest court in the land.

• Most Appeal Court cases will be reported.

• Some High Court cases will be reported.

• Only a few specialist court cases will be reported (eg tribunals).

It's not the judges who decide whether a case is important or not, but the editors of the law report series.

Figure 2.1 shows the current hierarchy of the court system in England and Wales, with the seniority of the court decreasing as you go down the list.

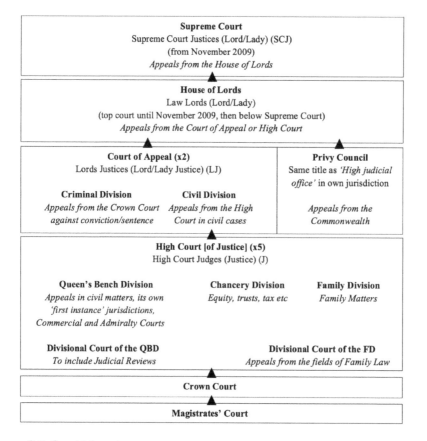

Figure 2.1 Court hierarchy

There used to be 11 law reports, each covering a different court's reports. There are now just four (Figure 2.2):

Appeals Cases (AC)	Contains Supreme Court and Privy Council cases. It *does not* contain Court of Appeal cases
Chancery Division (Ch)	Contains Chancery Division of the High Court cases, and cases appealed from there to the Court of Appeal
Queen's Bench Division (QB)	Contains Queen's Bench Division of the High Court cases, and cases appealed from there to the Court of Appeal
Family Division (Fam)	Contains Family Division of the High Court cases, and cases appealed from there to the Court of Appeal

Figure 2.2 The four law reports

The general rule is that any case reported in the preceding four law reports must be cited. If the case is not reported here, a case should cite the *All England Law Report* or *Weekly Law Report*. As you may guess, the Weekly Law Reports are reported much quicker and more frequently than the law reports, and volumes 2 and 3 have their content checked by the judge before they are then printed in a law report. So, if you see a citation like [2019] 2 WLR 123 or [2019] 3 WLR 456, check if the case has appeared in one of the four law reports.

All England Law Reports (All ER) also report judgments quicker than a law report, and they have reference to other sources of law: *Halsbury's Statutes* and *Halsbury's Laws*.

The next strongest authority is subject or specialist law reports published by ICLR (Incorporated Council of Law Reporting for England and Wales); they are Industrial Cases Reports, The Business Law Reports, and The Public and Third Sector Law Reports. There is a subsection of law reports which are not affiliated to ICLR which include Brewing Trade Review Licensing Law Reports, Criminal Law Reports, Lloyd's Law Reports, Industrial Relations Law Reports, Reports of Patent Cases, Bankruptcy and Personal Insolvency Reports, and Entertainment and Media Law Reports to name but a few. Each title will have a short abbreviated form (eg WLR, Crim LR, IRLR).

Cardiff University maintains an electronic database of specialist law reports and their abbreviated forms, available at www.legalabbrevs.cardiff.ac.uk, and a list of the most common law reports and common law abbreviations is on page 142.

Who's who in cases

Over time, the words used to describe parties in court have changed. Figure 2.3 shows the name of each party dependent on the court and when the case was heard.

	Criminal	Civil	Court of Appeal	Supreme Court
Has been wronged	*R*	Pre 1999 *Plaintiff*		*Respondent*
(First party named)	*Prosecution* Crown	Post 1999 *Claimant*	*Claimant*	
	v	*v*	*v*	*v*	*v*
Allegedly did the damage/wrong	*Defendant*	*Defendant*	*Defendant*	*Appellant*

Figure 2.3 The names of parties in different courts

Note: In criminal cases, only the defendant can appeal whereas either party can appeal in civil cases. At the Court of Appeal, party names may therefore be reversed from the previous court.

Performing searches

Your PQ, lecture notes or prior knowledge guide you to look up a case because you recall that is has some relevance to your case at hand. The following 11 results are returned from your search for *Douglas AND Hello* (Figure 2.4).

Compasslaw Database	Search terms: Douglas AND Hello	No. of Results: 11
Filter by **Default**		Page 1 of 1

1. Douglas & Ors v Hello! Ltd. & Ors [2004] EWHC 63 (Ch) (23 January 2004)
    ([2004] 2 Costs LR 304, [2004] EMLR 14, [2004] EWHC 63 (Ch); From England and Wales High Court (Chancery Division)

2. Douglas & Ors v Hello! Ltd. & Ors [2003] EWHC 2629 (Ch) (07 November 2003)
    ([2003] EWHC 2629, [2003] EWHC 2629 (Ch), [2004] EMLR 2; From England and Wales High Court (Chancery Division)

3. Douglas & Ors v Hello Ltd & Ors - Hello! Claims victory over Zeta Jones photos (S Howard)
    (2005) Independent 18 May 2005

4. Douglas & Ors v Hello! Ltd.& Ors [2003] EWHC 55 (Ch) (27 January 2003)
    ([2003] EMLR 29, [2003] EWHC 55 (Ch); From England and Wales High Court (Chancery Division)

5. Douglas & Ors v Hello! Ltd & Ors [2003] EWHC 786 (Ch) (11 April 2003)
    ([2003] 3 All ER 996, [2003] EMLR 31, [2003] EWHC 786 (Ch); From England and Wales High Court (Chancery Division)

6. Douglas v Hello! - An OK! result (G Black) (2007) 4:2 SCRIPT-ed 161 (2007)
    (Douglas v Hello! - An OK! result (G Black); From United Kingdom Journals;

7. Douglas & Ors v Hello Ltd.& Ors [2003] EWCA Civ 139 (12 February 2003)
    ([2003] EWCA Civ 139; From England and Wales Court of Appeal (Civil Division)

8. Douglas & Ors v Hello Ltd. & Ors [2005] EWCA Civ 595 (18 May 2005)
    ([2005] 2 FCR 487, [2005] 3 WLR 881, [2005] 4 All ER 128, [2005] EMLR 28, [2005] EMLR 609, [2005] EWCA Civ 595, [2005] HRLR 27, [2006] QB 125; From England and Wales Court of Appeal (Civil Division)

9. Douglas & Ors v. Hello! Ltd & Ors [2007] UKHL 21 (02 May 2007)
    ([2007] 19 EG 165, [2007] 2 WLR 0920, [2007] 4 All ER 545, [2007] BPIR 746, [2007] Bus LR 1600, [2007] EMLR 12, [2007] EMLR 325, [2007] IRLR 608, [2007] UKHL 21, [2008] 1 AC 1, [2008] 1 All ER (Comm) 1, [2008] AC 1; From United Kingdom House of Lords Decisions)

10. Douglas & Ors v Hello Ltd & Ors [2003] EWCA Civ 332 (3 March 2003)
    ([2003] EWCA Civ 332; From England and Wales Court of Appeal (Civil Division)

11. Douglas & Ors v Hello Ltd & Ors - Show me the money! (A Caddick) (2007)
    N.L.J. 2007 157 (7276), 805

Figure 2.4 Search returns for *Douglas v Hello*

It is not unusual to return so many cases that are reported by different law reports. But how do you know which are the most authoritative and will make your point as strong as possible?

Earlier we discussed the authority of each law report, and these can be seen in abbreviations underneath the party names.

Looking at the years of these reports should help us, with the most recent case *probably* being heard at the highest court, and therefore carrying the most persuasion in your PQ answer, although as we'll see, there are some exceptions.

Task B11 – Some of these sources don't appear to be from courts. Which sources are they? What is the source of that information? How do you know?

Task B12 – Which of the court reports below would be the most authoritative, and which would therefore be chosen to support your point?

Task B13 – Put all the cases from **Figure 2.4** in order of most authoritative to least authoritative.

The key message is that it isn't the year of the case that is the most important, but where the case was heard. It would follow that a case progresses up the court hierarchy, but the date of that case doesn't necessarily mean the report will be published at the same time.

For law reports, the report in which the case appears denotes its authority. For example, the WLR, HRLR and NLJ were all published in 2007, yet HRLR is more authoritative than NLJ, and WLR is more authoritative than HRLR.

The general hierarchy of court citations is illustrated in Figure 2.5:

		UKSC/UKHL		
	EWCA Civ		EWCA Crim	
AC	Ch	QB		Fam
		WLR		
		All ER		
		Specialist ICLR		
		Non-ICLR Law Reports		
		Academic and professional journal articles		
		Newspaper reports		

Figure 2.5 Hierarchy of court citations and law reports

Newspapers and online news outlets report very quickly following a decision, but are a small proportion of all cases and in little legal detail. Some journals (New Law Journal and Solicitors Journal) publish summaries soon after. Specialist reports take a bit more time and are in more detail. Finally, the All ER and/or WLR publish a full report. A final authoritative version may take months to appear in an official law report.

Task B14 – There are nine law reports cited in entry nine of the *Douglas v Hello* results. Order them from most authoritative to least.

More information on the Incorporated Council of Law Reporting for England and Wales (ICLR) can be found at www.iclr.co.uk/knowledge/case-law /iclrs-law-reports-an-explainer/.

You may be wondering what the point is of listing where the same case was previously heard. It's a fair question as all student writers need to find out is the most recent decision. Or is it? If you are a practising lawyer, you'll also be researching for your own arguments, your opponents' arguments, and ways to defeat those points from the opposing side. Looking for weaknesses in your own points is good practice so you can know how to defend them. It is the same with researching for PQs.

You probably know that a more recent case is likely to incorporate previous cases in its judgment which form the ruling. The reason that a lot of old cases are cited is that they were the first, or made an important distinction in the ruling about a particular set of circumstances that rulings today now follow. For example, *Lampleigh v Braithwaite* is a commonly cited contract law case from 1615, which has set a precedent for current cases that essentially a promise to pay after the performance forms a contract. It was actually cited in *Benedetti v Sawiris* in the Supreme Court as recently as 2013.

Imagine you are researching a case on how much a construction company should be paid where the parties disagree on how to work out the formula set out in the contract. You find the case of *Chartbrook Ltd v Persimmon Homes Ltd* where the Claim being discussed was how to interpret the contract – as an isolated document or within the everyday usage of building houses.

Your search in a law database returns the following 29 results (Figure 2.6):

Findlaw Database	Search terms: Chartbrook AND Persimmon	No. of Results: 29
Filter by **Date Newest>Oldest**		Page 1 of 1

1. [2020] C.L.J. 79(1) 8-11
2. [2020] L.Q.R. 136 205-210
3. [2010] 1 All E.R. (Comm) 365
4. [2010] 1 P. & C.R. 9
5. [2009] UKHL 38
6. [2009] 1 A.C. 1101
7. [2009] 3 W.L.R. 267
8. [2009] 4 All E.R. 677
9. [2009] Bus. L.R. 1200
10. [2009] 7 WLUK 9
11. [2009] B.L.R. 551
12. [2009] 125 Con. L.R. 1
13. [2009] 3 E.G.L.R. 119
14. [2009] C.I.L.L. 2729
15. [2009] 27 E.G. 91 (C.S.)
16. (2009) 153(26) S.J.L.B. 27
17. [2009] N.P.C. 87
18. [2009] N.P.C. 86
19. [2009] Times, July 2, 2009
20. [2009] C.L.Y. 722
21. [2008] EWCA Civ 183
22. [2008] 2 All E.R. (Comm) 387
23. [2008] 3 WLUK 250
24. [2008] N.P.C. 30
25. [2007] EWHC 409 (Ch)
26. [2007] 1 All E.R. (Comm) 1083
27. [2007] 3 WLUK 74
28. [2007] 2 P. & C.R. 9
29. [2007] 11 E.G. 160 (C.S.)

Figure 2.6 Search returns for *Chartbrook Ltd v Persimmon Homes Ltd*

Task B15 – How have the aforementioned cases been ordered?

Task B16 – Which court and law report would you choose and why?

You can learn more about how to present case law and court citations from page 117.

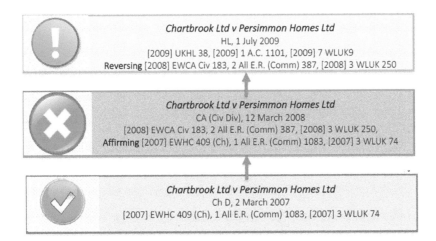

Figure 2.7 Graphic case history of *Chartbrook Ltd v Persimmon Homes Ltd*

It can be seen that the case from the Chancery Division was originally agreed upon and was given a positive judgment (green tick), meaning this ruling was approved and became binding. But then it went up the hierarchy to appeal, and the Court of Appeal ruling concurred with the lower court with one dissenting Lord Justice. At this stage, the case would have still received positive consideration (ie a green tick) as well as for the lower court.

However, when the House of Lords held that the Court of Appeal should be overruled, the green tick became a red cross to mean it should not be considered good law (or negative consideration). What has happened since the 2009 House of Lords judgment is that an aspect of the ruling has been varied or questioned (given mixed consideration). The ruling hasn't been changed and the decision is still binding, but an element of the ruling has been subject to further explanation. This can be identified by a cautionary mark (the orange exclamation mark (!)). Cases with cautionary marks are still technically 'good' law. Don't fall into the trap of seeing the green tick and believing that the other higher judgments are incorrect or not binding.

Many law databases use graphic case illustrations similar to **Figure 2.7**.

Despite the House of Lords ruling being the most authoritative, the earlier judgments are not thrown away. How is this 'unsound' law from the Court of

Appeal and Chancery Division useful to us as academic researchers, writers and lawyers?

The arguments used and therefore the interpretation in the two lower courts were found to be incorrect, so the dissenting Lord Justice from the Court of Appeal was actually correct according to the House of Lords. With this information, researchers can go back to the two lower courts to see the points of argument that the judges ruled against, and the correct interpretation of the one dissenting Lord Justice. These will be discussed in far more detail in the original court debate than the summarised version of the House of Lord's judgment.

Furthermore, the House of Lords may have actually decided on another point or points that swayed their judgment. Often, the *obiter dictum* offers researchers a useful summary of why a particular judge felt more inclined to find for one side over another. To read the House of Lords judgment would reveal that the contentious points were many. So, while they agreed with the dissenting Lord Justice on the one hand, they also found further points to dismiss the appeal, and award the judgment to Persimmon Homes Ltd.

The House of Lords rulings have more authority, but the arguments from the lower courts could also have a bearing on the points you are trying to raise in your own PQ answer. Remember that understanding failed arguments can strengthen your own position, or at least make you knowledgeable and prepared to defend weaknesses in your own points. Ultimately, understanding the full picture will allow you to qualify or alter your original position, thus strengthening it. When answering essays or PQs, knowledge and acknowledgement of your own argument's weaknesses will earn you extra credit.

In fact, in the instant case, the two higher courts make for interesting reading on how each judge has interpreted the findings of previous judges at lower courts.

The three courts above are given positive, negative and neutral judicial consideration, meaning that the decision is either good law, has been overruled by a superior court, or the court had considered a previous judgment, but didn't necessarily follow or apply that rule.

If the *Chartbrook* case were taken to the Supreme Court who sided with them, the court decisions above would have to be reversed to show the opposite, and the House of Lords and the dissenting Lord Justice would be overruled.

Positive, negative and neutral judgments

Law databases will have a description of the 'treatment' of a particular case to guide a researcher, telling them if the case is good law or not.

Task B17 – Here are some variants of positive, neutral and negative judgments. Decide which definition belongs to which category and place them accordingly in the boxes.

Fully followed (or partially followed) in a minority opinion of a subsequent court

Judicial review allowed

Judicial review denied

Leave to appeal denied by a subsequent court

Questioned by a subsequent court

Referenced in a dissenting opinion

Reversed, quashed or varied by a higher court

(For more detailed information on case histories and case treatments see www. lexisnexis.com/help/global/CA/en_ CA/docview_citatordoctips.asp)

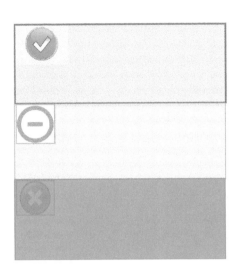

Database searching

Many databases use search terms that can be used not only in law databases, but many library catalogues and internet search engines. While there will be particular shortcuts for each database, the most common legal search terms are listed here.

Purpose	Shortcut key	Example search term
All terms must be present in a document to appear in the returns	& (or space)	offer & acceptance offer acceptance consideration intention
Either term must be present in a document to appear in the returns	OR	promise OR estoppel
The exact phrase must appear	" "	"Adams v Lindsell" "officious bystander"
Allow all word forms	*	frustrat* (returns frustrate, frustration, frustrating, frustratingly, frustrated)
Both phrases must appear in the same sentence in any order	/s	noise /s pollution
Both phrases must appear in the same paragraph in any order	/p	noise /p nuisance

continued . . .

cont.

Purpose	Shortcut key	Example search term
Words must appear in this order within the same sentence	+s	discretionary +s equity
Words must appear in this order within the same paragraph	+p	available +p market
Searches for the second word within words before and after the first	/n	duty /2 disclosure (returns duty of disclosure and disclosure duty but not duty of full disclosure as this is 3 words difference)
Searches for the second word within n words after the first	+n	mitigate +2 loss (returns mitigate any loss, mitigate some loss, mitigate all loss etc)
To exclude the second word	%	implied % express (would only include "implied" terms when searching within contract law)

Figure 2.8 Database search shortcuts

Search terms can be connected to make a string (eg restitution +s payment "advance" % mistake), but be careful using this method as you may inadvertently exclude an important return. It's advisable to add one search term at a time.

A further research aid is the "Key Cases Cited" or "Key Cases Citing" function of most databases. When searching from a case of interest from say 1990, the former allows you to see the precedent that was used in the arguments of your case that may have affected the outcome (pre-1990), while the latter shows you cases that have used your case as precedent in their arguments (post-1990).

Scenario

Here are some simplified PQs. Using legal databases such as LexisNexis or West-law, identify the key terms within each, and perform a search to see if the case that the PQs are based upon appears.

1 A husband left his wife and two children. They verbally negotiated that he would pay £50 per week as maintenance for the children, as long has his business was ok, to which they both agreed. After a few weeks, he fell into arrears due to ill health.

The key words from the PQ would be *oral* and *maintenance*. Requiring critical thinking (or joining the dots) on your part, the wider area of law is *contract*, so we can now add that as a key word. Entering these three words as in the 'free text' box returns 4727 cases. Far too many to read!

The next step is to narrow down the field of law. Including only Contract will reduce that number to 790, although there are sub-topics which are selectable (eg Breach, Remedies, Rights, Operation, Termination). As the PQ isn't that clear, they are left unselected.

Of the 790, only 279 have a positive or neutral Status (see page 35 for a reminder). This is still too large a number to do anything useful with. Selecting the jurisdiction as the UK reduces the number by just 14. On revisiting the PQ, the parties of the case strike me as a possible filter, so I look for *husband OR wife* (capital letters for "OR" are necessary – see page 35–6 for glossary of general database search terms) in the 'search within results' box. Result! There are now 47 which is far more manageable. But not quite good enough.

There is an option to sort by relevance or date, so relevance is selected, and the keywords and case summary or abstract are shown. The first return is *Soofi v Dykes*, a negligence case against a solicitor. This isn't relevant to my PQ, and by continuing to scan read noting my four highlighted terms amongst the case summary, I can read the context.

I'm also aware that as a married couple, they are *likely* to have the same family name. This information will help me narrow down the returns.

Another tip is to use the court as a search parameter. Selecting Supreme Court now returns four cases – far fewer case summaries to read. Now, one of the four on first glance seems like a good starting point. Alas, the case *Steadman v Steadman* relates more to the oral changing of terms of the pre-marital home. It is now wise to backtrack and now include only Court of Appeal cases.

Of the 14 Court of Appeal cases, reading each summary, the cases of interest are now:

- *Steadman v Steadman* again as the earlier Court of Appeal case
- *Balfour v Balfour* Wife sued husband for maintenance due following a verbal agreement.
- (notably) *Williams v Roffey Bros. & Nicholls* (a well-known contract case on payment of bonuses) contains a reference to *Williams v Williams'* enforceability of oral contract between spouses.
- *Gould v Gould* as above and intention to enter into legal agreement

Having already discounted *Steadman*, there are now three authoritative cases of interest that appear to be very relevant to the PQ – *Balfour, Williams* and *Gould*.

Academic skills – Identify the key words in the following PQs, log into your preferred law database, and narrow your search using the techniques mentioned earlier. Note that the PQs have been shortened to allow you to focus on the facts of the case.

2   Wheely Goods manufactures after-market alloy wheels for cars with copies of the original manufacturer's registered designs. Hamilton's, which is a small car company, sees its designs available on WG's website and believes them to be their own designs.

```
Key words



```

3   Helen runs a market stall selling fabrics. She asks her friend Vanessa to look after the stall for a short while to deal with a family emergency, leaving instructions to only allow a maximum 25% discount off the marked price, if asked. Vanessa sells stock for half the marked price.

```
Key words



```

4   On a mountain biking course, Craig, an experienced downhill cyclist, crashes his bike which then collides with Sophia, who is attending the course for the first time. She sustains cuts and concussion. An ambulance is phoned, and Richard, a junior doctor at the hospital, doesn't ask if she is allergic to any medicine. Unfortunately, the medicine given causes severe reactions leaving Sophia in hospital for two months.

```
Key words



```

5   Luigi's restaurant is not making profit, so he decides to sell it. Lana enquires about the restaurant's accounts and Luigi says his accountant has them, but not to worry as he makes a healthy profit every month. Lana decided not to proceed with the purchase.

```
┌─────────────────────────────────────────────────────────────┐
│ Key words                                                    │
│                                                              │
│                                                              │
│                                                              │
│                                                              │
└─────────────────────────────────────────────────────────────┘
```

6   James is an artist whose work targets current issues. On the side of his gallery, he is working on his current project which appears to be encouraging people to damage local council property in protest against some recent changes.

```
┌─────────────────────────────────────────────────────────────┐
│ Key words                                                    │
│                                                              │
│                                                              │
│                                                              │
│                                                              │
└─────────────────────────────────────────────────────────────┘
```

7   Barry produces organic soaps which he thinks smells similar to a famous luxury brand, Martha's. In order to attract a bigger audience, he lists a comparison table on his soap packaging allowing customers to read which of his soaps correspond to the scent of Martha's.

```
┌─────────────────────────────────────────────────────────────┐
│ Key words                                                    │
│                                                              │
│                                                              │
│                                                              │
│                                                              │
└─────────────────────────────────────────────────────────────┘
```

8   Claimant Boris, a racing enthusiast, pays and takes his own motorbike on a racetrack for a one-hour driving session. The same track is being shared between amateur racers, such as Boris, and Unlimited Cars Ltd, a company that has also hired the track to allow its non-expert customers to drive its own sports cars under instructor supervision. One of Unlimited's cars has a mechanical failure during a first 'sighting' lap, into which Boris crashes at high speed, causing serious injury.

```
┌─────────────────────────────────────────────────────────────┐
│ Key words                                                    │
│                                                              │
│                                                              │
│                                                              │
│                                                              │
└─────────────────────────────────────────────────────────────┘
```

Academic skills – Use the table that follows to keep a record of how the number of results decreases as your search terms become more specific. This is good practice for keeping a record of your search history. Use the example PQs as practice.

Search term(s)	Number of results

Turning research into Law

This section only splits into two: **Beginner's Tasks** and **Extension Tasks** for students who are familiar with UK university study. Choose the most appropriate level for yourself.

Now that you have identified discussion points in the PQ, you have to eliminate the irrelevant Claims, leave the important Claims, and possibly expand Claims that are too big to discuss in a single point.

There are two main ways to go about your research at this stage:

1   Take your initially identified 17 claims, reduce them to six combined areas which will help us to focus our research on a particular legal element. These are then transferred into a table which will help us to identify the corresponding law by group. These were labelled a–f on page 23 as follows.

   a)   What is Jack's role as a seller? (Point 1)

   b)   The nature of the advert (Points 2, 4, 5)

   c)   The item being sold (Point 3)

   d)   Does the nature of the correspondence matter (revoke, offer, accept)? (4, 6, 8, 9, 10, 12, 14, 15)

   e)   Communication methods (6, 7, 8, 10, 11, 12, 13, 14, 16)

   f)   The timings of the communications (7, 13, 15)

2   Transfer those 17 claims *individually* into a different table (left column) to help to isolate and identify the corresponding law.

Tip: Practice each style and see which one is your preference.

Task B18 – (Extension) Using your existing contract law knowledge, continue identifying corresponding case law. Review your own or given source of Law and consider the relevance and importance of each claim (as **Task B9**) by noting a tick (√) for key (major) Claims a plus sign (+) for minor issues and leave blank if the Claim is of no importance or relevance.

(Sub) Claims	Law
1 "A private watch collector." Not selling as a professional	Research establishes this point is not relevant
2 "Specialist . . . watches website." Check if this is still shown to 'the public'	Not relevant
3 "Pre-owned." Not new, so less buyer protection for Peter?	Not relevant
4 "Sees the post." Not stated if the advert is an offer. How can it therefore be accepted to form a contract?	ITT or Offer. *Carlill v Carbolic Smoke Ball Co* – an advert may be an offer if it is sufficiently certain and shows intent. *Partridge v Crittenden* a magazine ad was ITT unless made by manufacturer.
5 "Online." Is this different to seeing it in a shop, magazine?	
6 "Immediately emails/Next day, Peter revokes." Timing – Is there a cooling off period?	
7 "Peter . . . emails Jack." Delivery of communication (email) versus letter	
8 A £200 reduction is requested by Peter. How does this impact if it's an offer and how it can be accepted?	
9 "Revoke." Does the purpose impact any communication method?	
10 "Method of communication of withdrawal to home address"	
11 Home v business address – which is the correct correspondence address?	

continued . . .

cont.

(Sub) Claims	Law
12 How should a withdrawal be communicated? Same as first communication or is any method acceptable? This isn't a price renegotiation.	
13 Jack doesn't read the email the same day/time as it's sent.	
14 "Jack . . . posts." Jack doesn't accept by the same method as the email.	
15 Jack hasn't yet received Peter's letter of withdrawal.	
16 Withdrawal is sent by letter.	
17 Advise only Jack (seller/offeree) not Peter (buyer/offeror)	

You will note that Claim 4 contains two sources of law that would be relevant in discussing and clarifying if the advert is an ITT or an offer.

Beginner's Task – Need help completing the Law column?

If this is your first venture into PQ writing, it is essential that you don't feel down or become disillusioned by thinking this is too difficult for you – this is a common feeling amongst those who see it for the first time because they feel lost and overwhelmed.

Next are 12 cases that would be relevant to the given PQ. If you are unfamiliar with any of these, a quick internet search (or law database if you are a university student) of the case parties will give you a wide choice of summaries, opinions and full judgments.

It isn't necessary to read the whole judgment, but a simple internet search will return critiques, or if the internet isn't finding suitable material, try www.bailii.org/.

Tip: For those who are fresh from A-Levels, new to legal studies or who come from jurisdictions overseas, you will be expected to know the principles of key cases, such as the ten in **Task B21**. Use the flashcards on page 192 as a model to create your own to help you learn, remember and revise case law, legal processes and vocabulary.

Task B19 (Beginner's Task) – It is strongly advised that you take your time here. Choose one of the cases and read its summary or case notes. Think about how its content relates to, or is similar to the *Jack v Peter* case, particularly the Claims and sub-Claims identified in the first column. Concentrate on getting one Claim right in the first instance.

Task B20 (Extension) – Use your existing contract law textbook to find additional cases, laws and commentary which could be used to complete the Law column.

Task B21 – Make notes on the space on the right to summarise what each of these ten seminal cases is about. Once you have filled in the principles, you should be able to decide if they are relevant to the case. The next stage is to see how their principles can be applied. A completed version is in the Answers as Flashcards on page 205.

Adams v Lindsell [1818] 106 ER 250	
Brogden v Metropolitan Railway Company (1877) 2 App. Cas 666	
Carlill v Carbolic Smoke Ball Co Ltd [1893] 1 QB 256	
Felthouse v Bindley [1862] 142 ER 1037	
Fisher v Bell (1961) 1 QB 394	
Harvey v Facey [1893] AC 552	
Hyde v Wrench [1840] 3 Beav 334	
Partridge v Crittenden [1968] 1 WLR 1204	
Pharmaceutical Society of GB v Boots (1953) 1 QB 401	
Routledge v Grant (1828) 4 Bing 653	
The Brimnes [1975] QB 929	

Task B22 (Beginner's Task) – Once you have completed a summary or case notes of these 12 cases, use this information to see what elements of the cases could help answer the questions set in the Claims column on **Task B18**.

Order, order

There are a few essay structures (think of your standard introduction, main body, conclusion essay organisation) that can be used for answering PQs. But as you may imagine, not one structure suits all PQs. This largely depends on *you* and how you want to address the question.

In simpler cases, such as *Jack v Peter*, there are only two parties, and the Claims surrounding the transaction are relatively basic contract law concepts.

More complex PQs will involve multiple parties who may have been wronged, or where advice needs to be given to each party (eg the shipowner, shipper and bill of lading endorsee).

Highly complex questions will involve many parties and multiple Claims to navigate. A very difficult PQ that meets these criteria would be:

JUST TO SHOW A HIGHLY COMPLEX PQ

Chip Shipping Ltd (the shipowners), who are represented by GLB Shipping & Trading Ltd, entered into a contractual agreement for the supply of bunkers with AB Bunkers Ltd (the contractual suppliers) who then engaged the services of SUB Bunkers Ltd in a sub-contract to buy the bunkers. The sub-contractors then entered into a contract with Like-A-Bunk (the physical suppliers) for the supply of bunkers to be delivered to the shipowners.

The physical suppliers delivered the bunkers as agreed and issued the delivery receipt and invoice which incorporated the contractual terms and the terms and conditions generally used by the physical suppliers. Both the delivery receipt and the invoice were signed, but the signor has not been identifiable.

The contractual suppliers then declared bankruptcy. The shipowners paid in full for the bunkers to the bank to which a number of debts due to the contractual suppliers had been assigned. Due to the ripple effect created by the bankruptcy of the contractual suppliers, the physical suppliers remained unpaid by the sub-contractors for the bunkers delivered.

Advise each party.

This example would be something a PhD candidate would be researching, and would base their thesis upon, so you needn't be overwhelmed or discouraged. Remember that you are on the first steps of your journey into law, and English may not even be your mother tongue!

The good news is that most of the PQs written by your lecturers will be based on real life cases. Therefore, good reading habits and subscribing to newsletters and professional magazines will pay you dividends.

Tip: Universities pay money so their students can access databases for free (such as Westlaw and i-law). You can often choose to be updated with lawyers' interpretations and analysis of cases within your area.

Your writing will be much more structured, cohesive and readable if you plan ahead and decide which structure you will use from the outset.

Let's consider the PQ being worked through – the sale of Jack's watch.

There are three possible ways that an answer could be ordered or structured. Each has their own merits and limitations. You may realise that the steps that follow are relatively vague if your interest is contract law – this is because tort and criminal law have much more rigid, defined writing structures, but learning this organisational flexibility early on can help you with future writing as you will have the knowledge to identify and select the best structure for your PQ. Contract law needs the flexibility to adapt its answers.

A strong indicator of which structure should be used can be found by looking at the question prompt in the PQ. Question prompts we have seen so far have ended with phrases like *Advise Jack*. Together with the number and type of Claims identified, you should be able to work out which structure is the most appropriate for that particular writing task.

Figure 2.9 introduces three main methods which can be used to structure your answer.

A - By Party	B - By Issue	C - By CLEO
Claim	Claim	CLEO – Claim 1
Law – Claim 1	Law – Claim 1	CLEO – Claim 2
Evaluation – Claim 1	Law – Claim 2	
Law – Claim 2	Evaluation – Claim 1	CLEO – Claim 3 (...and so on)
Evaluation – Claim 2	Evaluation – Claim 2	
Outcome	Outcome	Summary outcome

Figure 2.9 Structure of each CLEO style

The eagle-eyed among you may realise that there are similarities between the Party (structure A) and CLEO structures (structure C). This essentially is true, with the exception of Party only having one Outcome section for the whole answer. Party structures are therefore more suitable when there is a theme running through the PQ, so your answer is closely linked to one point of law.

Think of CLEO as being suitable for PQs of two or more question parts. The differences between the By Issue structure (Structure B) and CLEO structure are that CLEO takes each question within the PQ in turn and deals with each individually – like mini-essays. Its outcome therefore brings together all the outcomes to answer the PQ, or to give final advice to the client.

The By Issue structure takes the whole PQ and addresses it like one very large essay. Bear in mind that one By Issue answer may contain just one Claim, Law, Evaluation and Outcome section, which is exactly as in one By Issue within a CLEO structure. In other words, one whole By Issue answer is almost the same as one section of a CLEO answer, without a summary outcome.

The simplest structure, one which could be well utilised in the example of Jack's selling his watch to Peter, would be CLEO with one Claim and a summary outcome (or simply using a By Issue structure with one Law and one Evaluation section).

By comparison, the late submission of work answer on page 14 is written By Issue.

To see how these three PQ organisations work in practice, look at the Resources section of this book where you can compare and decide on the suitability of each structure for your particular PQ (Figure 2.10).

By Party		By Issue		By CLEO	
Pros	Cons	Pros	Cons	Pros	Cons
Good for simple, multiple party issues	Outcome section can be tricky if complex issue	Best for complex issues	Hard to prioritise issues	Best for novices, a single issue and overall flow	Stronger possibility of arguing the facts, not the law
Good when there's a link between issues (eg offer and acceptance)	Unsuitable for certain PQs (eg if only two parties)	Can be used regardless of connection between issues	Students can get too bogged down in one section	Good for one linked issue, and one scenario one multi-PQ (especially criminal and tort law).	Vague structure, especially for contract law questions (a positive and a negative!)
Good flow at paragraph level as each issue is dealt with in turn	Can lack flow at essay level and potential for weaker Outcome	Most likely structure to be used for university LLB and LLM tasks	Danger of repetition if the same issue affects multiple parties	Saves repetition when same issues affect multiple parties	Danger of (unnecessary) repetition

Figure 2.10 Advantages and disadvantages of each CLEO style

An outline of the three structures used for *Jack v Peter* is given in Figure 2.11 with some suggested subheadings. The subheadings suitable for your answer are underlined.

By party	By issue	By CLEO
Claim	Claim	CLEO – offer or ITT
<u>Jack v Peter</u>	Law 1 – <u>offer or ITT</u>	CLEO – the postal rule
Law – all applicable points of law	Law 2 – <u>the postal rule</u>	
	Law 3 – <u>revocation</u>	
Evaluation – all applicable		
Not applicable as there are only two parties	Evaluation 1 – <u>offer or ITT</u>	CLEO – revocation
	Evaluation 2 – <u>the postal rule</u>	
	Evaluation – <u>revocation</u>	
Outcome	Outcome	Summary outcome

Figure 2.11 *Jack v Peter* by each CLEO style

No doubt, there are other CLEO structures that could be used depending on the party numbers and complexity of the Claims within the PQ, but these three main types will offer a good basic grounding into writing more complex answers.

Claim

In this chapter you will learn how to:

- Approach and develop your answer to each PQ section
- Identify the purpose of each key sentence within each PQ section
- Evaluate which CLEO structure is more appropriate in context
- Differentiate between legal and factual issues
- Identify the different stages within a sample Claim answer
  - And have an end of chapter test

Another way of considering the Claim is to think about what action could be taken. When you plan your answer, you can cross-reference these elements with those in the question rubric to help decide whether you need any detailed discussion of them.

Using this slower and more deliberate strategy will ensure that you do not miss any important points. For example, for an essay question on *duty of care*, you may start writing immediately on *breach of duty* without first identifying *negligence* or *breach of statutory duty*. Speeding through without adequate planning would leave the PQ reader confused, and you might miss points such as the element of causation or the other elements for the tort of *negligence*.

The facts in the question may also make issue of other torts.

However, having done a lot of the groundwork, you can then write a short, succinct Claim paragraph which summarises in a few lines each of the main elements that you have identified in the PQ.

Simpler PQs may only have one main Claim to identify, but as you advance through your course, you will have to identify and discuss each of the legal elements that are in dispute.

To clarify: when you see lawyers in films, they tend to make opening statements that seem a bit long-winded, verbose and full of unnecessary legalese. Consider these two settings: a police station and a courtroom. In the police station, a man has just been arrested for theft. In the interview, his opening statement would likely be "I haven't stolen anything," "You've got the wrong guy," or "I'm innocent."

Your writing also needs to be unlike the lawyer that you've seen in countless courtroom dramas. In opening statements, the lawyer sets the scene for the judge or jury, and doesn't go head-first into a denial as a layperson client may do in an interview. The lawyer would open with "Our defence is that the witnesses who identified my client are mistaken because he was nowhere near the scene when the theft took place. In fact, he was 50 miles away. This is a simple case of mistaken identity."

As academic writers, these sorts of approaches need to be avoided. In academic writing, it needs to be reformulated into the correct academic register, for the correct audience (reader), with the correct purpose. Register is the style and format of writing that is expected of a student writing for university, which generally means avoiding personal pronouns *I, you, he* and *she*; writing in the passive voice; and using complex sentences. The formality employed will be formal academic, so while it is good practice to use synonyms to show your wide vocabulary, make sure you don't slip into colloquialism such as *pinch, rip off* or *nick*. Your legal knowledge will be put to use as dictionaries will list *robbery, fraud* and *larceny* as synonyms. Be careful as the first two deal with other crimes separate to theft, and larceny is an American word which in the UK is an umbrella term for theft related crimes.

Consideration of who the audience is requires the writer to think about who will read your answer. Of course, it will be your law lecturer, but it is important to have audience in mind when it comes to writing a letter to a client, a senior partner or a junior colleague. What depth of information they need, how much needs to be explained and what they already know are some important concepts to consider.

Finally, purpose of the text means you should appreciate why the text is being written. In a courtroom, the charge has already been established so there is no need to explain the elements that make up the offence, and the relevant sections of the Act.

However, in a PQ, the elements that make up an offence need to be outlined, even though your law lecturer will very well know this.

In the theft example, the main claim is 'is the client liable to a charge of theft' and the sub-Claim is 'mistaken identity'.

Your answer will follow the same structure.

To summarise, you should:

- Read the question prompt several times
- Identify all the elements of the cause
- Identify the topic and understand how the question prompt wants this topic framed (eg the scenario may be a collision at sea, the topic may be *negligence*, the framing could be either the company's, the master's or the crew's liability)
- Identify vagueness in the question. For example, following on from the previous item, if the question does not state that the ship's master was negligent, this allows you to answer two frames – the situation where he is negligent, and the situation where he is not – in the Evaluation section
- Cross-reference which of these elements are pertinent to the question
- Discuss these elements in detail
- Write a summary of the points of law that occur in the given problem. Use your existing knowledge to identify any legal cases that address the Claim. As your knowledge of case law grows, train yourself to think of similarities between that and the PQ, for example, if the question discusses a 'for sale' advert in a newspaper, you'll immediately think of *Partridge v Crittenden.*
- Note the differences between your presented case law and that given in the question, for example if the stock was limited or plentiful, then there is scope to discuss *Pharmaceutical Society v Boots* or *Carlill v Carbolic Smoke Ball Co.*
- In certain fields of law, such as maritime, human rights and international trade, you will need to identify the jurisdiction.
- Write an outline (basic plan) of your answer
- Each Claim needs to be explicitly stated

You should believe that each sentence in the problem will offer you an element to discuss, or further clarify a previous point of discussion later in the answer.

Also be aware that your encyclopaedic knowledge of *Carlill v Carbolic Smoke Ball Co* is of limited use if the question makes it clear that the scenario is about an ITT, rather than an Offer.

> *Tip:* The first starting point, especially for students enrolled on courses titled International X Law, is to identify the jurisdiction. If this is not explicitly stated, you should assume and state in your answer that it is English and Welsh law.

Signposting language for Claim

Using words to introduce and signpost the reader to what is about to be said is a good way to give your content structure and make your points clearer. Figure 2.12 is a non-exhaustive list of four types of signposting that are mainly used in the Law section to begin a sentence and to link two sentences. Do not become over-reliant on them as beginning every sentence with a signal word can make your work seem mechanical and unnatural.

Introducing	Ordering
The question is regarding…	The first issue is…
See *If*-clauses on page 91	Secondly,…
Should x be an offer, then…	Next,…
X will argue that… Three points now arise: A, B and C.	Finally,…
In advising X,…	

Figure 2.12 Signposting language for Claim

How to write the Claim section

You will have noticed how much time has been dedicated already to the Claim section. Your memory and analytical skills are tested here, so it is a good idea to make notes to help you plan your essay.

Looking at the example *Jack v Peter* question, you will have already identified that the broad area of law this concerns is contract law, and the significant Claim within this area are offer and acceptance (essentially, whether an offer has been made, and whether that same offer has been accepted).

The minor point (which depending on your answer to the major point could be irrelevant) is if the revocation (withdrawal) of the offer was lawful.

Importantly, the PQ in this case focuses on *if* there has been a contract formed. This is the key issue. However, some PQs will focus on another area of contract law, for example *breach of contract* or *misrepresentation*, where a contract must have been formed in order for there to have been a breach. In these cases, you don't need to discuss the formation of contract.

A BASIC PROBLEM QUESTION ON CONTRACT – EXAMPLE CLAIM PARAGRAPH

The question at issue is whether Jack has formed a contract with Peter. Initially, courts would need to establish whether the advert was an offer or an ITT (Invitation to Treat). Second, according to *Treitel*, four elements must be met to form a binding contract: offer, acceptance, consideration and intention.

CLAIM paragraph's structure

There are three main sentences that make up a Claim section, though the length and complexity of

each will depend on the actual PQ being addressed. They are essentially:

- o   What is the broad issue of the PQ?

- o   What are the general legal elements for that broad issue?

- o   Identify which element(s) will be focussed on

  - o   If there are multiple legal issues, then the preceding process can be repeated for each.

Figure 2.13 Claim paragraph's structure

More advanced PQs will give you multiple scenarios. For example, a company has Vessel A and B. Vessel A has had a collision, and Vessel B needs to be salved. Using the three structures that follow, you can see that some outlines are more suitable than others.

Critical thinking – Which outline is the better? A summary answer is offered later.

By Party (Structure A)	By Issue (Structure B)	By CLEO (Structure C)
C – collision and salvage	**C** – collision and salvage	C_1 – collision
L – Vessel A v Vessel B (collision and salvage)	**L** – collision	L_1 – collision
E – Vessel A v Vessel B (collision and salvage)	**E** – collision	E_1 – collision
O – collision and salvage	**L** – salvage	O_1 – collision
	E – salvage	C_2 – collision
	O – collision and salvage	L_2 – collision
		E_2 – collision
		O_2 – collision

One structure in the preceding is not generally more correct than another but by looking at the PQ carefully, it should be clear that one possible structure just does not fit the question type. Structure A would be unsuitable because there is one party in this PQ. There are two ships which belong to one company, and the two events (the salvage and the collision) are independent of each other. If it were cargo that needed to be salved, the same principle would apply. Structure A would be better suited if Vessel A had collided with Vessel B, regardless of their ownership; that is, there is some factual connection between the two parties.

So, with Structure A eliminated, where next? There may be overlapping issues between the two scenarios where the same law or points raised in case law apply to both. In that case, it would be permissible to arrange your structure By Issue (B) so the same arguments and evaluations aren't repeated.

It could be that Structure C (By CLEO) would be more suitable if there were two clearly separate issues. This is a judgement call on your part as to whether you'd answer the collision/salvage question as one problem/Claim or two. The main difference between Structures B and C is the latter has a noticeable reset between the first Outcome and second Claim because the themes of the PQ are too wide to combine into one. Depending on the depth and breadth of the overlapping issues, you must decide to what extent the issues are important, the thematic connections, and which style would best suit your answer.

Now, what about if the collision had been in a harbour where a member of the public had been killed? Which structure would you use then?

What about if she was a worker of the company?

What about if she were heavily pregnant?

As each question becomes denser and more information-laden, and the number of separate questions within the PQ increases, you'll be more likely to move from structure B to C. In the event that there are more parties involved in the scenario, it may be necessary to add another L and E section before the final Outcome when writing by Issue (Structure B), or add another whole CLEO section in Structure C (which would follow on as $C_3 L_3 E_3 O_3$ in the earlier model).

In summary, you need to have done your research and planning before thinking about the structure to be used. Once you have a handle on all the Claims and sub-Claims (as a minimum), you can then decide which structure best suits that PQ.

Tip: Your tutors will more often than not be happy to advise you if you approach them with a plan of your work. At this early stage of drafting, they will be able to see which structure chosen is better for the question they have set.

Task B23 – Consider which structure would be most suitable for these PQ summaries. Note the legal knowledge needed to answer increases as the questions progress. If you need help to establish the Claim, some pointers follow.

a   A shopkeeper displayed a flick knife with a price label in his shop window.

b   A company director sends letters to shareholders asking for money to grow the business. In truth, the money is to pay off company debt.

c   A second-hand car dealer was asked if there was a history of outstanding finance on a car, to which he replied he was not aware of any. While it was true the dealer wasn't aware of any, this was due to his lack of reading the car's history.

d   A fashion brand contracted all five members of a famous K-pop group to advertise their product. However, one suddenly left the group.

e   The Cargo Receivers brought a claim against the Carriers for the loss of two containers' worth of deer meat due to raised temperature caused by a supposed electrical malfunction. The Carrier argues that because Waybills were issued, Hague Rules apply rather than Hague-Visby by referring to Article 1(b), thereby significantly limiting their responsibility to 100GBP per container. The Cargo Receivers argue that each deer steak was a 'unit' for the purpose of the Hague or Hague-Visby Rules.

f   A shipment of soya was destroyed due to condensation. The cargo claimants argue that the loss and damage was caused by the negligence of the Carrier under Article III of the Hague Rules. The Carriers in turn are relying on exemption from Article IV Rule 2(m) of the Hague Rues, and pleading that condensation damage was inevitable.

g   George, a famous pop star and style-icon, entered into an agreement for a fashion store to use his image to publicise his new album. Shortly after, the store used a similar image on the next season's clothes. George is unhappy about his image being used without his consent.

h   Ahern (manufacturer) sold goods to Carling (wholesaler) with a binding agreement that Carling would not sell the items below the price given by Ahern. Carling also agreed to pass on the same pricing terms to their customers. Carling sold items to Frederiksen who sold the items at discounted prices.

Case law that the preceding PQs are based on

a   Has the shopkeeper offered the item for sale or is it an ITT? *Fisher v Bell* (1961)

b   Company law/Misrepresentation *Edgington v Fitzmaurice* (1885)

c   Misrepresentation *Notts Patent Brick v Butler* (1886)

d   Agency/Misrepresentation *Spice Girls v Aprilia World Service* (2000)

e   Maritime law/Damages *Kyokyou v A.P. Moller* [2018]

f   Maritime law/Damages *Volcafe Ltd v Compania Sud Americana* [2016]

g   Intellectual Property/Passing off *Rihanna v Top Shop* (2015)

h   Privity of contract *Dunlop v Selfridge* [1915]

End of Claim chapter questions

1   What is the purpose of each of the sentences in the Claim paragraph?

Exemplar paragraph – Deconstruction	Purpose
The question at issue is whether Jack has formed a contract with Peter.	_____ _____
Initially, courts would need to establish whether the advert was an offer or an ITT (Invitation to Treat).	_____ _____ _____
Secondly, according to *Treitel*, four elements must be met to form a binding contract: offer, acceptance, consideration and intention.	_____ _____ _____ _____

2   What is the broad area of law, and the topic? _____

_____

_____

3   What do you notice about the first use of specialist terms (ITT)? _____

_____

_____

4   What do you think *Treitel* is and why is it written in italics? _____

_____

_____

5   Will all four elements of contract formation be discussed? _____

_____

_____

6   Has Claims been written in order of importance, process or strength of argument?

_____

_____

7   What writing structure do you think will be used, Party, Issue or CLEO? ____

_____

_____

8   Why do you think that revocation of offer is not mentioned at this stage? ____

_____

_____

9   Factual or legal issue?

    a)   Can a child enter into a contract?

    b)   Under what circumstances are contracts with children voidable and unenforceable?

    c)   An academically gifted 10-year-old asks a professor for private tutoring.

    d)   Two parties dispute a contract that was agreed verbally.

    e)   When can an employee be fired?

    f)   What's the difference between an employee and a contractor?

    g)   Who brought the hazardous material onto the land?

    h)   Why did the employer fire the employee?

    i)   Did the company violate the national minimum wage?

    j)   Is a flick knife in a window of a shop next to a price tag offering the item for sale?

    k)   A car driver has a sudden medical emergency while driving.

    l)   Professionals must act within the rules of their governing body.

Law

In this chapter you will learn how to:

- Use case law to support your point
- Identify the organisation of Law sections
- Use previously found research to write the Law section
- Implement different styles of note-taking dependent on your learning style and preferences
- Identify the different stages within a sample Law answer in two different approaches
- Approach and develop your answer to each PQ section
  - And have an end of chapter test

Researching

Researching for a Claim has already been discussed in the previous section, so revisit this if necessary. This section of the book deals with what to do with those sources of law, and how to ensure they are relevant to the facts of the PQ.

> *Tip*: You can review the persuasive power of each source on page 26 of the book if needed.

Case law is also the most commonly used authority because:

- Of its wider availability (cases are being heard on a daily basis)

- It's based on precedent so cases that guide the current judgments are cited to help the researcher follow the logic in the court's decisions (eg the court's evaluation and lack of decision of the meaning of "practical benefit" from part payment of debt, which was set in *Foakes v Beer* 1884, but then doubted in the Supreme Court's dicta in *MWB Business Exchange Centres Ltd v Rock Advertising Ltd* 2018) 2018 can help you argue both sides of a relevant PQ.

- Of the ability to search for subtle differences in the outcomes of what are very similar cases (compare how the factual similarities in *The Wagon Mound 1* helped form the decision in *The Wagon Mound 2* – remoteness of damages/foreseeable loss)

- It is constantly evolving (think of how communication of acceptance has changed since the posting of a letter in *Adams v Lindsell* in 1818 to the receipt of an email in *Thomas v BPE Solicitors* in 2010)

- Of the ability to easily search electronic databases, and furthermore, in what you can search for:

  - Cases that add extra information, examples or explanations to the statutes

  - Cases that have similar facts to the given problem (eg acceptance by email, or advert on the internet)

  - Cases that are legally similar (eg cases that match your problem, such as the method of communication or revocation of contract)

When you are looking for cases, many students spend a lot of time reading and researching cases that are an exact fit for the situation presented in the PQ. This is not a good use of their time because, as stated earlier, the PQs are normally *based* on real cases. The PQ will usually be about an element of law from within an existing case, and the question will not be to write a Case Note. The background situation could include distractions (presented as facts in the PQ but not legally nor factually relevant), elements from other cases (such as a factually similar case where the contract was unilateral not bilateral), or other areas of law (for example, are there any tortious or criminal liabilities mentioned in the PQ – consider Lucy running away from the manor house with a mug in her hand. Despite this being a *prima facie* murder PQ, another crime committed could be theft).

The key message here is that there is not (usually) one case that will exactly match the PQ you are answering. Spend your time more wisely than looking for the 'golden case' which more likely than not does not exist.

Second, your classmates may have chosen a particular case to expand a particular point. Your case may be a completely different one, and you now are doubting whose is the most correct. The answer here is that they are both equally valid. Assuming the same point of law was discussed in court, for example if an advert is an offer or ITT, whether you choose *Carlill v Carbolic Smoke Ball, Fisher v Bell, Harvey v Facey* or *Pharmaceutical Society of GB v Boots* to exemplify and explain the rule is irrelevant.

Only if your PQ related to a connected fact (the sale of land or property in a bilateral contract in *Harvey v Facey*), or to the intention shown by depositing money possibly to pay for claims of catching the flu in a unilateral contract (*Carlill v Carbolic Smoke Ball*) would one case have a stronger persuasive argument than another.

If a law has two elements that need to be proven, and only one of these can be supported by the facts, the argument is lost.

Finally, many students assume that just mentioning a relevant case is enough to secure them a high grade. Unfortunately, this is not true. While you may gain credit for mentioning a factually or legally relevant case, you will score well in the Law section, but not necessarily for the whole essay. The majority of your grades will be weighted towards the Evaluation section.

Case law has three main functions:

* To supplement statutes that have been identified in the Claim (eg under which Act does self-defence escape murder, and how can this be proven?)

* To exemplify factually similar cases (a shop put an item in its window with a price tag)

* To exemplify legally similar cases (the standard of care of someone holding themselves to be an expert)

Writing the Law section

As with most law answers, read the following but allow some flexibility to allow for the nuances of the individual PQ, and the fact there may not be a law, precedent or exception to your point at this current moment in time, so you can use the organisation that follows as a general guide for writing your Law section. This section will work through the process of peeling apart layers of argument, and how these can be used in the Law section.

Following the Claim section, you will have already identified the main and subsidiary legal Claims that exist in the PQ, for example, the area of law is contract, and the focus of the PQ is whether a contract was formed, and if so, with whom was an offer first accepted.

The general Claim needs to be clearly identified in the first section before going into the Law in any detail.

The Law section expands upon the Claims already identified and adds detail of why or why not an offence has been committed, or if a contract has or hasn't been formed. The detail comes from sources such as Acts, common law definitions, and case law.

Your research will have shown you sources which support, partly support or disprove a Claim from the PQ. These grey areas need to be identified, before they will be explained and expanded upon in the Evaluation.

Tip: A common error is to write everything that you know about the law of contract formation, rather than addressing the specific circumstances in the question. This may seem an obvious point, but students who may not fully understand the law or the PQ or don't have confidence in the accuracy of their Claims will tend to lack clarity and focus in their answers.

In the organisation of Law section that follows, note that not all elements are needed, and some may need more attention than others, depending on the PQ. For example, a PQ on murder with a sub-question on self-defence clearly requires the student to address this aspect in greater detail.

For a murder PQ where the question asks if any criminal charges could be brought against the defendant, the organisation could be:

Organisation of Law section

General claim or legal statement and/or definition

Use a source with an outcome that is relevant to the PQ, and lead on to a point of legal/factual similarity/difference or contention/argument

Specific exceptions to the rule/cases with legal or factual conflicts

If discussing a line of cases to show similarities/differences, or how a legal principle has developed over the years, relate later cases to your general statement. Don't just write a list of legal principles/cases

Possible defences

A summary of the significance of the point(s) of law raised

Figure 2.14 Organisation of Law section

The cases you choose to include should be drawn from those resulting from your research which are:

- The first precedent or decisions from the highest court of legally similar cases

- The *obiter* statement (judge's verbal decision) of those cases

- The most factually similar to your PQ

By referring back to the **Task B18** on page 41, the thorough research completed in the Claims stage provides a good basis for the identification of Law. The irrelevant (sub) Claims from **Task B13 (grouped)** have been omitted to produce a more focussed framework. This student's key arguments are highlighted with a tick (✓):

> *Tip*: The same idea can be used for the individually listed relevant Claims identified.

(Sub) Claims (and point number) *Question to be answered*	Law (case or statute) and notes
The nature of the advert (2, 4, 5) *Is the advert an Offer or Invitation to Treat?*	*Carlill v Carbolic Smoke Ball* – an advert may be an offer if it is sufficiently certain, shows intent, limited stock. *Partridge v Crittenden* a magazine ad was ITT unless made by manufacturer (✓)
Purpose of the correspondence (4, 6, 8, 9, 10, 12, 14, 15) a. (if ad is offer) *Is Peter's email a counter-offer or is it merely a request for information?* b. *If a request for information, then is Jack's letter of 12th May acceptance?* c. (accept) *When is the acceptance deemed to have been made?* d. (revoke) *When is the revocation deemed to have been received?*	a. *Hyde v Wrench* The change in price cancelled the previous prices. b. *Stevenson v McLean* Request for further information does not cancel earlier offer. c. *Thomas v BPE Solicitors* Office hours receipt rule applies to emails. Instant acceptance once sent up to 6pm d. *Tinn v Hoffman* Method of acceptance was stipulated in the offer, but acceptable alternatives are allowable if as fast AND *Routledge v Grant* Revocation at any time before acceptance (*Routledge v Grant*) (✓)
Communication methods (6, 7, 8, 10, 11, 12, 13, 14, 16)	*Adams v Lindsell* Letter of acceptance posted, and deemed to have formed a contract at the time of posting

continued . . .

cont.

(Sub) Claims (and point number) *Question to be answered*	Law (case or statute) and notes
	Quenerduaine v Cole The required speed of acceptance can be implied by the means of the offer. *Byrne v Van Tienhoven* A postal revocation was sent before an instant telegram of acceptance. (✓) Acceptance was received first so contract was formed.
The timings of the communications (7, 13, 15)	*Hyde v Wrench* Only the last offer is capable of being accepted. See *Thomas* and *Byrne*

In the Law section, you cannot draw any conclusions about the PQ as you haven't yet discussed the facts, as this will be done in the Evaluation. Your conclusion will therefore be at the end of the Evaluation and further summarised in Outcome.

Signposting language for Law

Using words to introduce and signpost the reader to what is about to be said is a good way to give your content structure and make your points clearer. Figure 2.15 is a non-exhaustive list of four types of signposting that are mainly used in the Law section to begin a sentence and to link two sentences. Do not become over-reliant on them as beginning every sentence with a signal word can make your work seem mechanical and unnatural.

Comparing	Adding	Conceding	Exemplifying
In both cases,...	In addition,... / Additionally,...	However,...	For example
On the one hand... / On the other hand...	Moreover,...	... although...	... such as
... whereas...	Furthermore,...	Even though, ...	...illustrated by...
Although...	Also,...	Despite...	For instance,...
There are several similarities between...	...besides which...	Despite the fact that...	
Nevertheless, ...	...in addition to which...	Notwithstanding...	
Likewise,...		Nevertheless,...	
Similarly,...		Conversely,...	
While... / ...whilst...		The alternative argument is...	

Figure 2.15 Signposting language for Law

End of Law chapter questions

Task B24 – The main types of legal authorities are listed. Rank them in order of most to least persuasive.

1   Case law

2   Case law from other jurisdictions

3   Journal articles

4   Legal commentaries

5   Legislative papers

6   Public policy arguments

7   Statutes

Task B25 – Rank which of these imaginary sources would be the most authoritative for Jack's PQ.

Contractlaw.com

Davies, J., 'Contract Termination' [2019] Journal of Contracts 4864

Department for Trade and Business, *Doing Good Business Online* (ABJ 57, 2019)

Jones v SneakersReseller247 [2019] QB 7942

Joseph Smith, *The Australian Law of Contracts* (3rd edn, Any Publisher 2021)

Sales of Goods Act 2015

Task B26 – Which of these search terms are the most suitable for Jack's PQ?

offer   consideration   implied terms   termination
mistake   acceptance   revocation   warranty
damages   intent   unilateral offer   compensation
repudiation   offeror   breach of contract   good faith

Task B27 – Which search terms would you use for Jack's PQ?

Task B28 – The four sentences of this Law paragraph have been jumbled up. Look back at the box on page 51 for help to correct the order. Citations have been noted to show their positioning only.

1   In *Hyde v Wrench* CITATION the court held that there was no contract. The claimant rejected the defendant's offer when he gave a new offer.

2   If the offeree claims acceptance but attempts to alter the terms of the original offer or add new terms, he shall be deemed to have rejected the original offer and made a counter-offer.

3   One definition of acceptance is that an offeree finally and unconditionally accepts the terms and conditions offered by the offeror. CITATION

4   Cancelling and invalidating an original offer means it cannot be accepted again.

Task B29 – Read back over the preceding Law paragraph. While the content there is correct, you probably realise that it doesn't flow very well, or it's a bit clunky to read. What it needs is signpost words (otherwise known as discourse markers, conjunctions or linking words). Where can the three linking words that follow be placed to improve the flow and connection of the paragraph?

Hint: Remember they can go at the beginning or in the middle of the end of sentences, and punctuation may need to be changed. Academic writing tends not to use *Because* to begin sentences.

For example	Therefore	Because

> *Tip:* Use discourse markers/signposting language with caution. Many students overuse linking words as they mistakenly believe they are carefully guiding the reader though their points. In fact, incorrect usage or over-relying on them shows the reader that you are unable to choose when they are needed.

Task B30 – Identify the purpose of each of the sentences from **Task B28** and match them to the descriptions that follow.

a   Explain the source's significance to the PQ/General ruling

b   Introduce the point of contention, argument or exception, or possible defences

c   Make a legal statement/Overarching general claim

d   Reference an authority

Task B31 – The Law paragraph from **Task B28** has been further developed. Rearrange the sentences into the correct logical and fluent order, referring to the box of page 51 if needed. Consider the topic of each sentence if you need help ordering.

1   Although there is no precedent, some commentators CITATION argue that it is possible for the offeree to withdraw the acceptance through a quicker form of communication, possibly resulting in a situation where the offeror knows about the withdrawal before the acceptance.

2   For example, in *Hyde v Wrench* CITATION the court held that there was no contract because the claimant rejected the defendant's offer when he gave a new offer.

3   However if an offeree accepts and then asks about final terms or possibility of negotiation, it is not a counter-offer and the contract is deemed to be valid at this point CITATION.

4   If the offeree claims acceptance but attempts to alter the terms of the original offer or add new terms, he shall be deemed to have rejected the original offer and made a counter-offer.

5   In addition, an offer cannot normally be withdrawn once it is accepted ^{CITATION} although there are exceptions, such as withdrawal by post ^{CITATION}.

6   One definition of acceptance is that an offeree finally and unconditionally accepts the terms and conditions offered by the offeror ^{CITATION}.

7   Therefore cancelling and invalidating an original offer means it cannot be accepted again.

Task B32 – Can you identify any additional discourse markers in the previous, more developed Law paragraph? Where are they situated within each sentence? What is their purpose?

Task B33 – [Advanced task] Are there any **signposts** in **Task B31** that could be removed to improve the flow?

Task B34 – Identify the purpose of each of the Law sentences in **Task B31**.

a   Add further (point of law/fact) arguments from an additional source

b   Develop a point of law/fact from another source

c   Develop the point from the additional source

d   How is the source's outcome relevant to the PQ. Follow on to the point of contention/argument

e   Make a legal statement

f   Reference an authority to support the preceding point

g   Summarise all the sources' facts and outcomes

Task B35 – Look back at your answers to **Task B21**. Which of these seminal cases do you think are the most relevant to *Jack v Peter*?

Task B36 – Regarding the *Jack v Peter* case, which of these sources (a–h) would you consider as being the best suited to discussing ITT or offer?

• The first precedent or decisions from the highest court [imaginary cases]

   a)   *Colin Watchseller v Ronald Watchbuyer* [2016] EWCA Civ 999 (England & Wales Court of Appeal)

   b)   *David Watchseller v James Watchbuyer* (1840) 2 Beav 777 (Beavan's Chancery Reports)

   c)   *David Watchseller v James Watchbuyer* [1960] 1 WLR 111 (Weekly Law Reports)

- The *obiter dictum* (judge's verbal decision) fits your PQ's gaps

  d) "If I advertise to the world that my dog is lost, and that anybody who brings the dog to a particular place will be paid some money, are all the police or other persons whose business it is to find lost dogs to be expected to sit down and write me a note saying that they have accepted my proposal? Why, of course, they at once look [for] the dog, and as soon as they find the dog they have performed the condition." *Carlill v Carbolic Smoke Ball Ltd* [1892] EWCA Civ 1 (Bowen LJ) –

- The most factually similar to *Jack v Peter*

  e) *Fisher v Bell* – flick knife for sale in the window. Offer made when presented to cashier

  f) *Hyde v Wrench* – a counter-offer cancels the original offer

  g) *Partridge v Crittenden* – adverts are ITTs due to a limited number of items available for sale

  h) *R v Nedrick* – *mens rea* in murder

Task B37 – Match the brief statement in a student's answer (1–5) with the organisational structure (a–e) for a murder PQ with a Claim of self-defence.

Organisation of Law section	Student's answer
a General claim or legal statement and/or definition	1 Arguments of what is "proportionate" and what is "reasonable" self-defence, with case law to support
b Use a source with an outcome that is relevant to the PQ, and lead on to a point of legal/ factual similarity/difference or contention/argument	2 Case – self-defence against a burglar Case – self-defence in the household Case – self-defence when a household visitor became aggressive and picked up a knife
c Specific exceptions to the rule/ cases with legal or factual conflicts [If discussing a line of cases to show similarities/differences, or how a legal principal has developed over the years, relate later cases to your general statement.]	3 Self-defence allows reasonable force in defence of self, property, another person, prevention of crime (include relevant defence only)
d Possible defences	4 What is needed to be shown to fulfil self-defence requirements
e A summary of the significance of the point(s) of law raised	5 Common law definition of murder. Elements of self-defence

Note that very little time will be spent addressing the requirements for murder if the question focuses of self-defence as, presumably, the factual occurrence of murder is not contentious and is accepted by both parties. As such, the common law definition of murder, and definitions of *mens rea* and *actus reus* are excluded.

Alternative note-making styles

Next is a set of cases on a general contract law PQ. If you are unfamiliar with any of these, a quick internet search (or law database if you are a university student) of the case parties will give you a wide choice of summaries, opinions and full judgments.

> *Tip:* As you remember certain cases that may (or may not) be relevant, write them down. You can always discard them at a later stage.

Your research on the exemplar case may bring up the following sources (in no particular order) written in a *linear* style (figure 2.16).

Research notes for Offer and Acceptance Problem Question

Law
Consumer Rights Act 2015

Case law – Relevant CASES
Is the advert an ITT or Offer?
Partridge v Crittenden – advert in magazine is ITT
Carlill v Carbolic Smoke Ball – evidence to be bound = offer

Communication
Entores v Miles Far East Corp – instantaneous communication – contract complete when received by offeror
Adams v Lindsell – acceptance of offer – accepted immediately upon posting
Yates v Pulleyn – offeree can choose speediest method if not stated/unclear in advert

Revocation
Byrne & Co v Van Tienhoven – offers can't be revoked after acceptance (BUT commentators disagree and state exceptions)
Mondial Shipping v Astarte – message left on answering machine, offer revoked depending on when machine states the message will be listened to (does it state business hours)

Case law – Relevant FACTS
Establishing when communication is received
Thomas v BPE Solicitors – business email – sent in evening, received in office working hours

Treatises
Treitel on the Law of Contract – the elements to form a contract (offer, acceptance, consideration, intention)

Figure 2.16 Linear notes

The following section is to show you some other note taking systems that can be used (Figures 2.17–2.19). Each has their own pros and cons, so give each style a go and see what you think works best for you. Take an idea from one style and try it in another. There is no right or wrong way.

Source	Point (Claim underlined)	Use (Factual or Legal link)
Treitel on the Law of Contract	Have the 4 elements to form a contract been met?	Factual link. Only consideration missing in PQ
Partridge v Crittenden; *Carlill v Carbolic Smoke Ball*	**Is advert an ITT/offer?** advert in magazine is ITT evidence to be bound = offer	Factual and Legal link. To discuss the factual difference and consequences of if ITT or offer.
Entores v Miles Far East	**Communication** instantaneous communication – contract complete when received by offeror	Factual link with PQ. Peter sent instant message (email)
Adams v Lindsell	acceptance of offer – accepted immediately upon posting	Law link. Peter revokes via post
Yates v Pulleyn	offeree can choose speediest method if not stated in ad	Law link. No method stated in ad
Byrne & Co v Van Tienhoven	**Revocation** offers can't be revoked after acceptance	Law link. If received (*Entores*) cannot be revoked BUT *Treitel* disagrees and state exceptions
Mondial Shipping v Astarte	message left on answering machine, offer revoked depending on when machine states the message will be listened to (does it state business hours?)	Revocation is possible
Thomas v BPE Solicitors	**Establishing when communication is received** business email – sent in evening, received in office working hours	Factual. Time of email not given. Unclear if courts decide private people check emails more/less/as often

Figure 2.17 Tabular notes

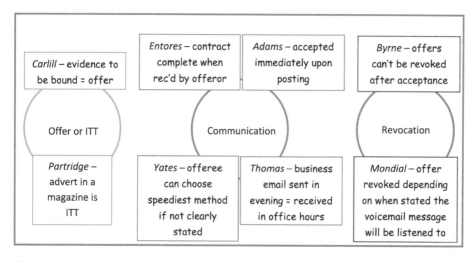

Figure 2.18 A mind map

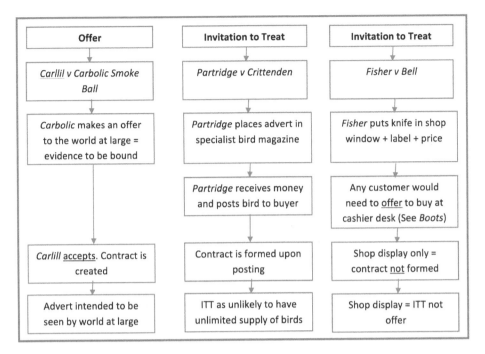

Figure 2.19 A flowchart

Self-check – Alternative note-making styles

Task B38 – The research notes that follow have been organised By Issue. Write the most appropriate subheading in the spaces before the cases by reading the short commentary to guide you.

RESEARCH NOTES FOR OFFER AND ACCEPTANCE PROBLEM QUESTION

Law

Definition of contract isn't defined in law. Refer to *Treitel*

Consumer Rights Act 2015 [no obligation to disclose faults]

11(2) of Electronic Commerce Regs – internet contracting (not email exchanges) take place "once recipients are able to access them".

Cases

a _____

    Partridge v Crittenden – advert in magazine is ITT

    Carlill v Carbolic Smoke Ball – evidence to be bound = offer

---

continued . . .

cont.   b   _____

    Brinkibon v Stahag – telexed acceptance

    Entores v Miles Far East – instantaneous comms – contract complete when received by offeror

    c   _____

    Adams v Lindsell – acceptance of offer – accepted immediately upon posting

    Yates v Pulleyn; Tinn v Hoffman – offeree can choose speediest method of acceptance if not stated/unclear in advert acceptance

    Thomas v BPE Solicitors – business email – sent in evening, received in working hours

    d   _____

    Byrne & Co v Van Tienhoven – offers can't be revoked after acceptance (BUT commentators disagree and state exceptions)

    Mondial Shipping v Astarte – message left on answering machine, offer revoked depending on when machine states the message will be listened to [in commercial contracts]

Having done the initial research, you must now select sources of information that are less relevant or persuasive than others, so only the most appropriate sources of information are included in your answer. All the sources uncovered are important, but you must answer the problem presented, meaning the discerning student will be able to discard those sources of less relevance to the given problem.

In terms of your researching cases, there is little discussion value in our PQ regarding revocation of contract other than on communication and timings, so minimal time will be spent on them regardless of the order you choose in your answer.

Task B39 – Some of the planned legal sources seem irrelevant to the given PQ. Which do you consider to be poor selections by the student?

Also, think about the logical order of your argument. It would be illogical to discuss communication timings before the communication method; likewise, discussion of revocation is only relevant if the offer has firstly been accepted.

Sometimes you will cite the facts or give the rationale of a particular case to support your point, but on other occasions it will be necessary to go into more details, for example where conflicting cases apply to your PQ. For instances where there is no dispute, such as where an offer has been undisputedly accepted, a citation can be made briefly.

Task B40 – Next are the sentence types that are normally seen in the Law section of a PQ answer. Reorder them so that they are presented in the most persuasive and logical order. Not all may be needed for every answer dependent on the nature of your PQ.

ORGANISATION OF LAW SECTION

Briefly recap the Claim to be discussed from the PQ

A summary of the significance of the point(s) of law raised

General claim or legal statement and/or definition

If discussing a line of cases to show similarities/differences, or how a legal principal has developed over the years, relate later cases to your general statement. Don't just write a list of legal principles/cases.

Specific exceptions to the rule/cases with legal or factual conflicts

Possible defences

Use a source with an outcome that is relevant to the PQ, and lead on to a point of legal/factual similarity/difference or contention/argument

---

Task B41 – Read the example Law paragraph that follows, and identify the different stages mentioned in the preceding box.

A BASIC PROBLEM QUESTION ON CONTRACT – EXAMPLE LAW PARAGRAPH – BY ISSUE

Is the advert an ITT or offer?

To establish the nature of the advert, courts would need to evaluate whether the advert was meant to induce parties into negotiation, or whether the offeror by signing is stating they are willing to be bound by the terms of the contract. There is no legal definition of what is an advert or an ITT, though key cases are helpful in distinguishing between the two. In *Carlill v Carbolic Smoke Ball*, a unilateral contract was held to be capable of acceptance without communication to that effect as the advert was to the world at large. Advertisements are normally considered ITTs (*Partridge v Crittenden*) for two main reasons: first, the wording of the advert lacks the required details needed by the offeror to make an informed decision, and second, the offeree normally has a limited supply of stock. It would therefore follow that the advert would be seen as an ITT by the courts.

Task B42 – Now identify the organisational stages in the Law section that follows.

A BASIC PROBLEM QUESTION ON CONTRACT – EXAMPLE LAW PARAGRAPH – BY CLEO

Method of acceptance

Peter sends Jack an email offering £2800 for the watch, which Jack is free to accept or reject. To be effective, any acceptance must be communicated to the offeror, which Jack does, by post, on the 12th.

In bilateral contracts, acceptance can be in any form as long as it is communicated to the offeree (*Taylor v Laird* citation). Here, a ship's captain voluntarily gave up his position and worked as a crew member on the return journey without telling or asking his employer. Upon return, he tried to claim wages, but it was held that he had not entered into a contractual agreement with the defendant and thus was unable to claim wages. Where the offer states a specific method must be used which is not adhered to, there is no contract (*Eliason v Henshaw* citation). Here, it was a term of the offer that an acceptance was to be sent to a specific company branch, but the plaintiff sent it to another branch. The plaintiffs received the acceptance and replied stating the same, but as they had not been correctly informed of their intention, had bought goods elsewhere. When the plaintiffs' delivery was not accepted, they unsuccessfully sued.

However, this American case seems at odds with English law where an alternative but equally speedy method of acceptance is used (*Tinn v Hoffman* citation) and that the offeror's objective remains (*Manchester Diocesan Council for Education v Commercial & General Investments Ltd* citation). It would seem that Jack's sole objective is to receive offers, so any specific reasons of limiting risk or for proof of tracking appear weak arguments.

Where no method of acceptance is given, but is implied, such as an online advert as in the instant case, it would seem logical that an email sent within the platform's forum or an address is copied and pasted into Peter's own email provider, is replied to in the same media. Additionally, *Quenerduaine v Cole* citation found that the speed of acceptance can be deduced from the medium of the offer, therefore an offer made by email should be replied to by equally expeditious means. This could be due to the nature of the goods being sold (ie it is a perishable good), or subject to price fluctuations or available for only a short time (*Chitty on Contracts* citation) none of which are relevant to Jack's watch.

cont.   In the given case, it would be difficult for Jack to justify his use of the
postal rule having received an offer via email, and it is therefore likely
that a court would find that at this point he had accepted the offer and intended
the offer to be accepted at that time. Whether or not he had communicated that
acceptance to Peter (as per *Taylor v Laird*) would be difficult to adjudicate as Peter
would no doubt argue that his offer should have been emailed back, whereupon
he would be unable to revoke his earlier offer.

Communication of revocation . . .

Evaluation

In this chapter you will learn how to:

- Best present your argument
- Identify the purpose and structures within an Evaluation section
- View the approach of opposite counsellors in their evaluation of the facts
- Argue on the facts and the law using previously discussed cases
- Use previously found research to write the Law section
- Identify the organisation and purposes of a sample Evaluation section
- Improve sample material through synthesising multiple texts
  - And have an end of chapter test

The third stage of the CLEO process is to relate the laws you have explained in the
previous section with the given situation. In other words, the factual analysis of the
PQ in light of the discussed law. Having planned before writing, you'll be clear why
each case and law was idenified in the Law section.

Even though the Law section may be more difficult in terms of time and effort
compiling research notes, it is the Evaluation which shows your legal abilty.

Here, you are making your thoughts about the relevance of the legal sources clear
to the reader. This means that you must explain how your given facts may (or may
not) meet the 'objective standards' identified in the Law section.

Image that you go to a lawyer about a dispute, and the information you get in the
meeting is just the history of previous cases (ie precedent). You would not be very
happy with your counsel as you would leave having no idea how this would be
relevant to *your* legal problem.

For the same reason, an Evaluation section would be incomplete without a Law section, and Law would be irrelevant without its complementary Evaluation.

A reminder:

Law = What does the legislation/case law say (eg what is negligence)?

Evaluation = law + scenario (eg do your client's actions constitute negligence?)

The facts may vary from one PQ to another, but the basic structure remains the same. By being explicit about the question, you can be explicit about the answer by using your legal judgement, but they must link and be logical.

The best way to make sure your argument follows a logical line of reasoning which is coherent and cohesive is to plan. By preparing an outline argument, the structure of your points and joined-up thinking will become clearer in your Law and Evaluation sections, meaning you writing will automatically become a lot clearer, rather than being disattached or fragmented if sufficient planning hasn't been done.

There are sample sheets on how to plan, think and link and connect in Part D.

Tip: The L section is how the law applies to all people, while the E section is how the law applies to the parties in the PQ.

In general academic English, your points will need to oppose and be stronger than your opponent's statements, reasoning, logic and research.

Critically, always identifying the central Claim (what is it exactly that's being argued) then, from strongest to weakest, by:

- Refuting the accuracy (ie finds the mistake and explains why it's mistaken)
  - Requires evidence to show their stance is wholly wrong
  - Opponents can still cling onto an opinion even in the face of contradicting evidence.
- Counter-arguing statements
  - Find a weak link in the opposite evidence, relevance or reasoning
  - Back up with your own reasoning and/or supporting evidence
  - Reason strongly to demonstrate your own points
- Partially conceding
  - Concede an opponent's point or an element of their position
  - Opponents can still cling onto an opinion even in the face of contradicting evidence.

EXAMPLE ARGUMENTATIVE TYPES

My stance – The bridge between England and Wales should no longer be free in order to generate income for the Welsh government to spend on projects such as infrastructure. Its customers would be the vast number of paying commuters, tourists, haulage lorries and business travellers.

Central Claim – Income from tolls goes directly to infrastructure projects, Welsh government has jurisdiction to spend that income wherever it chooses, consider cost and frequency of each car/bus/lorry that pays to cross the bridge.

Your opposing stance – The Prince of Wales bridge between England and Wales should remain toll-free becuase tolls stop the free flow of traffic, increase travel times, and add an unnecessary financial burden on commuters, tourists and transportation companies.

Using those three rebuttal types, I could counter your stance by:

Refuting the accuracy of your statement "*financial burden on . . . transportation companies*"

When tolls existed on the bridge, the majority of transportation companies displayed a pass in their windscreen, renewable annually. Annual passes were cheaper than the cost of paying daily. Regular users (eg buses and lorries) therefore benefited by paying annually.

Counter-arguing against the irrelevance of "*stop the free flow of traffic*"

Using existing technology (such as number plate recognition), advance purchasing allows travel through designated toll kiosks without stopping. The technology existed years ago for vehicles who displayed their badge in their windows, which was picked up by cameras allowing lorries and buses to pass without significant slowing down.

Tip: You can *rebut* an argument by stating, proving or showing it is wrong, but the correct verb to disagree or oppose is to *refute*. The correct usage is that you can rebut my subjective claim that Michael Jordan is the greatest basketall player ever by offering the names, stats and details of other players, but a claim that gravity is a force away from the earth can be refuted by dropping an object and watching it fall to the ground, so successfully disproving. According to Jowitt's Dictionary of English Law (5th edn) (2019) *to rebut* is to reply, contradict, defeat or take away the effect of something. Rebuttal is normally the intended word – acceptable synonyms include *dispute*, *deny* or *reject*.

> **cont.** To <u>partially concede</u> *"increase travel times"*
>
> For travellers who haven't bought a travel pass in advance (who will mostly be a small number of tourists without knowledge of the toll bridge), there will be a small time delay whilst paying. However, tourists would not disapprove of paying for a well-kept bridge and smooth road that brings employment and wealth into the local area.

Task B43 – Can you think of any arguments to refute the accuracy, irrelevance and conceding examples?

> *Tip*: There are whole books devoted to the philosophies of argument creation which are not covered here. Interested students should research syllogisms; fallacies; logic; adductive, inductive and deductive reasoning; and Atticus' patterns of persuasion: ethos, pathos and logos.

Writing the Evaluation section

In legal argument, in basic terms, here are some main ways in which you can start to shake the foundations of an opponent's argument. In the case of PQs, use these points to show how your argument can be made strongly and with the most persuasion, be aware of points that your opposing lawyer will make, and how these can be shown to be unsubstantiated by:

* Logically and clearly explaining connections between topics
* Clearly and directly stating causes, effects, problems and solutions
* Generalising critically, accurately and impartially
* Referencing disputed facts from an authoritiative source
* Refuting warrants (ie what links the legal grounds to the claim)
* Checking if the legal backing was dubious, outdated, appealed, or if judges dissented
* Challenging definitions (vocabulary) or language (eg modal verbs)
* Refuting grounds (ie is there misrepresentation, surpression of a fact, missing evidence)
* Falsely assuming
* Presenting ambiguous or unclear meanings
* Challenging legal authorities, findings and previous judgments
* Contradicting how the same law has been applied in a series of cases

> *Tip*: See https://grist.org/series/skeptics/ for hundreds of arguments against global warming skeptics' points. Consider which type of argument they are presenting to support their views.

However, legal English and PQs have both structures and are genres in their own rights, therefore you also need to incorporate elements that are expected of you when writing and evaluating.

Your goal in legal Evaluation is to explain to the reader that:

- Each element of your client's case can be argued by the facts
  - For example, the letter was incorrectly addressed, the member of staff wasn't an employee at the time, it was an ITT (Invitation to Treat) not an offer.
  - If a law has two elements that need to be shown, your argument is lost if you can only prove one.
- Some element of your client's case can be defeated because it either:
  - Fails to reach the legal standard put forward in the Law section
    - For example, a factor in defining the unlawful act hasn't been reached, such as the multiple elements needed to show contract formation, *mens rea* or allowable 'passing off'.
  - Is argued against successfully be the defendant
    - An example could be that a company's senior management was liable for corporate manslaughter due to 'substantial' duty of care failings. As 'substanital' isn't defined in the Corporate Manslaughter And Corporate Homicide Act 2007, it could be argued failings were minor and not systematic.
    - In defamation cases, a number of allowable defences have been provided for by the Defamation Act 2013.

Even though CLEO questions generally require you to advise one party, you must consider the validity of all the claims asserted as well as the defences of both parties. While playing the part of an 'advocate', it is important that you recognise arguments that may weaken your position, but then it is even more important that you can demonstrate how and why they do not apply to your case.

You must try to be as clear as possible in your discussion of the points. Very often, students skirt around the issues without being explicit about how the laws affect the PQ. Even the best students can struggle with this element, so you must guide your reader in a logical way through the arguments, so the Evaulation section can be deconstructed into these component parts:

THE AIMS OF AN EVALUATION SECTION

- Start with the general law and become more specific
- With each law, explain how this affects the case of your 'client' in the PQ (be this supporting or conflicting)
- Be as clear as you can as to how the action in the PQ relates to the parties
- Explain how this point sways any bearing a court may have when making a ruling

Remember that no one will think; process and interpret the PQ, facts and law; and evaluate the law in exactly the same way as you, so you must guide your reader through your thinking by being as clear, logical and methodical as you can.

And you should do so without repeating the facts of the cases given in the Law section.

> *Tip*: Even if the examiner disagrees with the outcome you have advised your client in contentious claims the better grades will be awarded to those who clearly outline the law, and how this relates to the case at hand through detailed and accurate Evaluation of the facts.

Signposting language for Evaluation

As earlier, using words to introduce to and tell the reader what is about to be said is a good way to give your content structure and make your points clearer. Figure 2.20 is a non-exhaustive list of four types of signposting that are mainly used in the Evaluation section to begin a sentence and to link two sentences.

Introducing a case/statute	Refering back to the PQ	Beginning to evaluate	Exemplifying
In both cases,...	In the given case...	Applying this principle...	For example,...
A similar/different rationale is used...	In the instant case...	In this type of case,...	For instance,...
In making a distinction between...	As mentioned above...	In the cases above...	...such as...
The court held that in [case name]...	In this type of case,...	With regard to [topic]...	Another example...
Accoding to [Judge], obiter,	In the present case	Despite the fact that...	In [case name]
[Case name] is...		Notwithstanding...	
The X Act (Year) provides that...		On the facts,...	

Figure 2.20 Signposting language for Evaluation

EXAMPLE EVALUATION SECTION – OFFER OR INVITATION TO TREAT?

PQ 1: Anna is selling her car. Bob sees the car and says he'd pay £500 less than the advertised price if he can pay by cheque. Anna says she will think about it. Bob says he will assume she has accepted unless he hears from her otherwise, to which Anna agrees.

On evaluating this claim, you need to note the intention of the parties. You need to establish the existence of an offer before any acceptance.

PQ 2: Anna is selling her car. Bob sees the car and offers £500 less than the advertised price if he can pay by cheque. Anna says she would discount only £200 for payment by cash, or the full asking price by cheque. Bob agrees and says he will assume she has accepted unless he hears from her otherwise, to which Anna agrees.

Despite these two different scenarios, the legal standard remains the same, but you have to identify the nature (type) of the advert, and which elements of contract formation have been met.

PQ 1's Evaluation – (Your position: you think the advert is an ITT.)

You would argue that the request to pay by cheque is for clarification. Assuming Bob didn't later hear from Anna, the unqualified acceptance has no definite contractually binding time. Also, you could mention silence does not amount to acceptance, however with Anna's agreement to this term, a court would be unlikely to allow this argument. The area of dispute would be at which time the contract became effective.

PQ 2's Evaluation – (Your position: you think the advert is an offer.)

If the advert is an offer, Bob's reply would very likely be seen as a counter offer due to the lower price offered. The discount offered for payment in cash could either be seen as acceptance, or another counter-offer. It would unlikely be accepted as an acceptance as there is lack of clarity on the terms (which price had been accepted; the £200 cash discount or full price by cheque), in which case no contract would exist. As in PQ 1, include acceptance by silence being inadmissible, and at what time the contract became legally binding.

Discussion

You would present broadly the same case law whether you believe the advert is an ITT or a contract, that is, to establish whether a contract exists under the elements of a contract.

continued . . .

> **cont.** There's also a case for you to discuss the contractual terms whether a price had actually been agreed, and if this has any bearing on a key term of the contract being uncertain. In PQ 1 and 2, there could be evaluation of acceptance and acceptance through silence, and both evaluations would need to discuss the intention of both parties by assessing Anna's and Bob's statements (or actions) and their contractual significance.
>
> Both PQs would need to identify the problems regarding if there was an offer available to be accepted, and secondly if acceptance of the offer had been completed lawfully.
>
> Parallels are then drawn between the facts of this case and the precedent already discussed in the Law section
>
> **Task**
>
> Consider the similarities between this and two courtroom lawyers where one is arguing the case for the advert to be an ITT, and the other for it to be an Offer.

From the preceding, you should be able to see how the Law remains the same, but the facts of the case have changed to suit the PQ.

> *Tip*: It may be appealing to answer a multi-problem scenario using a CLELE(LE)O structure, however there are several drawbacks to using this system. It is far more logical and clear to the reader to put headings or subsections within each stage.

See page 81–2 for an example of how headings or subsections look in a PQ answer, but remember to meet the formatting style required by your institution.

> *Tip*: A good answer will be able to bring together similarities and/or differences between cases. By arguing through analogies, you will be able to show you are a skilled writer . . . but of course this takes time and effort to master.

How to evaluate

After finishing the Law section, you'll have a good grasp of the Claims in the PQ, and also of the cases that you are using to present your argument. In the Evaluation section, you'll be showing how factual (what happened in the given situation) and legal elements from the PQ can be matched, and how the outcome of these cases was decided.

When you are writing your Evaluation, it would be advisable to follow this approach for each point you wish to make. For example, let's consider some cases relating to the communication methods used during contract negotiations in the context of *Jack v Peter*.

In the given PQ, here are the four communication purposes and corresponding media:

1   Peter emails an offer.

2   Peter revokes the offer by posting a letter.

3   Jack reads the email, and returns by post a letter of acceptance.

4   Jack then receives Peter's letter of revocation.

An example of this would be in our PQ, where there has been instant communication (email), but no case is an exact match to the circumstances. The nearest available is *The Brimnes* where a <u>withdrawal</u> of an offer was made by another mode of instant communication (telex), so there are two discussion points.

The first would be whether the nature of communication sent by email has any influence of the PQ. In *The Brimnes*, the nature of the communication was a withdrawal of an offer, but in the given PQ, Peter's emailed communication was a counter-offer or acceptance (a point that would need to be discussed before this worked example of an Evaluation).

Once this is discussed, the second point could be to discuss if the findings and definitions of instant communication could be applied to our PQ, and the evaluation of the strength of that argument, development of technology, speed of communication and different working patterns compared to the precedent case of 1975.

One way to organise your thoughts on how to evaluate a law or case it to break it down into the pertinent points, or the variables between one case and the next. By separating the Claims in a case, you can extract the key differences in order to discuss and evaluate them.

Let's consider *Adams v Lindsell* (the postal rule) as a potential case for use in the evaluation and consider how this compares and contrasts with our own *Jack v Peter* example.

Adams v Lindsell's method of offer (ie the first variable) was by post. At the moment, this bears little help to our case because the initial offer was made by email. In the same case, however, the method of acceptance (variable two) was also by post which now bears a factual similarity. A third variable (calling it purpose) was to accept an offer. The legal outcome was that acceptance of an offer is formed when a letter is posted.

There may well be more variables needed to distinguish one case and the next as the complexity of your cases increases, but this is a good way to start analysing and considering the differences of your sources.

Tip: An element of this differentiation will have already been done in your Law section. You can choose to do this deconstruction then or in the Evaluation. The same processes will apply.

Task B44 – Filling in the gaps where necessary, decide on the suitability of each case to support the *Jack v Peter* PQ, and consider how each case can help your evaluation by fact or legal principle.

	Method of offer	Method of acceptance	Communication purpose	Contract formed when	Legally and/or factually similar to *Jack v Peter*?
Jack v Peter	Email	Post	Accept an offer		
Adams v Lindsell	Post		Accept an offer		
Dunlop v Higgins		Post	Accept an offer		
Holwell Securities v Hughes				Upon receipt of letter when it's a contractual term	
Entores		Telex/Fax		Acceptance was received.	
Stevenson v McLean	Post	Post		When letter is delivered	
The Brimnes			Accept an offer	Received by offeror at that time and place	
Thomas v BPE Solicitors		Email			

Your research will have uncovered Law which clarifies the area of law, adds extra information, gives examples or further explanations to the statutes or cases, but additionally:

• Is legally similar, for example, the non-contentious Claims of:

    • The elements needed to show if the advert is an ITT or Offer

    • The nature of a breached term (a condition, warranty or innominate term), a short description and precedent to discuss

- A judge's *obiter dictum* (spoken words), such as the definition of defamation (*Sim v Stretch*)

- Where a previous case related to instant communication

- Has similar facts to your PQ, such as:

  - The acceptance was received by email, or the advert was seen on the internet, and is therefore usually an ITT (*Partridge v Crittenden*).

  - If the contract is unilateral rather than bilateral (*Carlill v Carbolic Smoke Ball*)

  - A man deliberately set fire to a house just to frighten the occupant, but they were killed. Did he have sufficient *intention* to be tried for murder? (*R v Nedrick*)

  - The degree of skill needed to perform a task or service (*Wells v Cooper; Bolam v Friern Hospital Management Committee*)

Note that any factual similarities you have will need to be discussed in the context of your PQ. It is unlikely that there will be an exact match of the PQ and a real-life case, but more likely to be based on real events, with some facts changed to help aid discussion.

State upfront if there are no facts to support a required element.

A discussion point which would show good critical and analytical knowledge would be whether Peter was wise to post a letter of revocation having already emailed. Your discussion here would be the problems he may have caused himself, why choose a slower method of communication, why change the method of communication, how could the evaluation be different had Peter changed one of the earlier points, and what precedent is there to support this?

Have a look at the Evaluation excerpt that follows to see how the points made in **Task B44** have been extrapolated and developed to make comparative and contrastive use of the case law identified in the previous section.

A BASIC PROBLEM QUESTION ON CONTRACT – EXAMPLE EVALUATION PARAGRAPH (SECTION ONLY)

Note – it will have already been discussed and concluded that the advert is a bilateral contract, and the advert is an ITT.

This has explicitly been written By Issue in order to identify and extrapolate the relevant sections.

continued . . .

> **cont.**   <u>Method of acceptance</u>
>
> Peter sends Jack an email offering £2800 for the watch, which Jack is free to accept or reject. To be effective, any acceptance must be communicated to the offeror, which Jack does, by post, on the 12th.
>
> Assuming that Jack's acceptance is unqualified, Jack could rely on the postal rule from *Adams v Lindsell*[8] where a contract is concluded once a letter is posted in a post box. However, Peter could argue that having emailed an offer, to receive postal acceptance is unreasonable given the difference in speed of the communication methods, and that the method of communication had changed from that which Peter sent.
>
> Jack's counter-argument would be that he is free to choose the method of communication unless there is a contractual term in the advert which stipulated the method of communication (*Holwell Securities v Hughes*).[9]
>
> In *The Brimnes*[10], the plaintiffs attempted to withdraw from a contract via the instant communication method of telex which was sent during office hours and read the next day. The Court of Appeal held that the telex was effective upon receipt as the plaintiff was told it was company practice to read telexes immediately.
>
> In the given case, there is no mention about when Peter's email was read, and there is also some doubt about the application of *The Brimnes* to Jack's situation. Jack is selling a watch as a person, not a corporate entity, so it is therefore questionable whether Jack would reasonably be expected to see and reply to an email during business hours, as a person would tend not to have designated office hours.
>
> However, in the 21st century, many people have email available on their mobile telephones as well as home and work computers, so Peter may try to argue Jack had the opportunity to read his email but chose not to read it. This may be a moot point and a weak argument as despite emails being accessible immediately, Jack is under no obligation to read it despite it not being good business practice, and the nature of business transactions and communications having changed since *The Brimnes* was heard in 1975, and the law has yet to catch up with technology in that sense.
>
> <u>Communication of revocation</u>
>
> As there is not yet any precedent on the use of emailed communication for offer and acceptance, the basic idea remains that any revocation must take place before its acceptance to become valid. An argument Peter may pursue is that by posting a letter of revocation, following the postal rule argument, the letter of revocation was actioned at the moment of posting . . . .

End of Evaluation chapter questions

Task B45 – Consider another case that you are familiar with (or you have just discovered) and consider its suitability for one of the elements discussed, following the *Adams v Lindsell* example.

	Method of offer	**Method of acceptance**	**Communication purpose**	**Contract formed when . . . .**	**Legally and/or factually similar?**
Jack v Peter	Email	Post	Accept an offer		
Adams v Lindsell	Post	Post	Accept an offer	Acceptance letter is posted into a letterbox	

Task B46 – Your PQ client has a contentious case or element. Can that element be argued against in the following ways? (True or false)

- The opposing argument fails to reach the legal standard.
- Facts can be argued against.
- The law is unclear on a legal element.
- Facts can be disputed.
- The judge needs correcting.
- Citing a legally similar case
- Citing a factually similar case

Task B47 – Name the three types of arguments you can make, and order them from strongest to weakest.

1   _____ (strongest)

2   _____

3   _____ (weakest)

Task B48 – Which is the most appropriate structure for writing each topic or element within an Evaluation section?

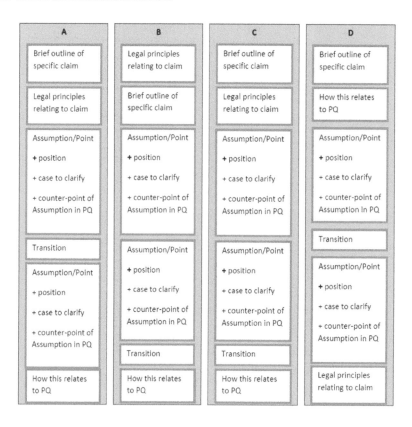

Task B49 – Match the pro-gun statements (1–8) with the relevant anti-gun view (a–h)

1 374 US citizens were killed in mass shootings in 2019.	a But if a thief knows or suspects a homeowner has a gun, they are less likely to target that house, so guns do equal protection.
2 Gun owners are more likely to accidentally shoot their family member than a burglar.	b In my country, it's my legal right to own a gun if I want.
3 Guns don't equal protection – it would be dangerous for a homeowner to stop, say, a burglar in their own home as they wouldn't know if the burglar was armed.	c It's not the gun's fault. People use guns as a tool (farmers), hobbies (sport) and collecting. Getting rid of guns won't stop violent and mentally ill people from shooting.
4 Houses and communities without guns are safer.	d Mass shootings are a wholly different issue to gun ownership.

continued . . .

cont.

5 Japan has some of the strictest gun laws in the world and one of the lowest death rates by guns. To get a gun, you must attend classes, pass a written exam, and complete a shooting range test before going on a register.	e Why does it matter because the majority of gun deaths are suicides?
6 Norway is a gunless and peaceful country.	f Firearms still exist and are needed by the police, and citizens should be allowed to defend themselves.
7 UK has 9th lowest firearm related death rate in the world.	g That's not true. Gun murder still happens regardless of their legal status.
8 Guns are meant to kill and are dangerous. They should be outlawed.	h Thousands of people die every year in car accidents, yet there's no talk of banning cars.

Task B50 – Identify the topic that connects the argument and the counter-argument. What argument style is being used by the eight counter-arguments (a–h) to rebut the original statement? Refutation, rebuttal, counter-argument, concession, or is the counter-argument unsound? One example has been done for you with the topic underlined.

Pairs	Argument style	Topic	Justification
1d	Unsound	There is no link between mass shootings and gun ownership.	There is too big a step to link the number of shootings (yes with a gun) in the whole of a country by mass shootings. Only a weak conclusion or correlation can be drawn.

continued . . .

cont.

Pairs	Argument style	Topic	Justification

Task B51 – Can you think of how you can counter the aforementioned anti-gun views? What research do you think you'd need?

Task B52 – Think of ways you could rebut (argue against) the following positions, the central Claim which of the three styles you use (see **Task B47**) and your argument against each of my points.

My position	Central claim	Counter-point type	Your counter-argument
The death penalty is a good deterrent against serious crimes.			
My employers should have no say in what I post about my private life on social media.			
Children should not be asked by a court which parent they'd like to stay with after a divorce.			
Information on the internet should be freely available to all.			
Marijuana has been decriminalised as a drug, and should now be legalised.			
Governments should have a minimum quota of immigrants.			
Employers shouldn't be forced to employ criminals recently released from prison.			

Task B53 – Read the counter-offer answer written By Issue. Identify the six structural elements from **Task B48** and include their sub-elements (assumption, position, case and rebuttal).

COUNTER-OFFER

Alex decided to accept Bob's offer at 3pm, but wanted the consideration to be paid in cash. The issue here is whether Bob changed the original offer if he paid in cash, or if this created a new offer which needed to be accepted. Under contract law,

---

> | cont. | when the offeror makes an offer to the offeree, the offeror may generally choose to accept or reject it. Once the offer is accepted, it will be subject to contract law. However, the offeree also has the right to bargain where any implied or express terms can be negotiated. Any acceptance of an offer at any stage of negotiation must be consistent with the terms of the offer, and any material alteration or alteration to the terms of the offer by the offeree does not constitute acceptance. *Hyde v Wrench* illustrated that if the offeree is unwilling to accept the offeror's offer, or the offeror changes the conditions of the offer, the offeree can reject or propose a new condition to become a counter-offer. Alex's initial offer to Bob did not specify the terms of payment. When Alex decided to accept Bob's offer, she wanted Bob to pay in cash. If Bob agrees to being paid in cash, then there is no objection and there is no counter-offer. On the other hand, if Bob does not agree to be paid in cash and discusses this with Alex, the key question is whether Alex has added a new term or merely requested clarification. The exact words used by Bob and Alex are not given, but there needs to be a counter proposal ie a specific offer or rejection rather than an answerable question, for example a delivery schedule. In *Stevenson, Jacques & Co v McLean* a telegram requiring clarification of a term was held not to be a counter-offer, so an original agreement remained valid. Without the exact wording, one cannot be certain, although it would likely be held by a court that an enquiry on the method of payment rather than a term on contract would be seen as a request for information. So, Bob can choose to accept or reject Alex's offer of payment in cash. Anything other than acceptance will produce a counter-offer which would need to be accepted in turn by Alex in order to be legally binding.

Task B54 – Notice the change in tense in each element and sub-element. When is past and present tense used?

Task B55 – The sentences used to explain the cases in Assumption 1 (**Task B53**) are poorly written. One word is repeated and overused. Paraphrase and improve the section.

Synthesising

Synthesising is an academic skill which goes beyond a summary (tell me the most important information from a text) and requires multiple summaries from multiple sources to be mixed and combined into one – the synthesis.

It is a powerful skill that can be used for all CLEO sections, particularly the last two. Synthesis is used not when looking at the wider, general view and comment of the PQ, but in the stages when you are pulling together information and sources to form a more specific and focused justification, argument or conclusion.

In law, it is likely that this will take the form of finding the point at which a case departed from its precedent, and how this affects the PQ.

In a PQ about consideration, the legal principles from the following cases clarified (or broke away depending on your argument):

- If a party is contractually bound to perform an act or service, extra benefit cannot be given as this is part of the original contract – *Stilk v Myrick* (1809), unless

- A party performs extra services beyond the original contract – *Hartley v Ponsonby* (1857), or

- Gain an extra benefit, in this case by avoiding a penalty clause – *Williams v Roffey* [1991].

The very quick brief outline plan in Figure 2.21 shows how the Law is summarised, but the Evaluation is synthesised in light of the three legal elements from each case. The Outcome then synthesises and summarises the facts evaluated, and draws a conclusion as to the likely court decision.

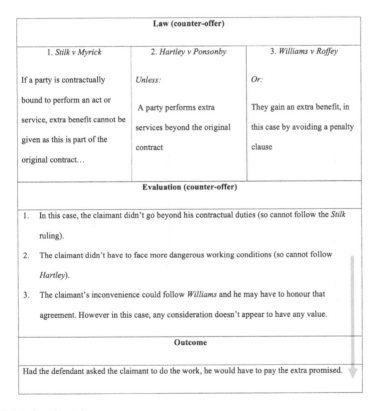

Figure 2.21 Synthesising

The following are cases where the latter case branched away from the precedent set by the former. Considering the argument techniques set out earlier (**Task B47**), how could a student use these cases to a) support a claimant and b) support a defendant? You may have to imagine or search for a PQ in order to give your plan/answer context.

Task B56 (Extension Task) – Plan your answer as synthesising the following cases:

Pao On v Lau Yu Long [1980] and *Williams v Roffey* [1991] following *Ward v Byham* [1956], and

Re McArdle [1951] following *Lampleigh v Braithwaite* (1615)

Outcome

In this chapter you will learn how to:

- Hedge your findings using assertive but cautious words
- Identify the purpose and structures within a sample Outcome section
- Recognise the organisation of an Outcome section
- Review your Outcome compared to the PQ and Claim section
  - And have an end of chapter test

The fourth stage of the CLEO process is where you will ultimately state how a court would decide on the Claims presented in the question. You will need to summarise all the points that you have made in the previous three sections, but you do not need to restate the Claim, Law, nor Evaluation. As a result, the Outcome section is likely to be the shortest.

During your analysis, you will have decided which Laws and Evaluation are the most persuasive in making your arguments, so it's the main points from these that you need to summarise for the reader. You do not need to explain why that party was successful, as this will have already been done in the L and E sections.

As a marker of scripts, I prefer my students' essays to slowly and logically explain their points, which ultimately leads to a finding or conclusion in the Outcome section. The reason is primarily that when an outcome is asserted in the Claim section, the reasons to support the claim are not given at that stage, and may materially be incorrect. When a conclusion is reached at the end of the answer, the area where the law has been applied or misinterpreted can be identified, and thus your law tutors can help with this or suggest a remedy, such as re-reading a particular case. As well as making your text easier to read and following your line of argument, delaying your conclusion until the end neatly summarises your previous arguments, and is delivered in one concise and meaningful section.

Hedging language

Because you are not (yet) a judge, the way that you present your Outcome needs to be fairly guarded and cautious. Just as a lawyer would never say to a client that their case was a certainty, students need to hedge their conclusions to protect against over committing. This can be done using key vocabulary and certain grammar structures and verbs, adverbs, adjectives and nouns, such as that shown in Figure 2.22.

Verbs	appear, assert, assume, claim, doubt, hold, indicate, seem, suggest, tend
Modal verbs	could, have to, may, might, must, ought to, should, will, would
Adverbs	certainly, mostly, often, possibly, probably, sometimes, usually
Adjectives	clear, probable, possible
Nouns	assumption, possibility, probability, tendency
That clauses	It could be argued that…. There is every hope that…
When / If / Should / Unless clauses (most certain to least certain)	If/When a letter was posted, a contract is formed OR A contract is formed if/when the letter was posted OR Should a letter be posted, a contract is formed [Zero conditional] If a letter is posted into a postbox, under the postal rule a contract will be accepted [First conditional] An offer stating a method of deliverty would be accepted if it met that criteria [Second conditional] If the letter had been sent by email and not text message (SMS), it would have been a valid form of acceptance [Third conditional]

Figure 2.22 Hedging language

Note: The word forms can change from one class to another (eg the verb *indicate* can transform into the noun form *indication*) so use this to extend your vocabulary (See vocabulary flashcards on page 192).

You'll also see that the *If*-clauses can be formed by starting with *If* followed by a comma after the object (If + subject1 + verb1 + object1 [comma] subject2 + verb2 + object2). In this case, the condition comes first, then the result.

Alternatively, the two clauses can be flipped and the comma removed (subject2 + verb2 + object2 + if + subject1 + verb1 + object1) so the result comes first then the condition (without a comma).

Task B57 – Complete the following table changing the nouns into verbs and vice versa. See flashcards for ideas on how to present this and expand to include pronunciation, adjective and adverb forms too.

Noun	Verb	Noun	Verb
acceptance		offer	
contract			repudiate
failure			supply
implication			terminate

Task B58 – Rewrite the following *if*-clause sentences so the result/condition changes order in the sentence. Some words and/or word forms may need to be changed or omitted for the sentence to be logical and retain the same meaning. There may be several alternative answers and structures.

We would be grateful if you could send the documents to us at your earliest convenience.	If you could send the documents to us at your earliest convenience, we would be grateful.
I am confident that if the goalkeeper had had a bonus clause in his contract, he would have stayed with the team.	
Had the company secretary not neglected the security of the documents for which he is responsible, we wouldn't have been named in the court summons.	
Legislation introduced in 2000 allows shareholders to be contacted electronically if they give their express permission.	
Should one partner go bankrupt, creditors can pursue the remaining partners for the whole debt.	
Unless directors have given personal guaranteees, they are not liable for the company's debts if they run the company lawfully.	

Signposting language for Outcome

As you know, using words to introduce to and tell the reader what is about to be said is a good way to give your content structure and make your points clearer. The main Outcome section signposts are:

Consequently, In conclusion, Therefore, Thus.

Writing the Outcome section

By now, you will have found and discussed similar cases, examined the strengths and weaknesses of your position in light of existing cases, and made an informed judgement about the merits of your client's claim. Your Outcome shouldn't and needn't inlcude more or new information. Your task here is to summarise the main point, drawing all the discussion from previous sections and paragraphs into one neat, and short, conclusion.

All key information will have already been discussed, so there shouold be no need to introduce new informtion at this late stage. Referencing previously cited research is acceptable but optional, and should be only to exemplify one or two key differentiating factors that are essential to your Outcome.

Tip: It is very rare for the question to contain too much to make it difficult to handle, or too little information to make a judgement on the Outcome. Examiners want an answer, not to unnecessarily trouble you.

A BASIC PROBLEM QUESTION ON CONTRACT – EXAMPLE OUTCOME PARAGRAPH

As Jack placed an ITT, was selling in a personal, not a corporate or professional capacity, he should not be expected to reply to emails within office hours (*The Brimnes*). Therefore, the email offering £2800 for the watch, duly accepted upon posting on 12th May, concludes a valid contract, and Jack will be able to have a claim for breach of contract if Peter refuses his consideration of £2800.

Tip: The final sentences have been guiding the reader towards your final answer. Do not simply repeat this information, but synthesise (ie pull together) all these conclusions and summarise them all in a short but meaningful manner. And don't forget to include your answer if the PQ demands it.

You may feel that this short conclusion is short and incomplete, but CLEO requires nothing excessive in the final section. You have given your opinion on the case, and related it back to the point raised earlier in the essay, so you are completing the circle.

A strange phenomenon of law PQs is that your conclusion may be different from another person's, yet you could both receive the same marks as the grey areas that allow for debate and discussion are deliberately contentious and down to interpretation. That's one of the great (and sometimes frustrating) parts of law!

As long as you have explained the Claims and supported those with legal or factual authority to evaluate the scenario, even if the marker disagrees with your conclusion, you will be scored the same as long as the arguments and cases used are relevant and logical.

Much like conclusions of other essay genres, the Outcome section of a CLEO answer will serve a similar purpose, that is: to tie up the arguments provided which confirm the liability of your client or the other party, dependent on the wording of the PQ.

Given that you will have followed the other sections of a CLEO essay, it will be highly likely that a reader will know, or at least be able to make an educated guess of your advice before reading the Outcome section.

Therefore, the purpose of an Outcome is to make it explicity clear to the examiner that what you have suggested previously forms the basis of solid advice to your client. Second, the clear advice given in Law and Evaluation will probably not be as clear as you think when read by someone else. The Outcome gives a strong cohesion to the rest of the essay, and unequivocally states whether, or to what extent, your client is liable or able to take action against another.

And much like other essay genres, there is a general style that can be used as a guide for answering the Outcome section. Although there is no fixed pattern, the following in Figure 2.23 can be adapted to suit your specific Outcome.

Organisation of OUTCOME section
• A legal statement on the primary Claim(s)
• Summary of main Claim(s) in relation to the discussed legal/factual similarity/difference or contention/argument without repeating the PQ
• Difficulties either party has in proving a point
• Possible remedies
• How a court would likely rule

Figure 2.23 Organisation of Outcome section

Tip: Some examiners read the Claim and Outcome first so that they have an idea of what to expect in the Law and Evaluation section. Before submitting your work, read these two sections and check that the Claim posed has been answered succinctly in the Outcome.

End of Outcome chapter questions

Task B59 – Identify the key elements from Figure 2.23 in the example Outcome paragraph (not all elements are always present).

A good way to check if you've answered the PQ is to evaluate whether, just by reading only the Outcome, you read a summary answer of the (contentious) points from the PQ and from your notes that you can check against (cross-reference). You can use this method to check whether you have answered the question fully, and how clear you have made it to the reader. Looking at the preceding, it can be established that:

> The advert is an ITT.
>   Jack is not a professional seller.
>   Peter's initial offer email isn't deemed to be received until it is read (because he's not a professional seller) – [note this is a very simplistic interpretation of *The Brimnes* as the case will have already been discussed at length].

Despite all the other acts of communication that go on in the PQ, the offer is completed and a contract formed on the 12th. All other permutations and *what ifs* will have been discussed in Law and Evaluation sections.

The advice to Jack is that a contract stands, contract stands, and Peter must fulfil his side of the contract.

Tasks B60–B64 – Identify the key elements of the following Outcome sections and colour-code as earlier (not all five always appear and the order can change to an extent).

TASK B60

In conclusion, it is in A's best interest to honour the initial contract with B, and he should be liable for the costs provided for by the agreement. However, A should be able to pursue a claim against C because A had continued to conduct his side of the contract by performance.

TASK B61

There appears to be two possible outcomes. A could sue B, but it would seem unlikely that B has enough money or insurance cover. Therefore, A could sue S who could be liable for B's actions under vicarious liability. This would likely be the best remedy as B is unlikely to be seen as an employee due to the degree of control of the employer, the nature of the payment and the employment contract.

TASK B62

In pursuing a claim of damages by misrepresentation, Z would be wise to use s. 2(1) of the Act. He would be able to claim for direct losses, and possibly for subsequent losses. An alternative available to him is suing for breach of contract, having relied upon M's expert status and relying upon his specialist advice to make a decision. The courts would balance these claims against M's argument that it was outside the contract, and that Z's previous experience made him less reliant on M's expert claims. While marginal, it would appear that the certainty of numbers and costs in the negotiations shows intention for the contract to proceed.

TASK B63

Sarah is highly likely to be found guilty of murder, and depending on her age at the time of the murder, could expect a sentence starting at 12 years if she was a

---

continued . . .

> **cont.**   minor at the time of the attack, or a minimum of 15 years if she was over 18 years of age.
>
>
> ### TASK B64
>
> It would seem that W's contract with O would more likely be voidable for misrepresentation than for mistake. The difference in *Shogun* and the instant case is that the contract of immediate vicinity was not formed face to face, and therefore W would have to bear his losses. That said, there has been criticism of the 3–2 majority decision in its fairness and the seller's position to better protect himself against risks, so W could be advised to take a risk as O would have been in a better position to uncover his client's dishonesty.

Task B65 – Identify the key claim(s) purely from the five preceding Outcome sections. For example, Jack's Claim (see page 93) would be *Does Jack have a legally binding contract with Peter*. Consider if it were the same scenario and conclusions drawn, but the final words were *Advise Peter*, then the key Claim would be *Is there a way Peter can escape liability for his breach of contract*.

Hint: This is a similar skill used by the barristers who write law reports, so reading such sources will also help with your writing.

Task B66 – Identify all the different types of hedging language used in the Outcomes of **Tasks B60-B64**

SQE writing

Students who have a non-law undergraduate degree can from September 2021 take a UK law conversion test called the Solicitors Qualifying Exam (SQE). This part will concentrate only on the SQE rather than university writing; however because the SQE uses task material similar to that of PQs, you will be directed to and recognise relevant PQ sections where there is crossover.

Writing SQE1 answers

Each of the two SQE1 papers contains 180 multiple-choice questions, and each paper concentrates on particular fields of law: Business Law and Practice, Dispute Resolution, Contract, Tort, the Legal System, Constitutional and Administrative Law, EU Law, and Legal Services. The second paper comprises of questions on

Property Practice, Wills, Solicitors' Accounts, Land Law, Trusts, and Criminal Law and Practice.

Though the same basic interpreting skills are required in SQE and PQs from reading, comprehension and understanding the question, candidates must use their legal knowledge and evaluate those rules accordingly when deciding which provided answer is most probable.

As the Claim is given in the question, the greater emphasis of SQE1 is the assessment of the analytical elements from the CLEO Law and Evaluation sections, and being able to correctly identify and apply those rules.

SQE1 is a multiple-choice question. A situation is given, followed by a question and five potential 'best fit' answers to choose from, such as:

AN EXAMPLE SQE1 QUESTION

Paul is a hotel owner bidding at auction for two lots of bedding, both believed to be 1000 cotton rating, but Lot B only has a cotton rating of 300 and is worth considerably less. Samples have been given to bidders of just the higher rating. Both lots have been wrapped identically and bear the same hallmarks and stamps. Paul wins the auction.

In a claim for breach of contract, which type of mistake would the court most likely award?

A   Common mistake *Res extincta*

B   Common mistake *Res sua*

C   Common mistake as to quality

D   Unilateral mistake

E   Without actionable misrepresentation, the contract is valid

---

In terms of the content of this book, the Claim is already given by identifying the issue of a breach of contract and the topic of mistake. There is no Outcome section where the student needs to draw conclusions as to the best course of action or remedies available to the bidder. There is instead a hybrid Law-Evaluation whereby knowledge of the law of mistake and the critical analysis of the scenario results in a summary court judgment.

Writing SQE2 answers

SQE2 fields of law are broadly the same as SQE1 except for the exclusion of Constitutional and Administrative Law, EU Law, Legal Services, Solicitors' Accounts and the Legal System.

The SQE2 assesses oral and written practice: interview and legal analysis/note-taking, and advocacy in the former; and case and matter analysis, legal research, writing and drafting in the latter.

In terms of written output, the SQE2 closely matches the PQ in that synthetic material is provided as a scenario, and extra material is provided to candidates as an appendix. Depending on the field of law, this could be a witness statement, police interview transcript, a practice handbook extract, judgments, statutes, standard contract forms, schedules or statements. It more closely reflects the various documents needed by a solicitor to represent a client in the real world.

From the initial email (normally from a partner at your practice), the background is given, is followed by instructions by the partner on the next steps, and/or areas of law that needn't be explored, and steps that have already been taken (eg due diligence, no conflict of interest, client care matters).

Another common feature is the requirement to write your correspondence clearly, as all your SQE clients will either have limited experience and knowledge of the topic, be vulnerable or need to have things explained to them carefully.

The *Jack v Peter* PQ has been adapted to follow the genre and style of the SQE2 task.

JACK V PETER ADAPTED SQE2 QUESTION

From: Partner@lawfirm.co.uk

To: Associate@lawfirm.co.uk

Subject: New client

You'll recall I told you about a client, Jack, who has an interest in collecting valuable watches. He contacted us regarding a non-payment from a customer, Peter, to whom he claims a watch was sold for an agreed price of £2800. A Letter Before Claim was then sent to Peter.

Peter has instructed Spicer Ratbone LLP, who have responded claiming a valid revocation of contract was sent on 11th May (**see attachment A**).

> *cont.*   Enclosed (**Attachment B**) is a draft statement from Jack
>   which contains all the pertinent information regarding his
>   claim. You will notice a reference to an offer email received and
>   letter of acceptance sent on 12 May. We do not yet have a copy but
>   Jack has confirmed he will provide it, and we are to proceed as per
>   the terms stated in the draft witness statement.
>
>   Jack has instructed us to commence proceedings at the County
>   Court. **Can you draft the Particular of Claims form using Attachment
>   C?** Some fields have already been populated.

What is immediately noticeable is that the Claims details will be hidden amongst the attachments rather than in the PQ text. Also, the disagreement has moved on from a PQ's *what is the claim and how could it be resolved* to the real-world *complete the documents in order to get the issue started in the legal process.*

Due to space constraints, how to answer SQE2 tasks won't be addressed in this book, however the parallels between the two assessment methods are significant, and therefore training for drafting a Claims form, for example, can be found in this book (in bold below) next to the example structure of the *Jack v Peter* claim form:

1   Claimant name(s) and interests (**Identifiable from the PQ**)

2   Brief detail of initial instruction/contract (**see Claim**)

3   Element of the contract that is in dispute (eg payment schedule if a payment by instalment is missed) (**Claim**)

4   Each step of the dispute is clearly stated chronologically, noting payment and/or cumulative balance owed (**Chronology**)

5   Completion, discharge or acceptance of the contract by one party (**Chronology**)

6   The full outstanding amount (**Evaluation**)

7   Correspondence requesting payment and details of that received (**Evaluation**)

8   Summary of what the defendant owes (**Outcome**)

In the model answers, the SQE has provided sample answers structured **By Issue** regardless of law topic. Where the topic is a breach of contract, the email from your firm's partner would follow roughly the same pattern, contain reference material, and may include more detailed instruction for the correspondence to the client, for example the four Claims that follow:

BREACH OF CONTRACT SQE2-STYLE QUESTION

From: Partner@lawfirm.co.uk

To: Associate@lawfirm.co.uk

Subject: Lauren and Rhod – new clients

Background information

. . .

Lauren and Rhod need advice on:

i   The type of breach of contract evident from the statements (**Attachment A**)

ii   Options for the pair following the notice of repudiation (**Attachment B**)

iii The 'reliance principle'

iv   Any changes to the terms, warranties or conditions (**Attachment C**) you recommend going forward that would benefit the couple with their next supplier

As they are new to owning and running a business, bear this in mind as you explain your advice. Mention advantages and disadvantages of each option so they fully understand their options before instructing us further. Use case law or judge's *obiter* to support your position where appropriate.

Note: You should assume that Rhod and Lauren own the company 50/50.

As earlier, the topic (breach of contract) is easily identifiable, yet there is a lot more focus on the Evaluation stage in this SQE-type question than the first, and the frequency of legal vocabulary is higher in this example. Additionally:

1   There is the presumed knowledge of the type of breach mentioned in the attachments which needs to be stated (anticipatory, material or immaterial) (**Claim**)

2   The impact of both remedies on the clients (take the notice of repudiation as discharge of contract, or to wait until their performance of the contractual obligations was due, and the consequences of both actions) (**Evaluation**)

3   Knowledge of the reliance principle (**Law**) and how it affects the given situation (**Evaluation**)

4   The differences between a term, warranty and condition (**Law**), identifying these in the given contract (**Claim**), and advising the couple of any which may give another party too much of an advantage (**Outcome**)

5   There may also be direction to refer the client to previous case law to support
     your assertion (**Law**)

Further detailed SQE test information, training providers, data and sample material
can be found at www.sra.org.uk/sra/policy/solicitors-qualifying-examination/.

Note: At the time of writing, the format of the SQE is still under discussion, so
the previous commentary is given having read and researched the available pilot
material, sample tests and examiner feedback. *SQE Prep & Practise* (OUP) will be
published in July 2021, and the first SQE exams will be held in November 2021.

PART

C Good academic practice

Part C aims

In this chapter you will use authentic sources to:

- Learn what plagiarism is, what needs to be cited and other forms of academic misconduct
- Directly quote, paraphrase and summarise
- Understand how to correctly cite and format the most frequently used sources of research in the academic legal style for footnotes and the bibliography
- Follow step-by-step instructions to correctly format your own sources
- See how search returns on law databases appear from case law and judgments
- Deconstruct and understand neutral, traditional and international citations and abbreviations
- Identify key elements within judgments
- Recognise and understand court hierarchy and abbreviations
- Understand statutes and their abbreviations
- Understand judges' abbreviations
- Adapt your writing to incorporate source information fluently and coherently
- Recognise and understand law reports and abbreviations
- Correctly order your bibliography
- Notice and correct errors in footnote and bibliography entries
- Practise the aforementioned using exercises to check your learning and understanding
- See examples of different types of assessment that you may be asked to do at university

DOI: 10.4324/9781003125747-3

Plagiarism and types of academic misconduct

Like many areas of law, there is not one singular, all-encompassing definition of plagiarism. Some definitions include:

> Plagiarism is presenting someone else's work or ideas as your own, with or without their consent, by incorporating it into your work without full acknowledgement.
>
> www.ox.ac.uk/students/academic/guidance/skills/plagiarism

> Plagiarism is defined as using, without acknowledgment, another person's work and submitting it for assessment as though it were one's own work; for instance, through copying or unacknowledged paraphrasing. This constitutes plagiarism whether it is intentional or unintentional.
>
> https://myuni.swansea.ac.uk/academic-life/academic-regulations/
> assessment-and-progress/academic-misconduct-procedure/

- to steal and pass off (the ideas or words of another) as one's own: use (another's production) without crediting the source
- to commit literary theft: present as new and original an idea or product derived from an existing source

                                          www.merriam-webster.com/dictionary/plagiarize

Plagiarism can easily be avoided, and there is no reason to commit plagiarism. More importantly, a law student (and medicine, accountancy and dentistry students too) will risk their registration to practise by the regulatory body if a student has been excluded from university because of unfair practice, such as plagiarism.

Your career in law could be over before you even graduate. It is that serious!

Other types of academic offences for assessed work (not examinations) include:

- collusion – unauthorised group work in order to present the same or similar work as their own
- commissioning – asking, getting or paying another to complete work for submission on their behalf
- falsification – changing or creating results from laboratory work, data collection or analysis
- self-plagiarism – submitting work for assessment that has already been submitted for other tasks

Your institution will have their own exact wording of these types of academic offences, so use the preceding as a rough guide.

Citing and referencing

A reference is an *acknowledgement* from the writer that they have read someone else's work, and believe that information to be so worthwhile, it is important to use in their own work to support a point.

Many students are unaware of the severity of plagiarism, and that recognising another author's work is not a bad thing. It is actually a good thing because it shows the reader that arguments have been well considered and backed up by another work. A cited work shows wide reading and provides evidence to support points, especially if this is a legal authority which the reader can check for themselves.

The key point is that any work you do use must be referenced with a citation. Not acknowledging the work of others in your own work could make you liable of committing plagiarism.

OSCOLA (Oxford University Standard for Citation of Legal Sources) is the most common format used to present the details of referenced sources in law. The current edition (4th) of OSCOLA is 55 pages long, and a summarised version and self-test questions are provided throughout.

Generally, OSCOLA referencing dislikes the use of Latin and punctuation marks, but likes the use of abbreviations.

In law essays (both PQs and standard essays), you are very likely to be instructed to use a numbering system to record your sources. Any source of information you use in your essay (paraphrased, summarised or directly quoted) will be followed by a citation number[1] (ie the number 1 formatted in superscript) immediately after the full stop of that sentence. That same citation number then appears in the footnotes along with further information to help the reader cross-reference and identify the source referred to in the essay. Roughly the same information is presented in the footnote as in the bibliography at the end of the essay, but be aware that the referencing format changes slightly between the two.

Bibliographies contain the same sources as is contained in the footnotes of your essay, but are written alphabetically rather than in the order they are presented (numerically). Additionally, bibliographies have subheadings for each type of source, that is, if it is a book, journal, law report, judgment, statute or statutory instrument.

The details required in the footnote and in the bibliography change depending on the type of source, and whether these were accessed on a paper copy or, as most likely, electronically. Legislation also varies depending on when it was enacted, as does legislation from other jurisdictions and devolved nations.

Those electronically accessed are the most frequently cited source types in academic writing, and the following pages will take you through these in detail. Stages of each will be described and any special formatting will be brought to your attention.

Advice on when a reference is needed or not often errs on the side of caution, meaning it is better to cite when you are unsure if it is needed than risk plagiarising by not referencing a source. That said, your writing can become clunky, awkward and lack fluency if it interrupts the readers' flow because of over-use of citations.

Task C1: Consider which of the following 12 sources in the box need to be cited and which do not, and place them into the appropriate column:

The exact words of a judge   The maximum sentence of a particular offence

Your own opinion   A commonly known fact

Paraphrasing of a dissenting judge's *obiter*   A case name

Your own opinion which develops another author's work

Your own opinion from a previous essay

Summarising a case (eg a case brief)   A statute

Combine two authors' points by paraphrase and summary

Memorising and reproducing the exact words of a judge

Reference needed	Reference not needed

As you can see, the majority of the preceding examples require a reference. You may think there is a fine line between 'a commonly known fact' and 'the maximum sentence of a particular offence' which, depending on your field, may be true. Even if you memorise a passage from someone else's work in an exam or for an essay, you must still reference the source. Criminal lawyers could reasonably be expected to know the maximum custodial sentence for fraud, but an employment lawyer may not. Your criminal law lecturer will definitely know this, and could consider it common knowledge, but to another student, a lay person or a family law lecturer who may read your work, this information needs to be supported and would therefore need to be cited. When you use another person's idea and then further develop it with your own thoughts, the basis of that idea needs to be cited. Synthesising or assimilating (ie combining) many people's work and rolling it into your own new original sentence which doesn't appear in any of those source texts needs to be referenced. This is because the source ideas within your new idea are not yours, and will need to be referenced.

Many help websites will give examples where if a number or percentage appears, the given rule is to cite, however in law, data-based essays are fairly uncommon. You may encounter opposing arguments of the same point which may both be common knowledge (eg global warming is (not) happening). But the detail which is extracted from the source will need to be cited because it goes beyond what is common knowledge. In this case, the argument from those who don't believe in climate change may be *for millennia the Earth has gone through ice age cycles every few thousand years.* As a general argument, this would not need a citation, although it would be good practice. A more detailed assertion: *the sun's rays are warming up Earth as a temperature rise is also happening on Mars too* would need citing as this is probably outside most people's common knowledge. It is common knowledge that President Trump is a climate-change denier, and his quote that it was a hoax can and should be attributed to his Twitter feed. Martin Luther King's famous *I have a dream* speech still needs to be correctly cited.

So, to summarise, cite information other than common knowledge. Common knowledge is:

- Information most people already know and accept
- May be particular to a country, race or culture
- Known be members of a certain field
- Cannot normally be attributed to a particular source
- However, common knowledge to one academic discipline, country, race or culture may not be common knowledge in another.

> *Tip*: If in doubt, cite it.

Correct formatting of OSCOLA references is important, as is consistent referencing. What you may notice in your university feedback is that some lecturers are more forgiving than others when it comes to the formatting of your references.

And some lecturers may like you to present your references in a particular manner that doesn't exactly match the requirements of OSCOLA. What is presented here is the most up to date edition (the fourth), and the most common types of sources used by university students.

The following pages will illustrate citations and bibliographies for different sources of information, as well as show you the formatting required to check your presentation is correct. Check with your lecturers if a bibliography for your PQ is needed as these are typically only reserved for longer pieces of work such as dissertations and theses. It is good practice that they are included in all assessed writing tasks.

While accurate use of citations, spelling, grammar and punctuation only usually accounts for around 10% of an essay's grade, this small amount could be the difference between a 2i and a first-class honours certificate.

Tip: For such minimal effort, getting your citations correct is time well spent.

Task C2 – Should the following statements be accepted as factually true, contentious or common knowledge, and which would need to be referenced?

a   There is gold on the moon.

b   Jesus Christ was born on 25th December.

c   There are four elements needed to create a binding contract in English law.

d   A little-known fifth element needed to create a binding contract is *capacity*.

e   The legal system in Turkey is civil law.

f   Around 70% of the earth's surface is covered by water.

g   The death penalty still exists in America.

h   The death penalty still exists in 30 American states.

i   The death penalty hasn't been used in over a decade in 11 states.

j   *Death Row* is the name of the special jail cells where prisoners facing the death penalty in America are held.

k   Another word for the death penalty is capital punishment.

l   Some people oppose the death penalty.

m   The Northern Irish Assembly, Scottish Parliament and Welsh Senedd enjoy different levels of legislative autonomy.

n   The Northern Irish Assembly, Scottish Parliament and Welsh Senedd's funding is worked out by the UK government using the Barnett formula.

o   The Scottish Parliament makes best use of its funding.

p   A *unicorn* is the name given to a privately started company which is now valued at over $1bn.

q   Deliveroo, Revolut and Just Eat are examples of unicorn companies.

Task C3 – Identify the following eight parts of this student writing

Direct quotation   Footnotes   Citation   Citation number
References   Quotation marks   Sourced material   Subheading

Xxxxxxxxx xxx xxx xxxxx xxxxxxxxxx xx xxxxxxx xxxxxxxxx. Xxx xxx xxxx xxxx xxxxxxxxx xxxx xx xxxxxx xxxxx xxxxx xxxx xx xxx xxxxxx. Xxxxxxx xxxxxxxxxx xxx xxxxxxxxx xxxxx xxxxxx xxxxxxxxx xxxxx xxx xxxxxxxxxxxx xx xx xxxxxx xx xxxx xxxx 'xxxxx xxxxx xx x xxxxxxxx xxxxxx xxxxxx xxxx xxxxxxxxxxx xxxxx xxx xxxxx xxxx.' [1] Xxxxx xxxx x xxxxxx xxxxxxx xxxxxx xxxxxx xxxxxx.[2]

---

[1] Initial Surname, *Title* (edition, Publisher Year) page

[2] Initial Surname, *Title* (edition, Publisher Year)

────────────────────new page────────────────────
Bibliography

Books

Initial Surname, *Title* (edition, Publisher Year)

Journal

Surname Initial, 'Title' [Year] Volume(Issue) Abbreviated.Journal.Name First page

---

Citations

Footnotes are the OSCOLA equivalent of in-text citations. You may have seen citations such as (Brown, 2021) being used in APA or Harvard. OSCOLA citations use a numbering system called footnotes which are positioned at the bottom of each page where there is a citation number, rather than immediately after the cited work.

Each source is given a number in the order it is presented in your work. The citation number is positioned immediately after the cited work (without spaces). If the acknowledged material ends with a punctuation mark, the citation number comes immediately after it.

Citation numbers can appear mid-sentence or at the end of the sentence, normally dependent on if they are summaries or paraphrases of the source text. Regardless, the formatting and presentation of citation numbers can be presented in two ways:

> There are several ways parties can avoid costly and time-consuming litigation. In the UK, the options include mediation, arbitration and adjudication,[1] the ADR directive[2] to resolve contractual disputes between consumers and businesses in the UK and EU, and between members of the WTO.[3] The benefits of ADR . . .

- Final keyword + (punctuation mark +) citation number + space + new word/ next sentence begins

In the following pages, citations with their accompanying citation numbers are marked in a red box, and the last box of each source type has a blue box which contains how all the cited material should appear in a bibliography.

Within each source title, each letter is capitalised except for prepositions (in, for, by, with), articles (an, a, the) – unless it is the very first word of the source.

Citation numbers are always written in superscript when next to the key information in the text, and when listing the source in the footnotes.

Books

In this section, the same chunk of text from page 104 is used as the source of information to be cited and referenced in the bibliography. The formatting rules will stay consistent throughout each type of source illustrated in the OSCOLA style.

> Many students are unaware of the severity of plagiarism, and that recognising another author's work is... a good thing because it shows the reader that arguments have been well considered and backed up by another work. A cited work shows wide reading and provides evidence to support points, especially if this is a legal authority which the reader can check for themselves.[1]
>
> [1] Geraint Brown, *Problem Questions for Law Students: A Study Guide* (Routledge 2022) 104.

A **direct quotation** from this book would be (see page 139 for further advanced information):

- First name
- Surname,
- Book Title in *italics*

- (edition – exclude if 1st, Publisher, Year of publication)
- Page number if paragraph numbers are unavailable + full stop

The footnote for a **paraphrase** of the same quoted text from this book would be:

> Many students enter university unaware that committing plagiarism is a serious academic offence. The benefits of avoiding plagiarism include demonstrating research skills, using support from other published texts or legal authorities, providing evidence to support arguments, and helping the reader locate the same source.[1]
>
> [1] Geraint Brown, *Problem Questions for Law Students: A Study Guide* (Routledge 2022).

- First name
- Surname,
- Book Title in *italics*
- (edition – exclude if 1st, Publisher, Year of publication) + full stop
- There is no page number for a paraphrase

Normally, paraphrases have the citation number at the end of the chunk of text where the source information ends (which may or may not be at the end of a sentence, whereas a summary of a larger chunk of paraphrased text will have the citation number at the end of the sentence.

Therefore, a **summary** of the same text would appear as:

> Many students are unaware of the seriousness of academic misconduct, such as plagiarism. However there are many documented benefits and educational resources for good academic practice.[1]
>
> [1] Geraint Brown, *Problem Questions for Law Students: A Study Guide* (Routledge 2022).

- First name
- Surname,
- Book Title in *italics*
- (edition, Publisher, Year of publication) + full stop
- Edition number not needed for a first edition
- There is no page number for a summary

Regardless of whether a direct quotation, summarised or a paraphrase was used, the **bibliography** at the end of the essay would have the entry:

> Brown G, *Problem Questions for Law Students: A Study Guide* (Routledge 2021)

- Surname
- First name's initial,
- Book Title in *italics*
- (edition, Publisher, Year of publication)
- Edition number not needed for a first edition
- There is no page number for a summary
- All entries in the bibliography omit a final full stop
- Bibliography entries are not numbered nor cross-referenced with their citation number, but appear alphabetically within subheadings to source type

2–3 book authors

- Author One's First name + Surname (, + Author Two's First name + Surname) and Last Author's First name + Surname,
- Book Title in *italics*
- (edition, Publisher, Year of publication) + full stop
- Edition number not needed for a first edition

> [2] David Ormerod and Karl Laird, *Smith, Hogan, & Ormerod's Text, Cases, & Materials on Criminal Law* (13th edn, OUP, 2020).
>
> [3] Paola Gaeta, Jorge Viñuales and Salvatore Zappalá, *Cassese's International Law* (3rd edn, OUP, 2020).

4+ book authors

Where there are four or more authors, same rules follow as a book except for the name of the first author is given followed by "and others".

So the five authors who wrote *Energy Justice and Energy Law* (Iñigo del Guayo, Lee Godden, Donald D. Zillman, Milton Fernando Montoya and José Juan González) would be cited in the footnotes and bibliography respectively as:

> [4] I del Guayo and others *Energy Justice and Energy Law* (OUP 2020).

del Guayo I, and others *Energy Justice and Energy Law* (OUP 2020)

Contribution to a book

- Author's first name
- Author's surname,
- 'Article Title'
- in + editor's First name and Surname (ed),
- and + second editor's First name and Surname (eds) (if 2nd editor given),
- *Book Title*
- (Publisher Year)

[5] Michael Sturley, 'Can Commercial Law Accommodate New Technologies in International Shipping?' in Baris Soyer and Andrew Tettenborn (eds), *New Technologies, Artificial Intelligence and Shipping Law in the 21st Century* (Informa Law, 2019).

[6] Baris Soyer and Andrew Tettenborn, 'Autonomous Ships and Private Law Issues' in Baris Soyer and Andrew Tettenborn (eds), *Artificial Intelligence and Autonomous Shipping: Developing the International Legal Framework* (Hart, 2021).

Bibliography

If the preceding six books were to be used in an essay, the bibliography page would look as follows:

BIBLIOGRAPHY

Books

Brown G, *Problem Questions for Law Students: A Study Guide* (Routledge 2021)

del Guayo I, and others *Energy Justice and Energy Law* (OUP 2020)

Gaeta P, Viñuales J and Zappalá S, *Cassese's International Law* (3rd edn, OUP, 2020)

Ormerod D and Laird K, *Smith, Hogan, & Ormerod's Text, Cases, & Materials on Criminal Law* (13th edn, OUP, 2020)

> **cont.**
>
> *Soyer B and Tettenborn A, 'Autonomous Ships and Private Law Issues' in Soyer B and Tettenborn A (eds), Artificial Intelligence and Autonomous Shipping: Developing the International Legal Framework' (Hart 2021)*
>
> *Sturley M, 'Can Commercial Law Accommodate New Technologies in International Shipping?' in Soyer B and Tettenborn A (eds), New Technologies, Artificial Intelligence and Shipping Law in the 21st Century' (Informa Law 2019)*

Task C4 – Complete the following statements in your own words

1   Source types (eg books, journals, cases) are placed under their own _____ in a bibliography.

2   Authors' names are different in footnotes and bibliographies because _____

_____.

3   _____ are the final characters in footnotes and are omitted in bibliographies.

4   Whether the source was used as a a) _____, b) _____, or c) _____ it will appear in the bibliography.

5   The sources appear alphabetically by surname in _____.

6   In footnotes, the sources appear _____

_____.

7   The name order of multiple-authored texts appears _____.

8   What effect does del Guayo's surname of two names have on the order of the bibliography? _____

_____

Journal articles

> [1] Paul Davies, 'Rectification Rectified' [2020] 79(1) C.L.J. 8.

- Author's first name
- Author's surname,
- 'Article Title'
- [year] if volume given, or (year) if no volume given
- Volume(Issue)

- Abbreviated.Journal.Name.

- First page

The majority of journals now volumise their content so the year will more frequently appear in square brackets. If there is no volume, the year should be placed between round brackets (2004). The round brackets indicate that the pages continue running (much like the running citation number of your PQ answer).

There is no space between the volume number and the bracket of the issue. Note that the issue can be a number, a season, month or quarter, or could be non-existent.

More information on the most common abbreviated journal names can be found at www.legalabbrevs.cardiff.ac.uk and cited according to their preferred or alternative forms, for example Berkeley J Intl Law (See **page** 143 for a list of journal names' abbreviations). If they are not listed here, write the journal name in full.

If directly quoting from a journal, the page number of the citation comes at the very end. There is a comma after the first page number, then the cited page. For example:

---

2 David Barrett, 'The Importance of Regulators and Inspectorates to the Realisation of Equality and Human Rights: Ensuring Compliance and Supporting Mainstreaming' [2020] Jan P.L. 56, 69.

Task C5 – What two structural differences are there between the Davies and Barrett articles?

A journal article may contain the name of a case as well as its best report. In which case, the footnote will follow the same structures as the preceding footnote but may appear strange at first, but actually contain lots of abbreviations and punctuation marks you are already familiar with:

---

3 John Taggart, 'Powers of Attorney and 'Lack of Capacity' under the Mental Capacity Act 2005: A Narrowing of the s 44 Offence? R v Kurtz [2018] EWCA Crim 2743' [2020] 84(1) J.C.L 74, 75.

Task C6 – Journal articles as sources

1   Which words within the article title are written in inverted commas and why is this?

2   What do you think 's' means, and what does it refer to?

3   Look at the case name within the citation. How is it different when it is part of a journal article title compared to if it were a case name you were presenting to support your point?

4   Has source 3 been directly quoted from? How do you know?

Note: Some law databases will present journal names in semi-abbreviated form, eg J Crim L.

Online journal articles

Online journals should be cited as per a paper journal. However online journals should only be used if no paper copy of the journal is produced. The majority of established and peer-reviewed journals that you access through law databases will have paper copies, even if they are accessed online through Westlaw or LexisNexis. The type of online only journal may be specialist, from another jurisdiction, or contain a single theme across multiple jurisdictions.

---

[4] Jotte Mulder, 'A Constitutional Reflection on the Economisation and Modernisation of EU Competition Law: A Case Study from the Netherlands' [2019] 14(1) The Competition Law Review <http://clasf.org/browse-the-complrev/> accessed 27 July 2020.

Pinpoints should be placed between the journal name and the beginning of the website.

Note the name of the journal is written in full because is it not one of the most frequently used. As a general rule, if the journal name has an abbreviated form (see page 143) it is accepted as a high standard and authoritative source for the majority of fields of law.

Websites starting www. do not need to include http:// or https://; just those which do not begin with www (such as clasf.org earlier) need have the full address.

This website provides a link to a folder system where it is not possible to go directly to the PDF file required. If a link takes the user to the full file or website (ending in .pdf, .doc or .html for example) use this. As a result, full website addresses can be very long. Don't be concerned if this is the case. Do not shorten the website using specialist web tools, eg if the Horder source that follows had conveniently but incorrectly reduced to https://tinyurl.com/y6h5os5r, nor a DOI (eg 10.5539/mas.v13n4p94) the source in the shortened link would have lost its provenance and authority.

[5] Jeremy Horder, 'The Court's Development of the Criminal Law and the Role of Declarations' [2020] 40(1) Legal Studies <http://eprints.lse.ac.uk/100812/1/ THE_COURTS_DEVELOPMENT_OF_THE_CRIMINAL_LAW_AND_THE_ROLE_OF_ DECLARATIONS.pdf> accessed 28 July 2020.

The formatting of online journals is:

- Author's first name
- Author's surname,
- 'Article Title'
- if volume given [year] + Volume(Issue), or (year) if no volume given
- Full Journal Name
- <full URL>
- "accessed" + date last accessed

You may find that an online journal you wish to use has a DOI (Digital Object Identifier) or ISSN (Internet Standard Serial Number) for other online media. If this is the case, OSCOLA states that you should cite and footnote it as a paper copy journal if a paper copy exists, or if not and for other online media, use the formatting.

It is good practice to leave the website as a live hyperlink so that you and your lecturers can have instant access to the reference. The live hyperlink is placed between two angular brackets.

"Accessed" simply means the date at which you last visited the website. This is primarily done because websites can be changed easily whereas print ones will remain as originally published. Most authoritative websites will state that a web page has been updated since it was originally published, so readers can see that some information may have changed. It is always worth protecting yourself. For example, I know that today 27 July 2020, the aforementioned website was working. When you read this book and access the link, an update in website design or each article having its own separate web page may have happened in the interim period. By giving the date, I have protected myself against claims of fabricating the source and reliance on its evidence.

Bibliography

In the bibliography, journal articles will be under their own subheading, in alphabetical order not numerical, and contain broadly the same information as in the footnotes, except: directly quoted page numbers are removed; the first name becomes an initial and their positions swapped:

JOURNALS

Barrett D, 'The Importance of Regulators and Inspectorates to the Realisation of Equality and Human Rights: Ensuring Compliance and Supporting Mainstreaming' [2020] Jan P.L. 56

Davies P, 'Rectification Rectified' [2020] 79(1) C.L.J. 8

Horder J, 'The Court's Development of the Criminal Law and the Role of Declarations' [2020] 40(1) Legal Studies <http://eprints.lse.ac.uk/100812/1/THE_COURTS_DEVELOPMENT_OF_THE_CRIMINAL_ LAW_AND_THE_ROLE_OF_DECLARATIONS.pdf> accessed 28 July 2020

Mulder J, 'A Constitutional Reflection on the Economisation and Modernisation of EU Competition Law: A Case Study from the Netherlands' [2019] 14(1) The Competition Law Review <http://clasf.org/ browse-the-complrev/> accessed 27 July 2020

Taggart J, 'Powers of Attorney and 'Lack of Capacity' under the Mental Capacity Act 2005: A Narrowing of the s 44 Offence? R v Kurtz [2018] EWCA Crim 2743' [2020] 84(1) J.C.L 74

Case law

UK cases post-2001

Citation of cases depends on whether the case has a neutral citation or not. Older cases (before 11 January 2001) will not have a neutral citation in order to help researchers identify cases published on the internet but not necessarily in a law report.

- *Party names + (Ship's Name if appropriate)*
- [Year]
- Court
- Case number
- Law report citation
- Full stop

In cases without a ship, exclude the ship name.

Include a comma between the Case number of the traditional citation and the year of the law report citation if the law report is available.

---

¹ *Transfield Shipping Inc. v Mercador Shipping Inc (The Achilleas)* [2008] UKHL 48.

² *Shogun Finance v Hudson* [2003] UKHL 62.

³ *Nisshin Shipping Co v Cleaves & Co Ltd* [2003] EWHC 2602, [2004] 1 All ER (Comm) 481.

⁴ *HIH Casualty and General Insurance v Chase Manhattan Bank* [2003] UKHL 6, [2003] 2 Lloyd's Rep 61.

Hint: Where you see the jurisdiction listed (UKSC or EWCA Crim) indicates if the ruling extends to the whole of the UK or just England and Wales. Neutral citations will include this information, and refer to the judgment itself, not the law report.

You will notice that footnotes 3 and 4 both appear to have two court citations whereas the others don't. Some cases will state the neutral citation <u>and</u> the 'best' (ie most authoritative) law report where the case was reported, presented in that order.

Neutral citations are now used much more frequently because transcripts of judgments can be uploaded to the internet and databases so quickly. It gives lawyers the chance to use precedent which has not been printed yet through an authoritative law report.

Neutral citations according to court

Supreme Court	[year] UKSC + number
House of Lords	[year] UKHL + number
Privy Council	[year] UKPC+ number
Court of Appeal (Civil Division)	[year] EWCA Civ + number
Court of Appeal (Criminal Division)	[year] EWCA Crim + number
High Court (Chancery Division)	[year] EWHC + number (Ch)
High Court (Family Division)	[year] EWHC + number (Fam)
High Court (Queen's Bench Division)	[year] EWHC + number (QB)
High Court (Administrative Court)	[year] EWHC + number (Admin)
High Court (Admiralty Court)	[year] EWHC + number (Admlty)
High Court (Commercial Court)	[year] EWHC + number (Comm)
High Court (Patents Court)	[year] EWHC + number (Pat)
High Court (Technology and Construction Court)	[year] EWHC + number (TCC)

Figure 3.1 Neutral citations according to court

Database search returns

A database search of recent cases may provide results similar to:

CompassLaw Database

1. R v Jensen (Annette) 3 January 2020 Court of Appeal (Criminal Division) [2020]
   EWCA 6834, [2019] 3 WLUK 27   Analysis | Judgment

   Negative treatment   Guidance

   Subject: Criminal procedure

   Keywords: Defences, Jury directions, Possession of explosives

2. Phizz Shipping Ltd v AWKS SA 6 February 2020 Queens Bench Division (Commercial
   Court) [2020] EWHC 1685 (Comm), [2020] EWHC 1347 (Comm), [2020] 7 WLUK 777
   Analysis | Judgment

   No substantial treatment

   Subject: Civil procedure, Damages, Shipping, Contracts

   Keywords: Breach of contract, Charterparties, Loss of profits

3. Hiraeth v Ni Hao *(The Coracle)* 5 February 2020 Queens Bench Division [2020] EWHC
   3959 (QB), [2020] EWHC 3458 (QB), [2020] 9 WLUK 99   Analysis | Judgment

   Positive judicial treatment   Significant

   Subject: Negligence

   Keywords: Employees, Risk Assessment, Supervision, Vicarious liability

---

It should be relatively simple to identify the key elements of the preceding cases. See Researching Skills from page 25.

Treatment has been detailed on page 35, but in brief, positive treatment has been affirmed by a higher court whereas cases with negative consideration have been overruled.

A case is *Significant* if it clarifies, extends or overturns previous judgments (ie creates precedent). A case can be significant regardless of the court, and a judge can label a case of general importance.

Cases labelled *Guidance* give legal or procedural clarification, again, regardless of the court.

Both labels are mutually exclusive.

There are three hyperlinks on the database search returns: the case name, Analysis and Judgment.

Selecting the case name or Analysis will take you to a summary written by a barrister or a court reporter (see later in this chapter) and will contain:

- Where the case is reported as a neutral citation (if available) and most authoritative report, or a complete list of law reports reporting the case
- A summary of the point of law and the ruling in brief
- The PQ/background
- The court's decision detailing
  - Any Lords dissenting
  - Each point of law worked through methodically citing case law
- Case history and status (positive, negative or neutral)
- All and key cases cited in the case
- Key cases citing this case (where this older judgment has affected the argument in newer cases)
- Legislation cited
- Commentary from other sources (eg journals and books)

For example:

Case analysis	Johnstone v Pense & Co	Positive/Neutral Treatment
- Law Reports [2010] 9 WLR 4	House of Lords	**House of Lords**
[2010] 4 AC 1	Lord Ace of Townsville, Lord Bass of Upperton and Lady Mallett	**Judgment** 16 March 2010
+ Judgements	2009 July 11, 12, 15; 2010 Mar 16	**Citation** [2010] 9 WLR 4, [2010] 4 AC 1
+ Primary References	*Company – shareholder – action by company for damages for breach of duty*	
+ Commentary	*Damages – contract – whether damages for breach of mental distress and anxiety recoverable*	
+ Precedent	**Judgement**	
	Lord Ace of Townsville	
	My Lords,	
	1. There are two parties before us contesting…	

In the preceding example, Lord Ace would give his judgment, followed by Lord Bass and then Lady Mallett. Paragraphs are numbered and follow the same structure as the previous Queen's Bench judgment, which may or may not be subheaded.

Task C7 – Where on the preceding figure can you find the following information?

A journal entry about the case   Judges hearing the case   Keywords (or catchwords)

Legislation cited   Previously cited authorities   Court name

Date of the judgment   A law report of the case (which one would you choose?)

Case judgments

The **judgment** hyperlink, if available, will direct you to the full decision of the court, will vary slightly depending on that court and will contain roughly this information:

James Dean Construction Ltd (in liquidation) v EVH Contractors Ltd

Guidance   Significant   **Positive/Neutral Treatment**

Judgment Date: 14th February 2020

High Court of Justice and Property Courts of England and Wales

Technology and Construction Court (QB)

[2020] EWHC 1648 (TCC), 2020 3 WL 5555

Representation: Mr A of Company A for the Appellant, and Mr B of Company B for the defendant.

Judgment: Mr Justice X (with whom Mr Justice Y and Mr Justice Z agree)

Following the judgment, subheadings are written in numbered paragraphs for ease of reference, structured in a way which you may think looks similar to a PQ answer:

- Claim(s)
- Background
- Legal Framework/Procedural History
- Legal Issue A
  - Summary of the question for the court to rule upon
  - Legislation – relevant sections of the law are clarified
  - Answering each of the questions in turn
  - Issues within each question are addressed
  - Evaluation
- Legal Issue B etc . . .
- Outcome

Hint: Reading judgments is a really good way to learn how to approach a PQ, and to read how professionals answer PQs.

Law reports

Selecting a law report of the most persuasive authority

Mince Ltd v Wacka & Co	Positive/Neutral Treatment
Supreme Court	**House of Lords**
Lord Ace of Townsville, Lord Heart of Upperton, Lord Diamond, Lord Spade and Lord Jack JJSC	**Judgment** 2 December 2015
2015 Oct 7; Dec 2	**Citation** [2015] UKSC 56, [2015] AC 6485
Company – shareholder – action by company for damages for breach of duty	
Damages – contract – whether damages for breach of mental distress and anxiety recoverable	
A commercial lease singed by Mince, a director of his company, stating "rent was payable…."	

There will be some differences due to the court, age of the law report and possibly the barrister who wrote it, but the preceding structure remains constant on the whole.

- Factual claim and procedural history
- *Held* – the ruling of the last court
- Key authorities referred to
  - Which judges agreed with the lower court's decision in the application of the precedent
- Decision of this court
- List of cases referred to in the judgments
- Additional cases cited in argument
- More detailed background from previous court
- Main argument of the **claimant**
- Main argument of the **defendant** and response
- Date of the final judgment
- Continues as per judgment including paragraph numbers

Your search results will have hyperlinks on either side of the main judgment text. More information on this can be sought from www.iclr.co.uk/knowledge/case-law/iclrs-law-reports-an-explainer/

Academic skills – Have a look through a judgment with which you are familiar and identify the subheadings that follow. Are there any differences, or has the judge broken down further (eg if an act was performed in a unilateral rather than bilateral agreement, any practical difficulties, and repetition of what the Claim is etc)?

UK cases pre-2001

Before 11 January 2001, cases were written without neutral citations so the reader was directed to the law report citation. Only the 'best' law report is needed.

- *Party names + (Ship's name if appropriate)*
- [Year] OR (Year)
- Volume
- Law report abbreviation
- First page or Case number
- Abbreviated Court name
- Full stop

---

[5] *C Czarnikow Ltd v Koufos (The Heron II)* [1969] 1 (AC) 350.

[6] *Overseas Tankship (UK) Ltd v Morts Dock and Engineering Co Ltd (The Wagon Mound) (No 1)* [1961] AC 388.

[7] *Re Selectmove* [1995] 2 All ER 531.

[8] *R v Clarke* (1927) 40 CLR 227.

[9] *Karsales (Harrow) Ltd v Wallis* [1956] 1 WLR 936.

[10] *The Wagon Mound (No 1)* (n 6).

[11] n 9.

Notice that the footnote for citation 6 has changed between its first mention and its second at the tenth citation. If 6 wasn't a shipping case, it is perfectly acceptable to just write the 'n' number, as per citations 9 and 11 (See page 145). Also be aware of the brackets around *Ship Names* depending on the year of the case.

Note that the first time a case is cited in the main answer of your PQ or essay, the party names must be stated in full, but subsequent mentions can be shortened, so the aforementioned could be "in the *Karsales* case" or "in *Karsales*". Footnotes needn't follow after the initial mention unless more information is added, such as pinpointing a direct quote.

Criminal law can be shortened even further to "in Clarke" or "in the *Clarke* case". The difference in the *italics* is to distinguish between the person called Clarke who was involved in the case, and the *Clarke* case itself.

Shipping cases can simply state the ship's name eg "*in The Heron II . . .*" or "In *The Achilleas . . .*"

Cases starting *Re* mean 'in the matter of' and tend to involve claims in adoptions and estates.

The *Table of Cases* subheading within the bibliography for the aforementioned ten citations (see UK cases pre- and post-2001 for footnote entries) will again appear alphabetically not numerically, so:

CASES CITED

C Czarnikow Ltd v Koufos, (The Heron II) [1969] 1 AC 350

HIH Casualty and General Insurance v Chase Manhattan Bank [2003] UKHL 6; [2003] 2 Lloyd's Rep 61

Karsales (Harrow) Ltd v Wallis [1956] 1 WLR 936

Transfield Shipping Inc. v Mercador Shipping Inc. (The Achilleas) [2008] UKHL 48

Nisshin Shipping Co v Cleaves & Co Ltd [2003] EWHC 2602; [2004] All ER (Comm) 481

Overseas Tankship (UK) Ltd v Morts Dock and Engineering Co Ltd (The Wagon Mound) (No 1) [1961] AC 388

R v Clarke (1927) 40 CLR 227

Selectmove, Re [1995] 2 All ER 531

Shogun Finance v Hudson [2003] UKHL 62

Note how Re Selectmove was altered in the bibliography

Task C8 – *The Wagon Mound* case was reported in [1961] UKPC 2, [1961] AC 388; [1961] 1 All ER 404. Which of the three given reports is the 'best'?

Task C9 – Why is the word *Harrow* in brackets in the Karsales case?

Cases from international jurisdictions

Non-UK cases should follow the citation pattern from their own jurisdiction. Here are some examples to show the differences and variations.

Antons Trawling Co Ltd v Smith [2003] 2 NZLR 23

Johnson v Capital City Ford Co. 85 So. 2d 75 (La. Ct. App. 1955)

Lefkowitz v Great Minneapolis Surplus Store, Inc. 86 NW 2d 689 (Minn, 1957)

Masters v Cameron [1954] HCA 72

Siemens Industry Software v Lion Global Offshore Pte Ltd [2014] SGHC 251

Tercon Contractors Ltd v British Columbia (Transportation and Highways) [2010] 1 S.C.R. 69

Task C10 – Can you identify the jurisdictions of the preceding cases? Choose from Australia, Canada, New Zealand, Singapore and the United States.

Note that US cases should give the shortened state name unless it is from that state's highest court, in which case give the abbreviation of the state.

Task C11 – Some case citations cite a law report, others the traditional citation, and others a neutral citation which may include both. Identify the following parts of each citation in the box and place into the left column of table that follows. Then identify its corresponding from the two given cases.

Case number	Claimant	Defendant
First page of report	Party names	Report name
	Year + court	Year + volume

Full citation	***Nisshin Shipping Co v Cleaves & Co Ltd** [2003] EWHC 2602, [2004] 1 All ER (Comm) 481.*	***HIH Casualty and General Insurance v Chase Manhattan Bank** [2003] UKHL 6, [2003] 2 Lloyd's Rep 61.*

Tasks C12 – Which part(s) of the preceding table can create i) the case name, ii) the neutral citation and iii) the law report?

Case name		
Neutral citation		
Law report		

Task C13 – Look up a case or law report that interests you. Identify the elements within it.

UK statutes

Cite Acts of parliament using its short title and give the year numerically. Note the capital letters for each main word in title, but not for prepositions (in, for, by, on, with), conjunctions (and), or articles (an, a, the). Acts do not begin with *The*.

Sale of Goods Act 1979

Pharmacy and Poisons Act 1933

Contracts (Rights of Third Parties) Act 1999

Police and Criminal Evidence Act 1984

Once you have stated the Act's name in full the first time, it can then be abbreviated to SGA 1979 (or SOGA 1979), PPA 1993, CA 1999, PACE 1984. PACE and SOGA are more frequently cited statutes, thus have been altered slightly from their true first letters to become an acronym (pronounced 'pace' rather than P.A.C.E.).

Be aware that some Acts can be similar when abbreviated, and you want to confuse your reader as little as possible, eg a commercial law paper may refer to the Companies Act and Competition Act, both abbreviated to CA albeit with different laws of enactment, so the use of the year is essential to differentiate between CA 1989 and CA 1998 (Companies Act 1989 and Competition Act 1998).

The police's powers of stop and search are provided by several Acts for a range of suspicions and reasonableness covering acts and circumstances such as road traffic accidents,[1] large-scale events[2] (ie football matches), drugs[3] and terrorism.[4] The most commonly used[5] stop and search power is conducted under section 1 of the PACE 1984[6] which provides for police officers to confirm of dismiss suspicions without the need of arrest.[7] Stop and searches under the Criminal Justice and Public Order Act 1994, s 60(3) differ from PACE as searches must be authorised by an officer ranked superintendent or higher.

---

cont.

---

[1] Road Traffic Act 1988, s 163.

[2] Criminal Justice and Public Order Act 1994, s 60.

[3] Terrorism Act 2000, ss 43 and 44.

[4] Misuse of Drugs Act 1971, s 23.

[5] Ministry of Justice, 'Stop and Search' (7 August 2020) <www.ethnicity-facts-figures.service.gov.uk/crime-justice-and-the-law/policing/stop-and-search/latest#by-ethnicity-and-legislation-over-time> Accessed 20 August 2020.

[6] Police and Criminal Evidence Act 1984, s 1.

[7] So long as the officer has reasonable grounds to stop and search a person of vehicle for prohibited articles. This power was extended by s 60 CJPOA 1994 where the power to stop and search is granted without the need for suspicion, provided other conditions are met.

Citations can also be written in a style of footnotes where substantive information is recorded inside the footnote (see citation number 7). It can break the flow for the reader, and you may be instructed to include this information in the main body of the text. Check your university's guidelines.

UK STATUTES

Criminal Justice and Public Order Act 1994

Misuse of Drugs Act 1971

Police and Criminal Evidence Act 1984

Road Traffic Act 1988

Terrorism Act 2000

As with previous bibliography entries, the list of statutes is presented alphabetically, without the section(s) or part(s) referred to in your text or footnotes.

Task C14 – Under which bibliographic subheading would you place citation number 5 and 7?

Parts of an Act

Statutes are divided into parts, sections, subsections, paragraphs and subparagraphs, and can be supplemented by schedules.

Task C15 – Match the abbreviation to the type of division.

		para/paras pt/pts s/ss sch/schs subpara/subparas sub-s/sub-ss
Acts are divided into	part(s)	
	section(s)	
	subsection(s)	
Schedules are divided into	schedule(s)	
	paragraph(s)	
	subparagraphs	

Statutory Instruments (SIs) are a type of legislation which follows an existing Act without the need of fully repealing or replacing it. SIs add detail to the framework given in an Act. They are cited as:

Full title

- Year
- SI
- SI year/SI number

The Motor Vehicles (Tests) (Amendment) (Coronavirus) (No. 2) Regulations 2020, SI 2020/790

The Consumer Protection from Unfair Trading Regulations 2008, SI 2008/127

As Acts are divided, Statutory Instruments are also further broken down:

SIs are divided into	regulation(s)	reg/regs
	rule(s)	r/rr
	article(s)	art/arts

Tasks C16–C20 are based on the preceding text "The police's powers of stop and search"

Task C16 – Find two ways that a section of an Act in the Stop and Search text was presented

Task C17 – Which Act has cited two sections and how is this presented in the footnotes?

Task C18 – Why is s 60(3) of CJPO not cited in the footnotes?

Task C19 – Is citation number 6 necessary?

Task C20 – Should citation number 6 appear in the bibliography under the Statutes subheading?

Task C21 – Look at the website legislation.gov.uk for assistance with the following questions

a   To what does Employment Rights Act 1996, s 1(4)(c)(ii) refer?

b   According to the Companies Act 1985, sch 1a what is 'significant control'?

c   Cite the statute that modified dates provided by the Stamp Duty Land Tax (Temporary Relief Act) 2020

d   Cite the statute that modified amount of tax paid under the Stamp Duty Land Tax (Temporary Relief Act) 2020 for residential homes

e   Cite the statute that modified amount of tax paid under the Stamp Duty Land Tax (Temporary Relief Act) 2020 for additional properties

f   How do you cite subsection (1a) of section 6 of the Unfair Contract Terms Act 1977?

g   How do you cite the words "except in so far as the term satisfies the requirement of reasonableness" from the aforementioned statute?

h   Does this section apply to consumer contracts? If not, cite the source of that legislation.

i   Which schedule should be researched if looking for guidelines on the test of reasonableness in UCTA 1977, and how should it be cited?

j   To what does Consumer Protection from Unfair Trading Regulations 2008, SI 2008/127, reg 6 (4)(d)(i) refer?

Websites

OSCOLA guidance on websites is relatively unclear due to the varied and increasing numbers of platforms available to researchers. Given that the latest OSCOLA guidance was published in 2012, and the FAQ webpage lists accessed dates from April 2014, it is hoped that any guidance is updated quickly and comprehensively. Therefore, the information presented next is a best guess by looking at OSCOLA as well as considering online sources frequently accessed by current university and college students. The basic information order is:

*   Name of the author or speaker (or organisation or their website domain)
*   'Title of document, website or programme'
*   (publication/broadcast date platform omit if none)

- <url> [exclude http:// or https:// if www follows)
- Insert start and end time if audio
- Accessed + date

Websites (an organisation's name as author, no date)

EUR-Lex 'Harmonising the Numbering of EU Legal Acts' <https://eur-lex. europa.eu/content/tools/elaw/OA0614022END.pdf> Accessed 19 August 2020

Websites (an organisation's full domain as author, no date)

Biicl.org 'Introduction to English Tort Law' <www.biicl.org/files/763_intro-duction_to_english_tort_law.pdf> Accessed 21 August 2020

Websites (from a person speaking/writing in an organisation's work, no date)

Mathilde Pavis 'Do Love Island contestants leave their legal rights at the door of the villa?' <www.bbc.co.uk/sounds/play/p07vkky1> Accessed 19 August 2020

Websites (directly quoting a person speaking/writing in an organisation's work)

Jessica Boyd 'Shagang Shipping Company Ltd (in liquidation) (Appellant) v HNA Group Company Ltd (Respondent) (16 June 2020) <www.supreme-court.uk/watch/uksc-2018-0173/160620-pm.html> 34.45–35.01 Accessed 19 August 2020

Websites (from a government department, no author)

Ministry of Justice 'Stop and Search' (7 August 2020) <www.ethnicity-facts-figures.service.gov.uk/crime-justice-and-the-law/policing/stop-and-search/latest#by-ethnicity-and-legislation-over-time> Accessed 20 August 2020

Websites (newspapers)

Newspapers have a small addition to standard web pages

- First name and second name of the author(s)
- 'Headline'
- *Newspaper's full name*
- (publication location, publication date)
- <url> [exclude http:// or https:// if www follows)
- Accessed + date

TT Arvind and Lindsay Stirton 'The UK Supreme Court will not only decide Johnston's fate, it will declare whether Scotland's constitutional traditions still

matters' *The Independent* (London, 14 September 2019) <www.independent.
co.uk/voices/boris-johnson-brexit-supreme-court-scotland-parliament-sus-
pend-a9104446.html> Accessed 21 August 2020

Note that TT Arvind's name is initialised in the source material, therefore it should
be written as presented. TT Arvind is also an author of several contract law textbooks, and commonly goes by this name (think JK Rowling is likely more recognisable than Joanne Rowling).

Directly quoting from websites

The exact words used by any another source need to be placed between single
quotation marks with the full stop and citation number following. Further style
guidance is given on direct quotations on page 135.

> Stop and searches have decreased for all ethnicities across the UK's police forces
> but at different rates, yet 'almost half of all stop and searches took place in the
> Metropolitan Police force area in London'.[1]
>
> _____
>
> [1] Ministry of Justice, 'Stop and Search' (7 August 2020) <www.ethnicity-facts-figures.service.gov.uk/crime-
> justice-and-the-law/policing/stop-and-search/latest#by-ethnicity-and-area> Accessed 20 August 2020.

Because websites appear as one long page of text unlike pages from books or journals, there is no need to pinpoint directly quoted material sourced online.

Directly quoting audio from websites

> Boyd[1] argued that 'The minority, led by Lord Bingham, held that evidence should
> be excluded if there was a real risk it had been obtained by torture. The majority
> agreed with Lord Hope, that it should be excluded if torture was established on the
> balance of probabilities.'
>
> _____
>
> [1] Jessica Boyd, *'Shagang Shipping Company Ltd (in Liquidation) (Appellant) v HNA Group Company
> Ltd (Respondent)'* (16 June 2020) <www.supremecourt.uk/watch/uksc-2018-0173/160620-pm.html>
> 34.45–35.01 Accessed 19 August 2020.

Note: After the URL, the time given is the starting and ending time of the exact
words spoken, not the section of speech.

Note: The formatting I have used for the timing is hour'minute.second (without spacing). As an example, the whole excerpt of Boyd's Supreme Court speech would be 25.48–1'15.21.

As with the written word, no pinpointing (ie page number) is required; therefore this can be omitted if paraphrasing an audio clip.

WEBSITES

Arvind TT and Stirton L, 'The UK Supreme Court will not only decide Johnston's fate, it will declare whether Scotland's constitutional traditions still matters' The Independent (London, 14 September 2019) <www.independent.co.uk/voices/boris-johnson-brexit-supreme-court-scotland-parliament-suspend-a9104446.html> Accessed 21 August 2020

Biicl.org 'Introduction to English Tort Law' <www.biicl.org/files/763_introduction_to_english_tort_law.pdf> Accessed 21 August 2020

Boyd J, 'Shagang Shipping Company Ltd (in liquidation) (Appellant) v HNA Group Company Ltd (Respondent) (16 June 2020) <www.supremecourt.uk/watch/uksc-2018-0173/160620-pm.html> 34.45–35.01 Accessed 19 August 2020

EUR-Lex 'Harmonising the Numbering of EU Legal Acts' <https://eur-lex.europa.eu/content/tools/elaw/OA0614022END.pdf> Accessed 19 August 2020

Ministry of Justice 'Stop and Search' (7 August 2020) <www.ethnicity-facts-figures.service.gov.uk/crime-justice-and-the-law/policing/stop-and-search/latest#by-ethnicity-and-area> Accessed 20 August 2020

Pavis M, 'Do Love Island contestants leave their legal rights at the door of the villa?' <www.bbc.co.uk/sounds/play/p07vkky1> Accessed 19 August 2020

Many of the features of websites in the bibliography are shared with other source types, such as the reversal of name order and the comma after the first name initial.

The formatting of some sources may appear odd and imbalanced, such as the second source in the preceding box, but do not worry about the aesthetics. Where a domain name is given, this is up to the first slash (/) of the address, excluding the www. prefix.

Task C22 – How are the in-text citations for both Ministry of Justice sources different?

Task C23 – Would the Ministry of Justice source be cited once or twice in the bibliography under the Websites subheading?

Task C24 – Does the date in the Pavis source refer to the date the programme was first broadcast on radio, the date the programmes were uploaded to the BBC website as a podcast, the date I first listened to the audio, or the date I last listened to the audio?

Task C25 – Is Pavis the host of the show, an expert contributor or guest on the show?

Task C26 – Why is the EUR-Lex source URL (web address) different to the other websites?

Task C27 – Why is the Ministry of Justice source not given as Ethnicity-facts-fig-ures.service.gov.uk, gov.uk or anything in between?

Judges' abbreviations

Judges can be cited according to their full names or, for the sake of time and space, in their abbreviated forms.

Court	Name	Abbreviation
High Court	Mr Justice + Surname Mrs Justice + Surname Mr Justice Smith Sir John Smith Mr Justice Smith + Mr Justice Evans	Surname + J Smith J No abbreviated form - titles/peerages remain Smith and Evans JJ
Court of Appeal	Lord Justice + Surname Lady Justice + Surname Lady Justice Jones Unless a peer/title, or a barrister sitting as a judge Lord Justice Jones + Lord Justice Evans	Surname + LJ Jones LJ Lord Smith/Sir John Smith, Judge John Smith QC Jones and Evans LJJ
Supreme Court	Lord/Lady + Surname President Deputy President Master of the Rolls Lord Reed P and Lady Arden	Surname + SCJ Lady Arden/Lord Sales Lord Reed P Lord Hodge DP Lord Etherton MR Named individually - No plural forms are used

Figure 3.2 Judge's abbreviations

Citing a single judge is straightforward as listed in Figure 3.2, but changes slightly when citing two judges. Look at the following examples.

a   In *Brand v No Limits Track Days Ltd*[1] Mr Justice Southey QC held that . . .

b   Applying the ruling from *The Heron II*[2] Smith and Jones LLJ . . .

c   Denning MR (dissenting) . . .

d   Lord Reed P explained in . . .

e   Reeves and Mortimer JJ found in favour . . .

f   As Sales SCJ held . . .

g   In a strong *obiter dicta*, Sir John Smith and Lady Jones warned against . . .

h   Lady Hale P said it was unlawful if "prorogation has the effect of frustrating or preventing . . . parliament to carry out its constitutional functions."[3]

Task C28 – Identify the number of judges, the court, any titles of the judge(s) and their role within the court if applicable

a   How else could Mr Justice Southey be written?

b   Why are only three citation numbers given?

c   What does dissenting mean?

Task C29 – One of the most famous judges was Tom Denning who served in the High Court, Court of Appeal, House of Lords and as Master of the Rolls. Look through each of these cases and work out how his *obiter* should be cited.

> *Anglo Continental Holidays Ltd v Typaldos Lines (London) Ltd* [1967] 2 Lloyd's Rep 61 (maritime law)
>
> *Central London Property Trust Ltd v High Trees House Ltd* [1947] KB 130 (payment of debt)
>
> *Entores Ltd v Miles Far East Corporation* [1955] 2 All ER 493 (contract law)
>
> *J Spurling Ltd v Bradshaw* [1956] 1 WLR 461 (contract law)
>
> *Lewis v Averay* (1971) (Criminal law)
>
> *Mandla v Dowell-Lee* [1983] QB 1 (Human Rights)
>
> *Miller v Jackson* [1977] QB 966 (Tort)
>
> *Nettleship v Weston* [1971] 3 All ER 581 (Tort)
>
> *Scottish Co-operative Wholesale Society Ltd v Meyer* [1959] AC 324 (company)

Hint: As a custom, recognise the long service of a judge by stating which type of Justice they were at the time of the citation. This acknowledges that the judge has progressed, become more learned and authoritative, eg:

> In *R v Duffy* (1949), Devlin J (as he was then) . . .

Directly citing judges

Sometimes it may be necessary to directly quote a judge who has made a strong *obiter*, or when a point can be summarised better by legal experts. The examples on page 109 are wholly appropriate ways to introduce a paraphrase, but sometimes a direct quote can be more powerful, such as one of Lord Denning's famous quotes from *J Spurling v Bradshaw*. Did you find it? It's particularly useful and recognisable due to its visual imagery.

For this quote, the full paragraph would be something like:

For exclusion clauses in contracts, Denning LJ explained unusual clauses need to be made prominently:

I quite agree that the more unreasonable a clause is, the greater the notice which must be given of it. Some clauses which I have seen would need to be printed in red ink on the face of the document with a red hand pointing to it before the notice could be held to be sufficient.[1]

Note the citation number has now come at the end of the direct quote. For further rules on formatting of direct quotes, see page 139.

Direct quotes are known by OSCOLA as pinpointing, and the pinpoint appears as a number in square brackets after the court, which will be the paragraph number if available, or page number if not. Pinpointing follows on from the rules of the citing of cases, dependent on if they are pre- or post-2001 (ie neutral citations).

- *Party names* + *(Ship's Name)*
- [Year]
- Court
- Case number
- Law report citation,
- Page number
- (Judge's surname + Judge's abbreviated title).
- *Party names* + *(Ship's Name)*
- [Year] OR (Year)
- Volume
- Law report abbreviation

- First page or Case number
- Abbreviated Court name
- [Paragraph number]
- (Judge's surname + Judge's abbreviated title).

---

[1] *J Spurling Ltd v Bradshaw* [1956] 1 WLR 461, 466 (Denning LJ).

[2] *Sevilleja v Marex Financial Ltd* [2020] UKSC 31 [49] (Reed SCJ).

The cases are cited under the Cases subheading of the bibliography.

Judges citing judges

Judges refer to previous cases and commentaries to pick apart the differences and nuances between cases. In *Sevilleja v Marex*, for example, the principle of *reflective loss* was based on the relationship between the company shares and the value of its assets. The Claim being discussed was if non-shareholding creditors can bring claims against the company and its directors. This sample answer shows different ways for a Supreme Court judge to cite earlier judges:

The reflective loss rule established in *Prudential Assurance Co Ltd v Newman Industries Ltd*[3] provided protection for companies in mitigating against losses of a shareholder and shareholders who are also creditors or employees. The Supreme Court was unanimous in deciding the rule has no effect where the claim is from a creditor, not a shareholder, but disagreed on redefining the principle.

The majority view (led by Lord Reed) felt there was a need to distinguish between:

(1) cases where claims are brought by a shareholder in respect of loss which he has suffered in that capacity, in the form of a diminution in share value or in distributions, which is the consequence of loss sustained by the company, in respect of which the company has a cause of action against the same wrongdoer, and (2) cases where claims are brought, whether by a shareholder or by anyone else, in respect of loss which does not fall within that description, but where the company has a right of action in respect of substantially the same loss.[4]

Therefore, claims in the former will not succeed following Prudential whereas claims in the latter will succeed.

cont. Sales SCJ (with whom Lord Kitchen and Lady Hale agreed) preferred a
        less clear-cut distinction, arguing that following Prudential 'loss suffered
by the company *is the same as* the loss suffered by the shareholder'.[5] Flaux LJ
developed four elements justifying the reflective loss principle (based on *Lord*
Millett in Johnston v Gore Wood),[6] including loss to the claimant is caused not by
the defendant's wrongdoing but a company's decision (per Chadwick LJ in *Giles v*
Rhind).[7] Lord Sales in stating *obiter* that Johnston should not be followed raises
doubt as to the suitability of the current framework.

On past cases, Lord Reed [at para 89] said:

> I would therefore reaffirm the approach adopted in Prudential and by Lord
> Bingham in Johnson, and depart from the reasoning in the other speeches in
> that case, and in later authorities, so far as it is inconsistent with the foregoing.
> It follows that *Giles v Rhind, Perry v Day* and *Gardner v Parker* were wrongly
> decided. The rule in Prudential is limited to claims by shareholders that, as a
> result of actionable loss suffered by their company, the value of their shares,
> or of the distributions they receive as shareholders, has been diminished.[8]

The court's summary was that reflective loss rule 'had unwelcome and unjustifiable
effects' and if had been applied in this case 'would result in great injustice'.[9]

---

[3] *Prudential Assurance v Newman Industries Ltd* (No 2) [1982] 1 Ch 204.

[4] *Sevilleja v Marex Financial Ltd* [2020] UKSC 31 [79].

[5] n 4 [197] (emphasis added).

[6] *Johnson v Gore Wood & Co* [2001] 2 AC 1 [62] (Millett LJ).

[7] *Giles v Rhind* [2002] EWCA 1428.

[8] *Sevilleja v Marex Financial Ltd* [2020] UKSC 31.

[9] n 4 [95] (Hodge SCJ).

Notice how citation numbers 5 and 9 use a shortcut to an earlier citation number
(n) and can give further information. n 5 references a new page and added emphasis, while n 9 refers to a summarised quotation by Justice Hodge.

Task C30

a   What are the differences in the way long and short direct quotes are presented?

b   How do the case names change between first and subsequent appearances?

c   Write out the rules of the four different ways of directly quoting judges citing
    judges for in text and footnotes.

d   Do cases cited in earlier judgments need to be included in footnotes or the bibliography?

e   In the footnotes, why have the full case citation for numbers 5 and 9 been omitted and what has replaced it?

f   Write the chronological order of who cited whom in the sentence containing citation number 6.

g   Why is the final direct quote in two parts, and how is this cited differently to one continuous line? How else could this be written?

h   Of the four mentions of *Sevilleja*, why does only footnote 9 have the judge's name in brackets?

i   What does the final number in square brackets in the bibliography refer to?

j   What phrases are used to associate a judge with i) a paraphrase, ii) a direct quote and iii) a previous judgment?

k   Why does source citation number 8 not have a paragraph/page number even though it is a direct pinpoint quote?

l   If a judgment has a word italicised in the text or written in double or single speech marks, how should this be presented in your direct quote?

m   In which subsection of the bibliography would the preceding footnotes appear?

n   If citation 10 were to reference *Sevilleja*, which n number should be cited?

o   If citation 10 were to reference Lord Reed in *Sevilleja*, which n number should be cited?

p   What is the student trying to draw the reader's attention to by using emphasis in the fifth citation?

q   How would pinpoints or summaries stretching over multiple pages or paragraphs be written?

Quotations within quotations

> There is no disagreement within the court that the expansion of the so-called "principle" that reflective loss cannot be recovered has had unwelcome and unjustifiable effects on the law and that, if the facts alleged by Marex are established in this case, the exclusion of the bulk of its claim would result in a great injustice.[15]

> 'It is not a question, in this court, whether "two wrongs make a right" as Mr Choo Choy put it.'[16]

Compare the two methods of directly quoting material that has already been directly quoted.

In the first excerpt, the word "principle" is in double speech marks, whereas the whole quoted passage has no quotations marks. The fact it is a direct quote can also be identified by the margin indentation to the sides and justified text (ie the text takes the shape of a box). The party name *Marex* has not been italicised to stay true to the cited material.

In the second box, a quotation within a short quotation (fewer than three lines of text) would have single speech marks on the outsides, the margins are full-width and left-justified, and double speech marks for the quoted word. The final full stop here comes before the closing speech mark because a whole sentence is cited.

Adapting sources to suit sentence structure

Where a chunk of text is cited and incorporated into your own sentence, the order is altered to:

Single closing speech mark + punctuation + space + citation number:

... following *Prudential* 'loss suffered by the company is *the same* as the loss suffered by the shareholder'.[5]

When fragments (small parts) of a sentence are inserted, no capital letter is needed to begin the directly quoted material. The exception is if it is a complete sentence, then a capital is copied as per the original source.

Imagine a student's wishes to directly quote the following source but insert it into their own new and grammatically complete sentence:

Putting matters broadly at this stage, in *Johnson v Gore Wood & Co* [2002] 2 AC 1 the House of Lords purported to follow *Prudential*, but the reasoning of some members of the Appellate Committee was not clearly confined to circumstances of the kind with which *Prudential* was concerned.

When quoted material starts your sentence, the first letter should be capitalised as per the original text, unless your sentence begins in the source's mid-sentence. For example, the original text is:

> '[T]he House of Lords purported to follow *Prudential,* but the reasoning of some members of the Appellate Committee was not clearly confined to circumstances of the kind with which *Prudential* was concerned.'[17]
>
> ——————————
>
> [17] *Sevilleja v Marex Financial Ltd* [2020] UKSC 31.

The small t in *the* House of Lords has been changed to a capital letter to suit the student's essay structure. To show there has been some adaptation to the original source, a capital T is placed between square brackets.

See the next section for making the source material fit mid-sentence.

Long passages from previous judgments (case, book and journal)

Follow the same guidance for quotations of over three lines in length. This is Alderson B's original ruling from the seminal case *Hadley v Baxendale*:

> Now we think the proper rule in such a case as the present is this: – Where two parties have made a contract which one of them has broken, the damages which the other party ought to receive in respect of such breach of contract should be such as may fairly and reasonably be considered either arising naturally, i.e., according to the usual course of things, from such breach of contract itself, or such as may reasonably be supposed to have been in the contemplation of both parties, at the time they made the contract, as the probable result of the breach of it.

Lord Hodge wanted to refer to use it in his summing up:

> Alderson B famously stated the principle in these terms:
>
> > [T]he proper rule in such a case as the present is this: – Where two parties have made a contract which one of them has broken, the damages which the other party ought to receive in respect of such breach of contract should be such as may fairly and reasonably be considered either arising naturally, i.e., according to the usual course of things, from such breach of contract itself, or such as may reasonably be supposed to have been in the contemplation of both parties, at the time they made the contract, as the probable result of the breach of it.[18]

---

cont.

----

[18] Lord Hodge, *AG of the Virgin Islands v Global Water Associates Ltd* (British Virgin Islands) [2020] UKPC
   18 [21] citing *Hadley v Baxendale* (1854) 9 Ex. 341 [354] (Alderson B).

Thus the footnotes order is:

Title + Surname, + full case citation + paragraph/page number + citing + full original case name with party names *italicised* + first page + [page/paragraph of original quote] + (Original Judge's Surname + Abbreviation).

Note that (Alderson B) needn't be added here as his name appears in the sentence preceding the long direct quote. (Alderson B) would be obligatory if his name were absent elsewhere.

When the original source is **a book**:

---

29 More recently, Professor Andrew Burrows (now Lord Burrows) in
   "A Restatement of the English Law of Contract" (2016), in which
   he was assisted by an advisory board of academics, judges
   and practitioners, described the general rule on remoteness of
   damage in contract in these terms (p 20):

   "The general rule is that loss is too remote if that type of
   loss could not reasonably have been contemplated by the
   defendant <u>as a serious possibility</u> at the time the contract
   was made assuming that, at that time, the defendant had
   thought about the breach." (Emphasis added)

Student's text

The general rule is that loss is too remote if that type of loss could not reasonably have
been contemplated by the defendant <u>as a serious possibility</u> at the time the contract
was made assuming that, at that time, the defendant had thought about the breach.[19]

----

[19] Lord Hodge, *AG of the Virgin Islands v Global Water Associates Ltd* (British Virgin Islands) [2020]
   UKPC 18 [29] citing Andrew Burrows, *A Restatement of the English Law of Contract* (Oxford
   University Press 2016) 21.

Note that the emphasis has remained. Andrew Burrows wrote the original without underlining, Lord Hodge added the emphasis, and it has remained in the student's text as it is important for the argument.

The footnote order is:

Title + Surname, + full case citation + paragraph/page number + citing + original author's first name and surname + '*Title of Book*' + (Publisher, Year of publication) + pinpoint to pages if no paragraph numbers.

Hint: Generally, it is important for the student to access the original text and to cite that accordingly. However, in law, the weight of the argument would be weaker without including Lord Hodge's acknowledgement of the Burrows source.

When the original source is **a journal**:

The original text . . .

> Today it promises to distort large areas of the ordinary law of obligations unless drastic steps are taken to prune it.

. . . has had its capitalisation adapted in order to flow better with the student's work:

> Academics have warned that '[t]oday it promises to distort large areas of the ordinary law of obligations'.[20]
>
> ------------------
>
> [20] Lord Reed Sevilleja v Marex Financial Ltd [2020] UKSC 31 citing Andrew Tettenborn, '*Creditors and Reflective Loss: A Bar Too Far?*' (2019) 135 LQR 182, 183.

The footnote has been constructed as:

Title + Surname, + full case citation + paragraph/page number + citing + original author's first name and surname + '*Title of Article*' + (Year of publication) + Volume/(Issue) + full/abbreviated Journal Title + first page of the article, + page pinpoint.

Law report abbreviations

The majority of reports contain the following words and are therefore abbreviated correspondingly (Figure 3.3):

Criminal Crim	European Eur	International Intl
Journal J	Law/Legal L	Quarterly Q
Report(s) Rep	Review Rev	Yearbook YB

Figure 3.3 Common abbreviations in law reports

The most frequently used law reports do not need to be defined as their abbreviated form is frequently recognised (Figure 3.4). However, that may not help you if you are new to law and are unsure which report is frequently cited.

Full Law Report name	Accepted abbreviated title
Law Reports	AC, QB, Ch, Fam, P
All England Law Report	All ER
British Company Law Cases	BCC
Common Market Law Reports	CMLR
Criminal Appeal Reports	Cr App R
Criminal Appeal Reports (Sentencing)	Cr App R (S)
Current Law Yearbook	CLY
English Reports	ER
Estates Gazette	EG
European Court Reports	ECR
European Human Rights Reports	EHRR
Family Law Reports	FLR
Financial Times Law Reports	FTLR
Fleet Street Reports	FSR
Industrial Cases Reports	ICR
Industrial Relations Law Reports	IRLR
Journal of Planning Law	JPL
Justice of the Peace Reports	JP
Law Society Gazette	LS Gaz
Lloyd's Law Reports	Lloyd's Rep
Local Government Reports	LGR
Property and Compensation Reports	P & CR
Public and Third Sector Law Reports	PTSLR
Reports of Patent Cases	RPC
Session Cases	SC
Simon's Tax Cases	STC
Tax Cases	TC
Weekly Law Reports	WLR

Figure 3.4 Accepted abbreviated titles of frequently cited law reports

OSCOLA advises that any law reports not given in Figure 3.4 are checked on www. legalabbrevs.cardiff.ac.uk/ which will give a preferred abbreviation (if available) and an alternative, eg Lloyd's Rep. is the preference for Lloyd's Law Reports, and Lloyd L. R. is given as an alternative.

Be aware that some report entries may be duplicated, for example can also be abbreviated to Lloyd's Rep. and Lloyd L. R. which is the same preferred and alternative abbreviation as Lloyd's Law Reports. In the scenario where the two Lloyd reports were used, and to distinguish between them, maintain use of the main and most frequent report, and use one of the alternative abbreviations for the least frequent report which clearly shows the difference between Lloyd's and Lloyd's List, thus Lloyd's Rep. and Lloyd's List L. R. respectively.

Styling and formatting

Sources can be cited at the beginning, middle or end of a sentence. For example:

- Lord Sales[1] questioned whether . . .
- In a decision concurring with Lord Reed, Lord Hodge[2] held . . .
- . . . for the amount of damages due under Field J.'s calculations.[3]

Note that in the first two sentences, the citation number appears before the verb (*questioned* and *held*), and in the final example, comes at the end of the sentence.

Consequently, citation numbers can appear:

- After a case name
- After legislation
- At the end of the sentence where a source has been directly quoted, paraphrased or summarised
- After a key word or phrase

In the case of *R v Wallace (Berlinah)*[1] the Court of Appeal focussed on reasonable foreseeability and voluntariness following an acid attack, contrary to the Offences Against the Person Act 1861.[2] Could the defendant have reasonably predicted that the time of throwing acid and as a result of his injuries, that he would choose to end his life[3] and if Belgian doctors accepted an 'independent, free and voluntary'[4] request for euthanasia, this would break the chain of causation.[5] Had the deceased refused treatment and subsequently died, the chain of causation would not have been broken.

---

cont.

---

1 [2018] EWCA Crim 690, [2018] 2 Cr App R 22.

2 s 29.

3 *Wallace* (n 1). OR *R v Wallace (Berlinah)* + all n1. OR (n 1).

4 *Wallace* (n 1) [3]. OR fully repeat n 1 [3]. OR ibid [3].

5 *R v Wallace (Berlinah)* [2018] EWCA Crim 690, [2018] 2 Cr App R 22.

The formatting of the in-text citation (see earlier sections) is:

Source + (Punctuation mark) + citation number in superscript + space

Subsequent citations of a case

Note: The n number technique should only be used when both citation numbers are relatively close to each other as to make it easier for the reader to cross-reference the footnotes without undue effort.

For footnote 1, the name of the case is not given as the parties have already been provided in the text. An alternative would be to write "In *Wallace*,[1] the Court of Appeal . . ." and include the full citation (*R v Wallace (Berlinah)* [2018] EWCA Crim 690, [2018] 2 Cr App R 22.) in the footnotes. In criminal cases, the defendant's first name is italicised in brackets, which differentiates this case from the 73 other *R v Wallace* cases that are currently recorded.

Similarly for footnote 2, the Act is given as the root source so other sections can later be cited from it. When the root source is initially given, pinpointing and sections can easily be added.

Notice how footnote numbers 3–4 have very little information compared to 5 which is a full reference. The third citation tells the reader in three alternative ways to look at citation number 1 (n1) for the full citation.

Case law (footnote number 3) can be condensed to just the first party name, both parties, a repeated full citation or a referral to the original footnote number. Cases with popular names eg *Adams v Lindsell* establishing the postal rule case can be subsequently cited as (Postal Rule case) when this is added to the first occurrence in the footnotes. Further footnotes can simply state:

Postal Rule case (n 1).

The fourth citation contains a reference to the page or paragraph number (dependent on if the source is a law report or case citation) because it directly quotes from paragraph 3 of *Wallace*.

The Latin abbreviation ibid is used to mean "the same as above", however some universities prefer a full citation to be repeated.

In the footnotes, the formatting for repeated mentions following an already given source is:

- n + space + previous citation number
- at + paragraph number or page number if citing a direct quotation

For maritime law, cases involving ships can be footnoted as:

---

[8] *K Line Pte Ltd v Priminds Shipping (HK) Co Ltd (Eternal Bliss)* [2020] QBD (Comm Ct) [2020] EWHC 2373 Comm.

[9] *Eternal Bliss* (n 8).

Here, the subsequent citation can be shortened to the italicised ship's name + the earlier citation number

Task C31 – Next are the footnotes from a student answer. Connect the subsequent footnotes to the original citation

1   Copyright, Designs and Patents Act 1988 (CDPA 1988).
2   *Lucasfilm Ltd v Ainsworth* [2011] UKSC 39, [2012] 1 AC 208, [2011] 7 WLUK 792 (SC).
3   CDPA 1988, s 4.
4   *Conversant Wireless Licensing SARL v Huawei Technologies Co Ltd* [2018] EWHC 808 (Pat).
5   *Eli Lilly and Co v Genentech Inc* [2017] EHWC 3104 (Pat).
6   ibid.
7   G Bacon and K Rooth 'Justiciability and Litigation of Foreign Patents in the English Courts' [2017] JIPLP 12(10) 851.
8   n 7 [856].
9   n 4 [14].

Task C32 – Answer the questions about the preceding footnotes

a   Why is the use of ibid not permissible for citation number 8 referring back
to n7?

b   Could ibid be used for citation number 8? If so, when?

c   How would the 1998 Act be cited at citation number 10?

d   How would section 51 of the 1998 Act be cited at citation number 11?

e   Could citation number 10 be "n 1, s 52"?

f   Add paragraph 22 to the judgment of *Lucasfilm* from the UKSC

g   Add paragraph 28 to 29 to your answer (f)

Adapting judgments to suit

Direct quotations are when the exact words of a source are written in your own
essay. There is no harm in directly quoting a source and citing it, however your
answer may be severely limited if you rely only on direct quotation as it will show a
lack of understanding, critical thinking and answering the question.

That said, there are times when a direct quotation can be a useful academic tool. I
normally caution against direct quotations unless:

• A text contains essential information

• The wording is of paramount importance

• The phrasing and interpretation are critical to the meaning

• Someone else has said something that you cannot possibly improve

Examples may include a statute, a definition, a judgment and an explanation.
For example, the direct quotation from Lord Hodge:

> There is no disagreement within the court that the expansion of the so-called
> "principle" that reflective loss cannot be recovered has had unwelcome and
> unjustifiable effects on the law and that, if the facts alleged by Marex are
> established in this case, the exclusion of the bulk of its claim would result in a
> great injustice.

could be written:

> The court's summary was that *reflective loss* rule "had unwelcome and
> unjustifiable effects . . . [that] would result in great injustice".[1]

Notice how the student has used the pronoun *that* to connect the two ideas, written between square brackets. Other acceptable words to use between brackets are conjunctions, pronouns and linking words that help with the flow of the point.

Content words are not permissible unless they clarify a statement, such as the example that follows which associates the loss to a party:

> 'The [claimants'] loss is the loss suffered by a creditor of the company which, apart from its cause of action in deceit, is worthless'. [1]

Abbreviations in case names

In the names of cases, there are several frequently used abbreviations which, depending on your field of law, you will regularly use. In Figure 3.5 is a list of the most general and oft-cited.

&	and
Attorney General	A-G
BC	Borough Council
Bros	Brothers
CC	County Council
Co	Company
Corp	Corporation
CPS	Crown Prosecution Service
DC	District Council
decd	deceased
Dept	Department
DPP	Director of Public Prosecutions
HM	His/Her Majesty's
Inc	Incorporated
liq	(in) liquidation
Ltd	Limited
ors	others
plc	public limited company
Pty	Proprietary
R	*Rex/Regina* (the King/Queen)
Rly	Railway

Figure 3.5 Abbreviations in case names

Task C33 – Put the following names into the correct columns. Not all of the details in the author's name are needed.

Author's name according to book/website title	Family name/ Surname	First name/Given name
Geraint Brown	*Brown*	*Geraint*
Jon D. Reason		
Marcia Passmore-Evans		
MacCormick, John-Lee		
Montel RUSH		
Professor Simon Ace		
MOORMAN, George		
BBC		
Montell, Brook & Day LLP (Barristers at law)		
Dr. Francis del Pierro		
Ronald van der Westhuizen		
E. Alfred McCormick		
Larry Orsinger II Jr		
Pan Linwei		
John Shaftle MA		

Task C34 – Put the names into the correct order for a bibliography

Task C35 – Identify what is wrong, if anything, with the following citations and correct them

a   (*The Achilleas*) *Transfield Shipping Inc v Mercador Shipping Inc* [2008] UKHL 48

b   Bhanawat A 'Rotterdam Rules – Redefining and Introducing the Electronic Bill of Lading' (2020) <www.marineinsight.com/maritime-law/rotterdam-rules-redefining-and-introducing-the-electronic-bill-of-lading/> accessed 28 October 2019

c   Di Lieto G and Treisman D, *International Trade Law* (1st edn, Federation Press, 2018)

d   Electronic Commerce (EC Directive) Regulations 2002 (SI 2002/2013)

e   *Hadley v Baxendale* (1854) 9 Exch 341

f   Limitation Act (1980)

g   Mahafzah Q and Naser M, 'The Inadequacy of the Existing International Maritime Transport Regimes for Modern Container Transport' [2019] 13(4) Modern Applied Science < www.researchgate.net/publication/330933467_ The_Inadequacy_of_the_Existing_International_Maritime_Transport_ Regimes_for_Modern_Container_Transport> accessed 29 July 2020

h   Misrepresentations Act 1967 s 2(2)

i   Murray C, Holloway D, Timson-Hunt D, Dixon G *Schmitthoff: The Law and Practice of International Trade* (12th edn, Sweet & Maxwell, 2014)

j   Nikaki T and Soyer B, 'A New International Regime for Carriage of Goods by Sea: Contemporary, Certain, Inclusive AND Efficient, or Just Another One for the Shelves?' [2012] 30(2) Berkeley J Intl L 303, 305

k   van Haersolte-van Hof J & Holland R '*What makes for Effective Arbitration? A Case Study of the London Court of International Arbitration Rules*' in Peter Quayle and Xuan Gao (eds), 'International Organizations and the Promotion of Effective Dispute Resolution' (Brill Nojhoff, 2019)

Task C36 – Place those 11 sources into bibliography page giving suitable subheadings

Other forms of assessment

In the current climate, there has been a move towards more technologically based assessments and away from traditional essays submissions. Now that technophobic lecturers have been forced to embrace IT, the standard essay and exam assessments may no longer be the primary method of testing. Assessment is a huge area of educational interest and research, and in the following is a student-focussed brief overview of the types of assessment that can be expected in the UK.

Standard assessments were 'closed-book', meaning only the knowledge in your head could be written as an answer. Lecturers are now designing deliberately 'open-book' assessments where you are meant to use law databases and search engines to help form your answer. This has the advantage of meaning you may not have to remember as much information, but it is now testing your application and evaluation skills more than ever.

Tasks can also be given individually or as group work, especially so for larger project work or problem-based learning. At the beginning of the first semester, it would not be unusual for new classmates to get to know each other by allocating and sharing workload on one project.

You should be able to access your institution's grading schemata or matrix which gives you an idea of what the assessors will be looking for, and the weighting of each element, skill or component you are being assessed on. It is a good idea to read this and understand the requirements. Your lecturer or tutor will be able to give you advice on each point and how to improve.

Written assessments

Essays

No doubt you will have already had experience of answering other written assessment types, such as compare/contrast, problem-solution, advantage disadvantage, and for/against essays. To show the differences, the same topic is used but consider the variation in your answer depending on which pattern you are answering.

Judgments in protecting the colour purple have proved troublesome for IP lawyers . . .

a   What was the basis for the conflicting judgments in dismissing protecting GlaxoSmithKline's colour purple (Pantone 2587C) and allowing the Mars Petcare's purple (Pantone 248C)?

b   How can companies convince the ECJ that their shade of purple has protectable and distinctive character?

c   What are the advantages and drawbacks of preventing the monopoly of certain shades associated with industries or products?

d   Evaluate the arguments used in GlaxoSmithKline and Mars Petcare in protecting their respective shades of purple

e   Organic Petfood Products Ltd wants to know if they can use a similar colour packaging of their pet food to Mars Petcare's products.

Task C37 – Match the letter (a–e) to the following question pattern types:

> PQ   Advantage/disadvantage   compare/contrast
>   for/against   Problem/solution

Short answers

You will normally be faced with a scenario such as the *Jack v Peter* PQ to give context, or just given a short question on a specific element of law. Using *Jack v Peter*, a typical question would be:

•   Define a contract (1 mark)

•   Explain whether Peter's first email to Jack is an offer or an ITT (3 marks)

•   What is the difference between an ITT and offer? (3 marks)

•   Why is the mirroring of an offer and an acceptance necessary? (5 marks)

•   Does the postal rule have a place in the 21st century? (10 marks)

What you may notice is that the questions become progressively more challenging to answer, and require more detail so show depth of understanding. Allocated maximum marks noted next to each question suggest to you the amount of time and detail that should be spent on each question.

All the questions will be related to the given PQ, and can be thought of as a pre-staged answer to a CLEO answer as discussed throughout this book.

Short answers and long answers (next) may require you to answer a certain number of questions from each part of the task. For example, part 1 of the exam might require short answers for each of the five questions, but part 2 may have three PQs on contract formation, mistake and misrepresentation for instance, but only one of these three need be competed.

Long answers

Using the same PQ format as short answers (earlier), a long answer follows a given scenario and requires the production of a professional document. An example might be to assume the role of a company secretary and draw up a corporate governance policy, a lawyer arguing the merits of two conflicting cases relevant to the PQ, or simply write a report to the chair of the ethics committee regarding the situation. As per the short answer examples, there may be questions with mark available to guide you to what needs to be answered, and the detail in which that answer needs to be.

These are separate to an essay question because an answer needs to be given within the context of the given situation. Essays tend not to be PQs, although examinations can use a variety of the methods listed.

Case summary

A case summary is your brief understanding of a case in your own words. Details and extra information are omitted for the sake of writing the 'headline' information only. Imagine a senior partner at a law firm asks you what case x was about. Your answer would be short and to the point and exclude unnecessary detail. The same idea can be used for writing a case summary.

The content of a case summary would usually include an overview of the facts, current court and procedural history, judges, both parties' key arguments, judges' *ratio* and commentary, and overview of the decision.

The mnemonic FIJI (Fact, Issue, Judgment, Impact) outlines the structure.

A replication of a case summary to use as a model can be found in law databases such as Westlaw's Case Digest or Lexis' Case Overview.

Case notes

Case notes are very similar to case summaries except there is an extra element of critical analysis which gives the reader your understanding of the case and its wider impact.

Most law firms write case summaries in their areas of expertise, and you will see a broad range of styles that reflect the field of law and the firm's house style.

Likewise, your university will have a particular style (eg the use of subheadings) for writing case summaries and case notes.

Follow the rule of FIJI but critique by questioning the decision, use dissenting opinions to develop arguments in terms of consistency, contradiction and logic. If there was a move away from policy to reflect a change in technology or public opinion for example, highlight this. Finally, give reasons for your opinion, explaining how and why you agree/disagree with judges on the same or different points. Refer to past cases.

Online tests

There are many types of questions that can be used – consider the variation of questions this book has used – and computers offer more versatility and options. Computer-based tests can be easily constructed by lecturers and marked automatically by software, though paper tests can contain most of these question types. In an hour's test, around 50 questions can be expected, dependant on the styles used. Rather than using one type all the way through a test, lecturers will vary the style of questions. Nine of the main types of questions have been described in the following.

Multiple Choice Question

Simply, a cue is given, and usually three to five options. One answer will be correct or the 'best' answer, while the other answers are distractors.

a   MCQ stands for

i) Multiple Choice Question   ii) Many Constant Quality   iii) Measuring Computer Quality

Gap fill

Used in the comprehension of listening and reading tests, gap fills do not offer any word choices and it is up to you to think of the most suitable word, or find the exact word or synonym from the source material.

b   The assessment method _____ requires the student's own critique and evaluation of a particular case.

Or where a word is given in **bold**, but the word form (eg noun/verb/adjective) needs to be amended.

c   The purpose of _____ is to liquidate the assets within the business. **[bankrupt]**

Cloze gap fill

Similar to a gap fill, but an option of answers is provided.

d   Part 2 of the Proceed of Crime Act _____ allows the court to confiscate criminal proceeds from a defendant.

```
                    2001   2002   2003   2004
```

Given word choices can also appear in a drop-down menu in online tests. Note that a cloze gap fill may contain more words than there are spaces, and are more often used in longer texts.

It's possible that the cloze answers may be single words or full sentences, or that full sentences need to be placed into the correct position within a larger text (eg the placement of topic sentences in an essay).

e   If a trademark is not protected, _____(a) may accidentally occur, such as 'passing off'. Passing off is a third party's use of an unregistered mark in a way which _____(b) goods or services as their own.

```
(a) i.  breach       ii.  violation      iii.  infringement  iv.  abuse
(b) i.  symbolises   ii.  characterises  iii.  represents    iv.  indicates
```

Matching

Two parts of an answer need to be connected to make one whole. The two parts are mixed up, and the challenge is to correctly identify the two connecting parts. The focus is more on the detail than broadly categorising items.

f   Match the offence on the left with the description on the right

Assault   Breaking someone's nose (no surgery required)

Battery   Knocking someone's hat off while they are wearing it

ABH   Sending threatening text messages causing the receiver to avoid to sender

Categorising

Categorising is much like matching, except for the key difference in the number of answers to be placed. Categorising has multiple answers that need to be placed correctly whereas Matching requires just the correct placement of one. Gives a list of items that need to be placed into their correct place. In a computer-based test, this can be done with a drag and drop function. Paper tests will look like:

g   Put the topics in the blue box into the correct area of law

```
Murder      Flags of convenience   Negligence    INCOTERMS
Evidence    Vicarious liability    e-commerce    Leases
```

Criminal law	Shipping law	Tort

The instructions will say if not all provided answers need to be categorised and an answer(s) will remain (eg leases which doesn't fit into any of the three fields in the example question). The test will not try to trick you.

Ordering

Ordering tasks require the test candidate to rearrange the order items by time, importance, significance or any other variable. Like Matching, this can be done by drag and drop on computer, rewriting in full in the space provided or simply writing the answer in the correct sequence (where each of the following nine answers would be numbered/lettered).

h   Put the following stages of the law-making process into the correct order, starting with the earliest (from Bill to Act)

Committee stage	Second Reading	First Reading
Report Stage	House of Lords	Green Paper
White Paper	Third Reading	Royal Assent

True/False/(Not Given)

A statement is given, and the candidate must decide if that statement is correct or not correct.

i   True or False – Criminal liability consists of *actus reus*, *mens rea* and the absence of any defence.

Longer texts can include the trickier *not given* option which assesses deeper the comprehension and understanding of the source material, such as:

j   Driving with headlights on when the weather is good is optional in the UK, and new cars now automatically have less bright sidelights when a car is running. Yet the number of car accidents has not decreased. In fact, statistics from Scandinavian countries show that compulsory headlights at all times has done nothing to reduce the overall number of accidents. (True, False or Not Given)

Other foreign language abbreviations can appear in company party names which are used to state the company type, for example (Figure 3.6):

Company name	Country	Suffix meaning in English
AB	Sweden	*Aktiebolag* Limited company or Corporation
GmbH	Germany	*Gesellschaft mit beschränkter Haftung* Limited Liability company
KK	Japan	*Kabushiki Kaisha* Joint stock company
NV	Netherlands	*Naamloze Vennootschap* Limited Liability Public company
SA	France	*Société Anonyme* Public limited company
SpA	Italy	*Societa per Azioni* Public limited company by shares

Figure 3.6 Foreign language abbreviations in case names

Bibliography

The names Reference List, Bibliography and Reference page are used interchangeably to mean roughly the same thing – the page(s) at the end of the submitted work which list all the sources that have been referred to in the text. A bibliography can be used to mean books that are read but not cited in the text, whereas a reference has been read and used in the text. For consistency, bibliography is used throughout to mean the same thing.

That means all the footnoted sources need to be repeated in the references, however they are listed alphabetically rather than numerically. References are broken down into categories, thus your cases, legislation, journal articles and so on will be listed, alphabetically, under a subheading.

Notice how references are alphabetical but citations are listed in numerical order as they are presented. Names are presented alphabetically by first name, regardless of how the author's name is written in the source.

a)   There are some jurisdictions where it is illegal to drive without headlights on.

b)   Jurisdictions where daytime visibility is bad are the same jurisdictions where the use of headlights at all times is mandatory.

c)   Only careful drivers use their headlights where is it not law.

d)   Using headlights reduces the number of collisions.

Multiple answer

A question may have more than one answer, for example, *Who are the 12 judges of the UK Supreme Court?* requires 12 names in the answer. The same topic posed as *Name the current Supreme Court judges* gives no indication of the number of sitting judges. If there are options provided, the question is said to be a cloze multiple answer. There may also be distractors or *red herrings* – wrong answers provided for you to leave unselected, eg:

Select all the current (2020) Supreme Court judges

Lord Reed	Lord Hodge	Lord Kerr	Lady Black
Lord Lloyd-Jones	Lord Briggs	Lady Arden	Lord Kitchen
Lord Sales	Lord Hamblen	Lord Leggatt	Lord Burrows
Lord Sumption	Lady Hale	Lord Hope	Lord Dyson

Free-text entry

Consider this a mini-essay. Given the time or word constraints, your lecturer is not expecting an essay as detailed as a standard essay, but will generally want an outline of the key points in a specific area. The test may be open-book, but don't allow this to waste your time by over-researching. Unlike the previous question types, free-text is marked by humans, but the question pattern will be one of (or similar to) those listed in Essays. The type of question that can be expected is:

k   What were the reasons for the Consumer Rights Act (2015) superseding the previous unfit law?

Exams

Exams are time-limited situations which typically consist of a number of open- or closed-book questions and/or essays. The questions can be of different patterns, all on a particular topic, and may offer you a choice of which question to answer. For example:

l   Tort Exam Semester 1

Answer <u>all</u> questions from Section A and <u>one</u> question from Section B. Time **90 minutes**.

Section A (30 marks)

a) Explain breach of duty of care (10 marks)

b) Explain the principle of causation in the law of tort (10 marks)

c) Explain, with references, the Caparo three-part test used to decide whether a duty of care is owed (10 marks)

Section B (70 marks)

a) Problem question A . . . Advise James

b) Problem question B . . . Does any liability arise and against whom?

c) Analyse and evaluate the different types of damages in the law of negligence

---

A surprising number of students do not read the question and will attempt to answer all six. Only four questions need to be answered. Time management is the other issue.

How much time would you allocate to each section and question?

A basic rule is to look at the number of marks available and divide it by the time. Approximately 75% of the marks are awarded in Section B, so 75% of your time should be spent here. Three-quarters of 90 minute is just over an hour, so time should be spent proportionately to where the grades are. Around ten minutes is advisable in each of the three questions in Section A.

The marks available also tells you the depths to which you should answer the question. Clearly, the one Section B question requires much more thought and detailed answer.

Other variations include seen (ie given to candidates before the exam) or unseen papers, closed- or open-book (where a textbook, statute or judgment can be brought into the exam room with your annotations (notes) written), or open-book where you are given a clean copy of a text without your annotations. There may be compulsory and optional sections of the exam with instructions of how many questions from which sections should be answered (as shown earlier). Finally, you may be given allocated reading time to read a text before the exam begins, and you may be allowed to write on this text.

Timed questions

Where exams typically have all the candidates taking the same test in one computer lab or exam hall, timed questions have the luxury of being taken at the candidate's convenience, which could be the library, living room or bed (though not recommended!).

Deliberately manufactured to be open-book, I have used both an eight- and 24-hour timed-essay which is far longer than an exam. The counter-balance is that the question is normally far more detailed and a rigorous examination of your evaluation and researching skills, and lends itself well to the problem question.

Reflective tasks

Written in a less academic and narrative style, reflective tasks can be used for students to consolidate what they have learnt from case study, real-life practice or feeding back to the reader what they would have done differently and why. Reflective essays are more common in nursing and healthcare, but also exist for students returning from work placements or internships at law firms.

University VLEs

There has been a jump in the frequency of assessments on university's Virtual Learning Environment (such as Moodle, Canvas and Blackboard). The information written is shared with the lecturer and your classmates to see, comment on and offer feedback for you to act upon.

There are **blogs** which are your own work on a topic or theme, and run like a series of mini-essays as you grow your knowledge on a particular aspect. More tech-happy lecturers may alternatively ask you to produce **vlogs** (video blogs) or audio **podcasts**.

Sometimes, you are assessed on the questions you ask your classmates on their information, and the answers you provide to their questions on a **forum**. Lecturers also ask questions (and can be asked too) to deepen your knowledge and thereby pass it on to your classmates through **peer teaching**.

Lecturers provide quizzes for summative and formative learning which can include question types as detailed in the preceding, as well as being the platform used for end of term exams. You may be asked to use a lockdown browser which ensures that for a set time, only the web browser logged into your VLE and that single page is accessible for that time.

Leaflets and guides

Universities with external activities such as law clinics may advertise their services via leaflets or and guides. The transferrable skill being assessed is taking complex legal information (eg the law on being followed or stalked online) and changing the audience, genre and style into a help leaflet. An example would be changing the law on digital stalking from www.cps.gov.uk/legal-guidance/stalking-and-harassment and changing the audience, genre and style into a help leaflet

https://1q7dqy2unor827bqjls0c4rn-wpengine.netdna-ssl.com/wp-content/
uploads/woocommerce_uploads/2016/08/2009_Digital_Stalking_Leaflet.pdf.

Oral assessments

Law clinics

Following leaflets and guides, your university may offer public clinics on a particular field of law, giving students the chance to answer verbal problem questions. A real client comes in, and often with the lecturer's supervision, the student(s) will advise the client. Medical students are assessed using in OSCEs (Objective Structured Clinical Examinations) on how they communicate and take history, examine, explain how to use an inhaler or administer medicine, clinically evaluate and diagnose, and perform practically (eg insert a cannula), and a similar approach is used both in formative assessment and summatively as per the SQE2 Client Interview. The elements of hearing the client's background to the case, listening skills, asking probing questions, evaluating the content and offering accurate advice are similar parallels.

Posters

Even though a poster is a printed medium, the presenter spends time talking to the delegates who have come to look at the poster in the first instance explaining the aim, method, findings and conclusions of the research and using the poster as a supplementary aid rather than the focus of the research.

More commonly used in presenting medical, science or research in the arts, posters can have a place in focussing student understanding on a particular area. Universities have poster competitions for students, and also host competitions or conferences for students and academics from other universities to present their findings to people with similar interests. They are busy events with lots of people wandering around looking at poster titles that are of interest to them, and delegates will then chat to the presenter. Academic culture and etiquette dictate the viewer has a minute or so to browse the poster, and then the presenter opens the conversation with *Are you interested in X? Would you like me to explain anything in my poster? What field are you studying?* The poster serves as a point of reference that the host talks about and engages with the questioner in two-way dialogue. The same key information will then be repeated for the next person who comes along.

Academics present posters usually as a condensed version of (to be) published research, and they are a great way to learn about current research topics, find your own area of interest, ask questions of experts and to network. Examples on international/human rights posters from the Refugee Law Initiative can be found at https://rli.sas.ac.uk/annual-conference from each year.

Presentations

During a presentation, the speaker is at the centre of attention and the audience respectfully listen. Many people will listen to the explanation of the research once only, and the audience have the opportunity to ask questions at the end. Presentations can last from a few minutes up to an hour for keynote speakers and invited guests.

Assessed presentations can be done in front of the class, just the lecturer and via computer. Information is displayed using software such as Microsoft PowerPoint or Prezi, and rather than one static slide as a poster, presentations are more dynamic and include gifs, animations and transitions.

Students may be asked to present using just one static slide, discuss three slides in three minutes (3MTs are common in PhDs), or a *pecha kucha*. Academia has adapted pecha kucha to mean a certain number of slides of a certain length before automatically changing to the next slides, eg 20 slides of 20 seconds each is a talk of six minutes 40 seconds.

Some courses use a blend of these styles, or will build up towards one larger final presentation at the end of the course.

Mooting

Mooting is a great way to practise your court advocacy skills. In a moot court, you will be part of a team who represent one of the clients, and the lecturer is the judge/chair. Moots can replicate a criminal or civil trial which involves cross-examining and re-examining the witness. The key point is that each member of the class has a role to play, and their motivation and engagement make mooting a success or failure.

Similarly, a created situation can be created by your lecturers for negotiation or arbitration/mediation purposes which require different mindsets of being adversarial/cooperative and problem-solving.

A mock trial is similar to a moot, but mock trials include the testing of the evidence to establish case facts before presenting them to court. This step is bypassed in a moot.

Video presentations

Imagine a news report, or where a presentation has been pre-recorded and is 'broadcast' to the audience of classmates and teachers. In addition to the standard presentation, video presentations allow use of video editing skills to enhance the work with animations, transitions, voiceovers, video overlays etc just as you may see in a TV news report.

Viva

Used for, but not limited to assessing PhDs, a viva is an in-depth verbal interview by your supervisor and other experts about your work. You are asked questions and challenged on your work to prove to the panel that you know, understand and have written the thesis yourself. Vivas last for 1–4 hours so the panel can really understand the process, methods, results and findings, and critique you on the conclusions drawn.

Other assessment methods may use a diluted version of a viva as preparation for undergraduate and master's courses.

Resources

Student answers with lecturer commentary

Alex has decided to sell her samurai sword. She put a picture of it on a website along with the description reading:

> Samurai Sword For Sale. Pristine example – one owner. Surgical grade steel. Imported from Japan in 2012. Certificate of Authenticity. Manufactured 5/4/10. Serviced on 3/11/13 and 6/12/18. Curved blade with cover. £5000 or near offer. Please call at 26 Mumbles Street or phone Swansea 781246. The first person to agree a price WILL get it.

On Monday at 9am, Bob sees the advert while waiting for a dental appointment. He telephones Alex from work at 10am and makes an offer of £4500 which Alex says she would like to consider. Bob says that he will assume Alex has accepted unless he hears from her by 9pm that evening, to which Alex agrees.

At 11am on Monday, Callum calls at Alex's house but she is not home. He leaves a note: "Monday 11am. Saw the ad. Please keep it for me. Here is a cheque for £5000. Callum"

At 2.15pm on Monday, Dan sees the notice and within minutes posts a letter of acceptance and a cheque for £5000, using a post box at the end of the street. Unfortunately, Dan misaddresses the envelope so it only arrives on Friday.

At 3pm on Monday, Alex decides to accept Bob's offer and posts a letter to Bob's business address saying "I agree to sell on your terms. Because of your lower price can you pay in cash?"

At 9pm on Monday, Alex reads Callum's acceptance and immediately phones Bob's business address, leaving a message on the voicemail saying: "Ignore the letter you will receive. Deal off. Alex."

Bob is away on business and only listens to the tape on Wednesday evening.

Advise each party as to their legal position.

DOI: 10.4324/9781003125747-4

Better problem question answer by Party

The question at issue is whether Alex has concluded a contract with Bob, Callum or Dan. To establish a legally binding contract, it is necessary to follow the rules of formation of contract, and there are four basic elements which are: offer, acceptance, consideration and contractual intention. Of those four requirements, analyzing offer and acceptance is the focus at issue.

Identifies the wider area of law, the specific area, and the immediate issue that needs to be addressed

<u>Bob & Alex</u>

The question is whether the advertisement constitutes an offer or an ITT (invitation to treat). An offer is "an expression of willingness to be bound by certain terms"[1] whereas an ITT is "an invitation to the other party to make an offer".[2] An ITT is something that might appear to be an offer, but in fact is not. The main distinction between them is the intention to be legally bound. As usual an advertisement is considered as an ITT. In *Partridge v Crittenden,*[3] the High Court held that an advertisement in a particular part of a magazine which offers to sell protected birds was an ITT. However, it will not always be the case. Advertisements can also be offers. In the case of *Carlill v Carbolic Smoke Ball Co,*[4] an advertisement in a newspaper was held as an offer, on the basis that there is a sufficient intention to be bound in the situation where there was an amount of money deposited in a bank. In addition, another jurisdiction in the US [5] has also shown that an advertisement announcing a sale which are 'clear, definite and explicit' is an offer.

Identifies the first issue to address clearly before defining the key terms
Cases are concise, and relevant to the PQ
Offers alternative perspective

In the case at hand, Alex's advertisement on a website has a clear price, some

---

[1] Chris Turner, Unlocking Contract Law (4th edn, Routledge 2014)
[2] n 1
[3] Partridge v Crittenden [1968] 1 WLR 1204 (QBD)
[4] Carlill v The Carbolic Smoke Ball Co Ltd [1893] 1 QB 256
[5] Lefkowitz v Great Minneapolis Surplus Stores 86 NW 2d 689 (Minn, 1956)

specific information about the goods and the intention to be bound. Therefore, it is more likely to be considered as an offer. However, Bob considered it as an ITT while making an offer to Alex.

An acceptance is an unconditional and unequivocal response to an offer,[6] and it must exactly match the terms of the offer. A statement which adds new terms or intends to change the terms of the original offer is not an acceptance, but a counter-offer.[7] In *Hyde v Wrench,*[8] Wrench made an offer to sell his farm for £1000, but Hyde rejected the price and responded to pay £950. The court held that Hyde rejected the offer and made a counter-offer. In *Jones v Daniel,*[9] the response to the offer had the statement of the agreement and additional terms on the method of payment, then the court held that it was a counter-offer. However in the case of *Stevenson v McLean,*[10] in the response, the offeree accepted the price and other terms but was a little confused about the delivery. It was held by the court to be an enquiry about details, not a rejection of the offer. In addition, silence cannot show acceptance, and the court will reject silence as any representation of acceptance in this issue.[11] Therefore, in the Bob's offer, the term of the assumption of the silence is void.

Alex's reply firstly includes the acceptance of the price and appears to have added a new condition about the method of payment. If it is a counter-offer, there is no acceptance of it, so no contract is formed. However, it is likely to be considered as an enquiry about further information. In the meantime, Alex

Shows research but recognises its lack of persuasion

Relevant authority supports statements

You can't assume 'confusion': it could have been a mere representation

---

[6] n 1
[7] n 1
[8] Hyde v Wrench [1840] 49 ER 132
[9] Jones v Daniel [1894] 2 Ch 332
[10] Stevenson v McLean [1880] 5 QBD 346
[11] Felthouse v Bindley [1863] 142 ER 1037

accepted the offer and a contract might be formed.

It is a common question whether parties can change their mind in the negotiation. The legal position is that the offeror can, so an offer maybe withdrawn or revoked at any time until it has been accepted. In *Byrne v Leon Van Tienhoven*,[12] the offeror failed to revoke the offer because it was accepted before the revocation arrived. The general rule is that acceptances cannot be revoked, but some commentators argued that if the offeror can receive the notice of revocation before the acceptance and there are no harmful consequences happened, then the revocation of acceptance is allowed.[13]

In the case at issue, whether Alex's reply can be revoked depends on the arrival time of the revocation which is through voicemail at 9 pm. In general, instantaneous communication applies the receipt rule. In *Entores*,[14] the company accepted the offer by telex, the court held that the contract was actually concluded when the telex was received. However, there is a doubt in *Thomas v BPE Solicitors*[15] when an email received in the evening was read until the next working day. In this situation, the email is communicated when it is available to be read. Accordingly, Bob only listens to the tape on Wednesday evening, so it is likely that the revocation was received at that time. If Alex's acceptance by post arrived before that time, it cannot be revoked, then the

> Pulls the Law section (above) to draw a conclusion

> Appropriate academic style of writing and good specialist vocabulary used

> Considers an alternative argument where there is legal uncertainty

> Explains why these cases are important to PQ, not just decision

[12] Byrne & Co v Leon Van Tienhoven &Co [1880] 5 CPD 344
[13] T.T. Arvind, Contract Law (OUP 2017)
[14] Entores Ltd v Miles Far East Corporation [1955] 2 OB 327
[15] Thomas v BPE Solicitors [2010] EWHC 306 (Ch)

contract was formed when the acceptance was communicated. On the other hand, it is also likely that the revocation was received at 9 pm, because as the first offer said, it is reasonable for Alex to believe that Bob was able to listen to the voicemail at 9 pm. Therefore, the revocation might be valid, in this situation there is no acceptance and no contract.

Hedging language used to advise with caution

Callum & Alex

In the negotiation between Callum and Alex, the advertisement is deemed as a unilateral offer where acceptance and performance are seen as the same thing.[16] In *Carlill v Carbolic Smoke Ball*,[17] the court identified that in this case a formal acceptance was unnecessary since performing according to the terms of the offer was the acceptance. Hence, Callum's performance of leaving a note and a cheque for the full amount is likely to be interpreted as acceptance. Moreover, by reading it at 9 pm, and in accordance with the receipt rule, the contract was formed at 9 pm.

As the main claims have already been spelt out, the remaining parties' disputes discuss the same Law (already discussed) so needn't be repeated

Dan & Alex

If an offer is accepted by post, the acceptance is taken to have been communicated as soon as it is posted, even if the letter is lost during the mailing process or if it is misdirected.[18] In the case of *Adams v Lindsell*,[19] Lindsell misdirected the letter which led to a delay, the court held that the letter of acceptance took effect at the time of posting. Dan posted a letter of

Good paragraph structure – Point written first with relevant case to support in following sentence

---

[16] n 1
[17] n 4
[18] n 3
[19] Adams v Lindsell [1818] 106 ER 250

acceptance at 2.15 pm, but he misaddressed the envelope, resulting in a delayed delivery. According to the case above, it is considered that the acceptance was communicated at 2.15 pm, and the contract was formed at that time.

In conclusion, if the advertisement is deemed as an ITT, there is a contract between Bob and Alex only when Alex's reply of acceptance by post arrived before the notice of revocation which is considered to be communicated on Wednesday evening. If the advertisement is deemed as an offer, there could be a contract between Dan and Alex at 2.15 pm, or Callum and Alex at 9 pm. Because of the term in the advertisement which is "the first person WILL get it", a contract was formed between Dan and Alex.

> There is a good balance of assertion and caution in the Outcome section which follows good sources and evaluation

Lecturer's comments

You have chosen to structure your essay by party, which is a suitable organisation given the similarity of issues and the many parties involved. There is a good amount of referencing to authorities which are legally and factually suitable.

Discussion of the meaning of the words in the advert, and their legal weighting, isn't mentioned. There is perhaps a little too much reliance on case law to guide your answer, rather than your writing driving your thoughts and leading to your outcome.

That said, you lead the reader through a logical process for each party with whom there could have been a contract. A very good first attempt at writing a PQ answer, but there is one key legal element missing. Well done.

Poor problem question answer by Party

In the case at issue, the advertisement was put by Alex on the internet, the question discusses formation of contacts, especially the recognition of offer and acceptance of the same offer, consideration from both parties, and an intention to be bound by the terms of the contact. The question is whether Alex is contractually bound with Bob or Callum or Dan. This essay will show that Dan first formed a contact with Alex.

Too informal, not academic style – reads like a list

The outcome is given at the start

Alex and Bob

Alex decides to sell her samurai sword and posts a picture of it, along with a description, on an internet site. Her intention is to sell it as an ornament to the first person who makes an acceptable offer, based on her price of £5000. Alex's sword doesn't have a certificate so cannot be sold as a weapon, just an ornament, so it is unfit for purpose as a sword.

You are assuming her intention. Is this the purpose? If not its far from clear it is not fit for purpose

An offer is an acceptance by one party (offeror) to enter into a contact on specified terms with the intention of being bound immediately after the other party (offeree) expresses its acceptance.[20] The traditional rule is that priced goods offered for sale in an advert are not an offer, but an invitation to treat.[21] For instance, in *Partridge v Crittenden*[22], the appellant seed an advert stating that he had wild birds for sale, which stated the price but did not provide specific information nor quantities of birds available. The Court of

Repeats info already given in the PQ. Not needed unless discussing the legal 'loading' of words eg *"you WILL it"*

Check grammar

---

[20] E Macdonald et al (OUP 2018) 10
[21] Jill Poole, Textbook on Contract Law
[22] [1968] 1 WLR 1204

Appeal chucked out the appellant's appeal because the court held that the advert was not an offer but an ITT (invitation to treat).

A counter-offer is equivalent to a rejection of the original offer.[23] However, in some cases, the offeree merely requests clarification of the offer or further information about the offer. In such situation, the offer shall not be deemed to have been rejected and offeree may still accept the offer.[24] For example, in *Stevenson, Jacques & Co. v McLean,*[25] the offeror wrote to the offeree to offer $40 US per ton of iron and stated that the offer will continue until next Monday. On Monday morning, the offeree sent a cable to the offeree asked if a specific instalment term would be acceptable, or to suggest their own maximum term. The offeror did not reply and sold the iron to a third party. In the case at hand, following *Stevenson*, Alex's request that payment be made in cash will not be considered by the court as a counter-offer. At 3pm, Alex appears to have accepted the offer. As in *Stevenson*, the act of asking simply requests further information rather than rejecting an offer.

The postal rule is an exception to the general acceptance rule. A contact is formed when the offeree communicates the acceptance of an offer to the offeror by post.[26] For instance, in *Henthorn v Fraser*[27], the plaintiff had been negotiating with the defendant over the purchase price of the house and the defendant stated that the offer was valid for 14 days, but after the plaintiff had unconditionally accepted it by post, the defendant sold the house to a third party.

> Wrong court & informal. No ITT discussion.
>
> Discusses counter-offers but later admits this isn't relevant
>
> Repeated word "offer"
>
> The example case is described but not explained nor linked to the PQ
>
> The evaluation now seems lost and irrelevant
>
> Although the postal rule is discussed and a relevant case is cited, the relevance to this PQ hasn't been explained

---

[23] n20 Koffman & Macdonald's Law of Contract (9th edn, OUP 2018) 21

[24]

[25] [1880] 5 QBD 346

[26]

[27] [1892] 2 Ch 27

The court ultimately ruled against the defendant because once the postal service had been sent it, the acceptance was complete. However, if the offeror is not at a disadvantage, postal acceptance may be withdrawn[28]. In the case at hand, Alex's acceptance by post will be considered by the court as following the postal rule. I'm not sure whether Bob is disadvantaged.

Alex v Callum, Alex v Dan.

There are two general principles of acceptance, the one is in order to achieve acceptance (and contact), the offeree expressly expresses their intention or consent (by way of declaration or act) and must match the terms of the offer; the other is that acceptance is not effective until the offeror is notified.[29] In the case at hand, Dan and Callum's acceptance and payment of the £5000 cheque will be considered by the court as acceptance of the offer. As per the definition of acceptance, the terms of acceptance of the notice offeror were agreed upon when Alex check and saw the message left by Callum at 9p.m.

As mentioned in the postal rule, that the contact formation to be accepted via post, although the letter was late.[30] This principle was confirmed further in [1879] 4 Ex D 216[31] where documentation was lost in the post. The Court of Appeal decided that the contact had already been formed when the acceptance was sent by post. In the case at hand, when Dan sent an acceptance letter through the post to Alex, it would likely be deemed by the court to be a binding contact, formed when Dan sent the letter at 2.15pm on Monday.

Informal register using "I"
Explanation of Bob's disadvantage needed
Ok to link two parties if there is enough similarity
Use hedging language to make your statements less certain (eg may, would, likely)
If there is repetition (eg postal rule), consider if this would have been better dealt with using the Issue structure. Note this when rereading and redrafting

---

[28]
[29] n.28
[30] n 28
[31] Household Fire and Carriage Accident Insurance Co. Ltd v Grant

Finally, if the Alex's advert is an offer, then Dan and Callum acceptance by

conduct, then a contact is formed. If Dan's acceptance reached Alex on Friday,

then the contact formation. However, according to the postal rule, the contact

between Dan and Alex had been formed when Dan sent letter.

Outcome

Ultimately, for Dan and Callum and Bob, the law states that they have all

formed contacts with Alex. It depends on which person was the first to agree a

price with Alex has formed a legally binding contact.

> Your intro states that Dan formed a contract, but the conclusion ends vaguely

Lecturer's comments

It seems that the evaluation of the law was the weakest area, either because you weren't familiar with how to deal with it, or because you didn't understand it. The less relevant parts were discussed, and the more relevant parts were described but not analysed in terms of the PQs context.

The wording of the advert is key, and this wasn't discussed. If you state by default or omission that it is an ITT, use case law to confirm this too.

There were also stylistic errors (vocabulary choices, academic register etc) that you will develop, especially so with the referencing and citation. Proofreading your work will help spot spelling errors (eg contact not contract) and grammar (the past of 'see' is *seen*, not seed).

Writing your first PQ answer can be difficult to get your head around, so don't be too disappointed.

Better problem question answer by Issue

Under English law, there are four elements to form a contract: an offer, an

acceptance, consideration from parties and intention to form a contract. In

advising each party, is it necessary to discuss the offer and acceptance, and the key

issue is which party is eventually bound to purchase the Samurai Sword.

Alex's advertisement

In deciding whether the advisement constitutes an offer or an invitation to treat

(ITT), the advert's purpose and specific terms need to be explored. An offer is a

promise made by a party to enter into a contract. It should show that an offeror

has: good intentions, of no further bargaining, and the wording of the offer should

be specific and complete in order to have the basic terms of an agreement. The

purpose of ITTs is to let the other party make an offer because the wording of

ITTs are too ambiguous are not binding on offeror or offeree. As a result,

advertisers can choose customers by themselves. In *Harvey v Facey*[32], Harvey wanted

to buy a property owned by Facey and telegrammed him his lowest cash price.

Harvey responded "We agree to buy Bumper Hall Pen for the sum of nine

hundred pounds asked by you". Harvey claimed his offer had been accepted, but

the court held that Facey's first telegram was not an offer because there was only a

statement price in the response which, lacking the details and certainty of terms,

was incapable of being accepted.

However, this is not an absolute rule. In the special circumstance that

advertisement provides clear limits and specify terms, the advertisement can be an

---

Citation needed for the 4 elements.

Strongly stated the Claim that a contract has been formed.

Citation needed

"As a result..." this sentence is throw-away and contains little info. Support/ detail is needed

---

[32] [1893] AC 552

offer. In *Lefkowitz v Minneapolis*[33] there was an advertisement in the newspaper announcing for sale "1 Black Lapin Stole Beautiful, worth $139.50… $1. First come, first served". The court held that the advertisement was an offer because it was 'clear, definite and explicit'. In the case at hand, Alex's advertisement has clearly shown the conditions of the offer, announcing that the Samurai Sword is available for £5000 and the first person who agrees at that the price would get it. Additionally, the detail given in the advert such as the production date, appearance and provenance of the sword suggests it is more likely to be considered an offer because of the clarity of wording.

Valid argument but not a strong authority.

Carlill or *Boots* may have been suitable citations here to differ ITT and offer

Why do some words have an underline

Unqualified acceptance

The issue is whether Bob's phone call and Alex's voicemail constitute a counter-offer or an acceptance. Acceptance is a final and unqualified expression of assent to the terms of an offer. A counter-offer is when the offeree objects to the offer or changes the original offer in essence. What he communicated cannot be regarded as an acceptance but a counter-offer. In case of *Jones v Daniel*[34], the offeree sent a letter of acceptance, accepting all the terms of the offer but asking for a 10% deposit payment. The court held that this condition was not included in the original offer, so the offeree's letter did not constitute a commitment. In another case, *Crossley v Maycock*[35], Sir George Jessel distinguishes two kind of response: a counter-offer which added new conditions which had never been discussed or agreed, and a response which formalises agreed terms. The former would need to

---

[33] Lefkowitz v. Minneapolis
[34] Jones v Daniel (1894 2 Ch 332
[35] Crossley v. Maycock (1874) LR 18 Eq 180.

be re-accepted while the latter is a valid acceptance. Applying this to the instant case, Bob changed the price from £5000 to £4500, which changed the original offer in essence and constituted a counter-offer. Alex also further specified the method of payment in her response. If Alex's reply is a counter-offer, the message on voicemail at 9pm on Monday is not a revocation of an acceptance but an offer. Therefore, the reply was not binding on Bob and he could choose to accept or reject this new offer. Moreover, Bob receives this new offer and revocation of the offer at the same time on Wednesday, which means that this offer has been withdrawn successfully on Wednesday. In summary, there is no contract between Bob and Alex.

Effective acceptance

There are two rules about when the acceptance take effect, the reception rule and the postal rule. The reception rule means that acceptance takes effect when it has been brought to offeror's attention and offeror has the possibility of knowing it has been accepted. If the acceptance does not require notice, it shall take effect according to the trading habits between parties or the requirements of offer. In postal rule, if an acceptance is sent by mail or telegram, the offer is accepted as soon as an acceptance is posted into a post box. In *Adams v Lindsell*[36] the defendant provided an offer to the plaintiff, but the letter was sent to the wrong address, leading to a delay in it being accepted. The court held that, due to the negligence of the defendant, acceptance should be deemed effective as soon as the letter of acceptance was posted. The postal rule was established in this case. Similarly, in

> You are guiding me through the case step by step and it reads logically
>
> You are drawing me towards a conclusion but not explicitly stating who is bound – that's fine if it appears later*
>
> You have discussed the key elements here...

---

[36] Adams v. Lindsell (1818) 1 B & Ald 681

Household Fire Insurance Co v Grant[37], the court held that even if the acceptance had never been received, a contract exists because the acceptance was posted. In the case at hand, Callum left a note with Alex at 11am on Monday. However, Alex didn't notice it until 9 o'clock in the evening, so it is more likely that the acceptance takes effect then. Similarly, Dan sees the advertisement and posts a letter of acceptance. If the postal rule is applied in this situation, the acceptance takes place at 3pm on Monday. Otherwise, it takes effect on Friday.

There was no contract between Alex and Bob. Bob has the choice if he wants to accept Alex's counter-offer. Callum's message was noticed by Alex at 9pm on Monday, so this acceptance took effect at that time. In addition, if the postal rule is applied for Dan's acceptance of the offer, it becomes effective at 2.15pm on Monday, thus a contract is formed between Alex and Dan first, and Dan has the contractual right to the sword. By contrast, if the postal rule cannot be applied in Dan' s acceptance of the offer, the acceptance took effect on Friday because his letter of acceptance did not arrive until Friday. In which case, Callum is the first person who is contractually bound by Alex's offer to purchase the sword.

...and making a firm conclusion

Good hedging language

Previously discussed elements are now drawn together

*which it does here

Lecturer's comments

A good first attempt at a PQ. There were a few missing citations, and some lesser-known cases which shows you have researched, but importantly grasped the relevant laws and elements from the cases to evaluate against the PQ.

Most impressive was the way you guided me through the legal arguments under each subheading. I was able to follow your points which were clear and logical.

Your concluding sentences from each Claim were clear and guided me towards your final Outcome which stated who was bound. There was enough hedging to show there was hesitancy in your conclusions, but enough assertion based on previous research and arguments to persuade a reader that your findings would be supported in court.

However, as you develop your writing skills, you will learn how to address lesser authoritative cases swifter (eg Lefkowitz) to allow more attention for the more pertinent cases. Also, beware of your sentences which appear to be oversimplified maybe because the rule/case they enforce is not understood. If a law cannot be stated clearly, any evaluation that comes after it will be unclear to the reader.

Bank of problem questions

Next is a collection of PQs that will be of the type and style you will encounter on your law course.

The following two PQs will allow you to practise using the preceding content but give you the flexibility to formulate your own answer because the next two questions are based on *Jack v Peter*, and each PQ becomes increasingly more complex.

From page 189 you will find a bank of essay planning sheets to help you with the process of planning, researching, then writing an answer.

CONTRACT LAW – MORE DEVELOPED

Jack, who is a private watch collector, is selling one of his watches for £3000 on a specialist pre-owned watches website. Peter sees the advertisement and immediately emails Jack on the 10th to say he'd like to buy the watch for £2800.

The next day, Peter decides he'd like to revoke the offer, so he posts a letter to Jack's home address stating that he wishes to withdraw from the sale.

On the 12th, Jack reads Peter's email, and posts a letter to Peter stating that he'd like to accept his offer of £2800.

On the third day, Jack receives Peter's letter of withdrawal.

That same day, Jack receives a fax from Ben for the watch offering £1400. Jack thinks this is too low, so posts a letter to Ben rejecting the offer.

That evening, Jack decides to take Ben's offer for the watch, so sends Ben a text message (SMS) accepting his offer of £1400.

Advise Jack.

CONTRACT LAW – MOST DEVELOPED

Jack, who is a private watch collector, is selling one of his watches for £3000 on a specialist pre-owned watches website. Peter sees the advertisement and immediately emails Jack on the 10th to say he'd like to buy the watch for £2800.

The next day, Peter decides he's like to revoke the offer, so he posts a letter to Jack's home address stating that he wishes to withdraw from the sale.

On the 12th, Jack reads Peter's email, and posts a letter to Peter stating that he'd like to accept his offer of £2800.

On the third day, Jack receives Peter's letter of withdrawal.

That same day, Jack receives a fax from Ben for the watch offering £1400. Jack thinks this is too low, so posts a letter to Ben rejecting the offer.

That evening, Jack decides to take Ben's offer for the watch, so sends Ben a text message (SMS) accepting his offer of £1400.

Jack then speaks to one of his watch collecting friends that night, and verbally offers Sarah the watch for £3000. Sarah posts a letter to Jack early the next morning stating she'd like to accept the offer. However, on the 15th, Sarah changes her mind so phones Jack leaving a voicemail to the effect that she wishes to reject his offer of £3000. The next day (16th), Sarah's letter of acceptance arrives.

Advise Jack.

EMPLOYMENT LAW

David is a head teacher at a high school. One of his teaching staff, Geoff, went out to celebrate his 40th birthday with other colleagues and his friends on a Friday night. Over the course of the weekend, pictures of the night's events were posted on social media, and by Monday morning, students within the school were fully aware that Geoff had been drinking, partying, and dancing with friends and other staff members. Some parents of Geoff's pupils subsequently saw the pictures and complained to David about the content.

David approached Geoff on Tuesday morning and told him that his actions were inappropriate for a schoolteacher, and was fired on the spot. The next day he received a letter from David informing Geoff that he had been dismissed for gross misconduct.

Geoff has come to you for help as he fears he may not be able to get another teaching job.

IP LAW

Jamie buys a pallet of plain dinner plates and instructs a local printer to put images of famous, but now dead celebrities onto each item.

Thomas is now acting on behalf of all the celebrities' families who are upset that their relatives' images are being used without consent, licence or endorsement.

Advise Jamie. Refer to *Fenty & Ors v Arcadia Group Brands Ltd & Anor* [2015] EWCA Civ 38

CONTRACT LAW (BASIC)

Jonathan is an agricultural farmer who grows and sells lettuce, cucumbers and tomatoes. He has a contract to supply Elliot's shop with an agreed number of each. Due to a period without rain, many suppliers of summer vegetables and fruits were unable to fulfil their orders, including Jonathan. In the meantime, the price of said items had risen sharply due to the increased demand. Jonathan told Elliot that he was reneging on the contract and significant changes would be needed if Elliot wanted the contract to continue, including an increase in price and a decrease of the frequency of deliveries. The changes were presented as a 'take it or leave it' proposal. Elliot felt he had no choice other than to accept the changes.

Elliot has now issued proceedings against Jonathan, who requires your advice. *Refer to Kolmar Group AG v Traxpo Enterprises PVT Limited [2010]* EWHC 113 (Comm)

CRIMINAL LAW

In the early hours of the morning of 1 January 1992, Hefin was involved in a drunken fight outside a pub. He punched Kevin who fell to the ground, hitting his head on the pavement, causing serious head injuries. He was quickly attended to by paramedics and admitted to the nearest hospital.

Kevin remained in hospital. He was pronounced dead on 1 January 1993.

What criminal charges could Hefin face, and what defences are available to him for the charge of murder?

MARITIME LAW

A shipowner, Sarah, agrees with a shipper (Kelly) for the carriage of some goods from London to Piraeus. A bill of lading is issued to Kelly in London. After loading the goods, Kelly sells the goods to a third-party buyer by endorsing the bill of lading accordingly. Although not mentioned in the bill of lading, the goods were actually carried on the ship's deck, and on the voyage to Piraeus the ship encountered heavy weather and some of the goods suffered damage.

Discuss and consider the position of the shipowner, shipper and bill of lading endorsee.

IP LAW

Joan is a professional British artist whose works have been shown in galleries worldwide. One day while watching TV, Joan sees an advert for men's clothing with a logo which she feels is the same as one of her sculptures. She wrote to the company, Mark Rees Menswear, including a picture of her sculpture. She also posted the letter and photos of her sculpture and MRM's logo on her own blog so her followers could judge for themselves.

The story was picked up by ArtWurld magazine who published Joan's photo from her blog.

Discuss all the potential copyright infringements by all the parties mentioned.

CONTRACT LAW

Tony's company produces plastics for the food industry, and has newly formed a contract supplying food-grade trays and films to Peter Pratt Foods (PPF). An initial oral agreement was followed up with a purchase order, and delivery finally took place on 15 April, 14 days later than agreed. After delivery and inspection, PPF refused to pay for the goods, alleging that it was of a lower quality than agreed. Tony returned to inspect the items and confirmed PPF's suspicions of the defect, stating "the packaging supplied is not as bad as claimed". Tony offered to take the goods back to its warehouse to remarket themselves. PPF neither refused this offer, claimed damages nor a replacement delivery.

| cont. | On 15 July, PPF claimed the purchase price of the goods. Tony argues that the contract was avoided based on the delay in delivery and agreement between the parties. |

The agreement between the parties did not contain a jurisdiction clause, but their countries are parties to the Convention on the International Sale of Goods (CISG).

Advise PPF, referring to the Convention on Contracts for the International Sale of Goods, Art 1(1), 18(1), 29(1), 47, and 49.

TORT LAW

Ian and his friend Andrew meet up for a coffee. During their time at the coffee shop, Ian posts several updates on his social media accounts. His first update states, "Starbucks serves cold coffee."

As the conversation develops, Andrew tells Ian that he has contracted the disease tuberculosis, to which, Ian posts on his social media account "Andrew has tuberculosis."

While queuing for a cupcake, a Chinese tourist doesn't wait her turn and gets served before Ian, upsetting him, so the next post written by Ian is "Chinese people are rude."

Ian then sees a social media post giving the name of a professional footballer using illegal drugs, and he reposts it on his own feed.

Is Ian liable for any claims brought against him for the any of the four online posts?

COMMERCIAL LAW

Eco Choc Ltd is a company that produces, packages and sells ethical and sustainable chocolate. It was set established in 2018 by millionaire environmental campaigner Richard who is also one of the directors. The articles of the company state the company is for the development, production and sale of ethical and sustainable food and drink.

Invested money by shareholders has been spent mostly on research. At the start of 2019, the research department invented a more efficient way to grow chocolate

cont.   using chemical fertiliser. Due to the amount of money invested, Richard and the other directors agreed that they should start producing chocolate so the investors would start to see a return.

Declan is a shareholder in the company and a green activist. Having heard the recent news about the new growing process, he is against the company producing chocolate in this way.

Declan has come to you for advice, including whether he can prevent the company producing chocolate in this way and whether any action can be taken against the directors.

MIXED LAW

Wayne is an illustrator, and during his course of business, Paul approached him to design a company logo. Wayne's solicitor drew up two contracts – one for the commission of the work, and a second for the assignment of title of any work created to be the intellectual property of Paul. The contract for the commission of work was electronically signed by all three parties (Paul, his solicitor and Wayne), and has timestamps over the period of two days.

The work was duly completed to Paul's satisfaction, who paid Wayne the agreed amount in good time. Paul was keen to sign the second contract so he could use the new logo. Due to time constraint, Wayne was only able to assign the IP of the artwork to Paul via his computer, again using an electronic signature on the transfer of title contract.

Paul began using the new logo. A short time later, he received a letter from Wayne's solicitor telling him he was in breach of copyright.

Advise Paul on the validity of both contracts.

MARITIME LAW X3

Last month, Pryderi Wholesale bought 1000kg of dog food from Abehjerne Farmers to be transported from Denmark to the UK on an FOB contract. The nominated ship was *The Medusa*, and AF made the contract of carriage and procured a bill of lading. The bill of lading states that 100 × 10kg sacks of dog food are present, yet the contract between the parties was for 200 × 5kg sacks.

Advise Pryderi.

cont.   Last month, Pryderi Wholesale bought 1000kg of dog food from Abehjerne
Farmers to be transported from Denmark to the UK on a CIF contract.
The nominated ship was *The Medusa*, and AF made the contract of carriage and
procured a bill of lading. The bill of lading states that 100 × 10kg sacks of dog food
are present, yet the contract between the parties was for 200 × 5kg sacks.

Advise Pryderi on their rights.

Last month, Pryderi Wholesale bought 1000kg of dog food from Abehjerne
Farmers to be transported from Denmark to the UK on an FOB contract. The
nominated ship was *The Medusa*, and AF made the contract of carriage and
procured a bill of lading. However, upon arrival in the UK, the dog food was found
to have become mouldy and could no longer be sold.

Advise Pryderi against whom he should claim compensation.

COMPANY LAW

Two friends, Seren and Ffion, decided to open up a shop selling hand-made
jewellery. They approached a lawyer who drew up the Articles of Association
and submitted the relevant documentation for the creation of a company limited
by shares with two directors. Soon, a third friend, Eira, joined the board and at
Eira's request, varied the Articles which was signed and agreed by three ladies,
facilitated by the same lawyer.

Seren, Ffion and Eira consequently own all 100 shares, split 50, 25 and 25 respectively.

With the passage of time, the girls argue, and Seren and Ffion decide they want
Eira removed from the board.

The model Articles of the company have been amended to provide that:

"Under a proposal to remove a director at a general meeting, any shares held by
that director shall carry three votes per share."

Applicable statute from the jurisdiction states:

> Section 84 of the Newtonia Corporations and Companies Act 2019 – Removal
> of a Director

During a meeting of Directors, a Director may be removed before the end of his
contractual term, notwithstanding anything in the Articles, or any agreement
between the Director(s) and the Articles.

Advise Seren and Ffion if they can rely on the amended Articles of Association to
remove Eira.

Using a statute as problem question research

This simplified PQ will relate to the case of *Fisher v Bell* [1961] QB 394, where the sale of an ejector knife in a shop window was found not to be unlawful under section 1(1) of the Restriction of Offensive Weapons Act 1959. The brief reason was that the knife and a price tag was not deemed to be an offer, but an Invitation to Treat. That is, an offer is made when a customer presents the knife to the cashier with payment, and the cashier then accepts that offer when they take payment.

Therefore, the prosecution failed on the charge of *selling* or *offering for sale* because the shop window display constituted an Invitation to Treat.

Let's look at the legislation and see if you can pick out the exact wording (Figure 4.1).

Now imagine that you have the following PQ (which has been simplified for the purposes of this section).

Section 1(1) of the Restriction of Offensive Weapons Act 1959

Penalties for offences in connection with dangerous weapons.

(1) Any person who manufactures, sells or hires or offers for sale or hire, or lends or gives to any other person—

(a) any knife which has a blade which opens automatically by hand pressure applied to a button, spring or other device in or attached to the handle of the knife, sometimes known as a " flick knife " or " flick gun "; or

(b) any knife which has a blade which is released from the handle or sheath thereof by the force of gravity or the application of centrifugal force and which, when released, is locked in place by means of a button, spring, lever, or other device, sometimes known as a " gravity knife ",

shall be guilty of an offence and shall be liable on summary conviction in the case of a first offence to imprisonment for a term not exceeding three months or to a fine not exceeding fifty pounds or to both such imprisonment and fine, and in the case of a second or subsequent offence to imprisonment for a term not exceeding six months or to a fine not exceeding two hundred pounds or to both such imprisonment and fine.

(2) The importation of any such knife as is described in the foregoing subsection is hereby prohibited.

Source: http://www.legislation.gov.uk/ukpga/Eliz2/7-8/37/section/1/enacted Accessed 2 November 2020

Figure 4.1 Section 1(1) of the Restriction of Offensive Weapons Act 1959

A SIMPLE PROBLEM QUESTION – USING STATUTES FOR RESEARCH

B puts an ejector knife in his shop window along with a price tag of £10. The police want to prosecute A for selling or offering for sale a dangerous weapon.

Advise B

You may know now about the *Fisher v Bell* case, but remember it was tried in 1961, and the law may have changed in that time. Regardless, it would be a good idea to read the actual legislation yourself.

Section 1(1) Restriction of Offensive Weapons Act 1959	Section 1(1) Restriction of Offensive Weapons Act 1961
Penalties for offences in connection with dangerous weapons.	Penalties for offences in connection with dangerous weapons.
(1) Any person who manufactures, sells or hires or offers for sale or hire, or lends or gives to any other person—	(1) Any person who manufactures, sells or hires or offers for sale or hire, or exposes or has in his possession for the purpose of sale or hire or lends or gives to any other person—
(a) any knife which has a blade which opens automatically by hand pressure applied to a button, spring or other device in or attached to the handle of the knife, sometimes known as a "flick knife " or " flick gun "; or	(a) any knife which has a blade which opens automatically by hand pressure applied to a button, spring or other device in or attached to the handle of the knife, sometimes known as a "flick knife" or "flick gun"; or
(b) any knife which has a blade which is released from the handle or sheath thereof by the force of gravity or the application of centrifugal force and which, when released, is locked in place by means of a button, spring, lever, or other device, sometimes known as a " gravity knife ", shall be guilty of an offence and shall be liable on summary conviction in the case of a first offence to imprisonment for a term not exceeding three months or to a fine not exceeding fifty pounds	(b) any knife which has a blade which is released from the handle or sheath thereof by the force of gravity or the application of centrifugal force and which, when released, is locked in place by means of a button, spring, lever, or other device, sometimes known as a "gravity knife", shall be guilty of an offence and shall be liable on summary conviction in the case of a first offence to imprisonment for a term not exceeding three months or to a fine not exceeding fifty pounds level 4 on the standard scale
or to both such imprisonment and fine, and in the case of a second or subsequent offence to imprisonment for a term not exceeding six months or to a fine not exceeding two hundred pounds or to both such imprisonment and fine.	or to both such imprisonment and fine, and in the case of a second or subsequent offence to imprisonment for a term not exceeding six months or to a fine not exceeding two hundred pounds level 4 on the standard scale or to both such imprisonment and fine.
(2) The importation of any such knife as is described in the foregoing subsection is hereby prohibited.	(2) The importation of any such knife as is described in the foregoing subsection is hereby prohibited.
Adapted from: http://www.legislation.gov.uk/ukpga/Eliz2/7-8/37/section/1/enacted Accessed 2 November 2020	Adapted from: http://www.legislation.gov.uk/ukpga/Eliz2/7-8/37/section/1 Accessed 2 November 2020

Figure 4.2 Comparing current and previous Acts

Academic skills – Using your law databases or the legislation.gov website, you search for the Act. What is it that you discover?

Hopefully, you see that the law which the prosecution relied upon in 1961 has been revised by the Restriction of Offensive Weapons Act 1961. So, the law has changed since the seminal case.

The two statutes are placed side by side so we can evaluate the amendments, the exact legislation additions underlined and the formatting adjusted to make the differences more apparent.

Task D1 – What was the purpose of the changes in Section 1(1)?

Task D2 – How has this altered the advice you would give A in the PQ, compared to the advice given to the defendant in *Fisher v Bell?*

Using primary sources to answer a problem question

A SAMPLE PROBLEM QUESTION – CRIMINAL

Danielle is driving her car and using her mobile phone to film the scene following a serious car accident as she slowly drives past it on the motorway. A police officer witnesses her filming, stops her car and sees the mobile phone on the passenger seat in video mode. Danielle admits to filming the accident and apologises. The mobile phone is lawfully taken as evidence.

She later receives a summons to appear in court, answering the charge of using a hand-held mobile phone contrary to RTA 1988, s. 41d and Regulation 110 of the RVR 1986 (both in the following).

Advise Danielle.

Road Traffic Act 1988 s. 41d

Breach of requirements as to control of vehicle, mobile telephones etc.

A person who contravenes or fails to comply with a construction and use requirement—

(a)as to not driving a motor vehicle in a position which does not give proper control or a full view of the road and traffic ahead, or not causing or permitting the driving of a motor vehicle by another person in such a position, or

(b)as to not driving or supervising the driving of a motor vehicle while using a hand-held mobile telephone or other hand-held interactive communication device, or not causing or permitting the driving of a motor vehicle by another person using such a telephone or other device,

is guilty of an offence.

Source: https://www.legislation.gov.uk/ukpga/1988/52/section/41D#reference-c19271861
Accessed 2 November 2020

Figure 4.3 Road Traffic Act 1988 s. 41d

Amendment of the Road Vehicles (Construction and Use) Regulations 1986

The Road Vehicles (Construction and Use) Regulations 1986 are amended by inserting after regulation 109—

"Mobile telephones 110.

(1) No person shall drive a motor vehicle on a road if he is using—

(a)a hand-held mobile telephone; or

(b)a hand-held device of a kind specified in paragraph (4).

(4) A device referred to in paragraph (1)(bis a device, other than a two-way radio, which performs an interactive communication function by transmitting and receiving data.

(5) A person does not contravene a provision of this regulation if, at the time of the alleged contravention—

(a)he is using the telephone or other device to call the police, fire, ambulance or other emergency service on 112 or 999;

(b)he is acting in response to a genuine emergency; and

(c)it is unsafe or impracticable for him to cease driving in order to make the call (or, in the case of an alleged contravention of paragraph (3)(b), for the provisional licence holder to cease driving while the call was being made).

(6) For the purposes of this regulation—

(a)a mobile telephone or other device is to be treated as hand-held if it is, or must be, held at some point during the course of making or receiving a call or performing any other interactive communication function;

(b)a person supervises the holder of a provisional licence if he does so pursuant to a condition imposed on that licence holder prescribed under section 97(3)(a) of the Road Traffic Act 1988 (grant of provisional licence);

(c)"interactive communication function" includes the following:

(i)sending or receiving oral or written messages;

(ii)sending or receiving facsimile documents;

(iii)sending or receiving still or moving images; and

(iv)providing access to the internet;"

Adapted from source: https://www.legislation.gov.uk/uksi/2003/2695/regulation/2/made Accessed 2 November 2020

Figure 4.4 Amendment of the Road Vehicles (Construction and Use) Regulations 1986

Creating a CLEO plan from statute research

Academic skills – Look up the Defamation Act 2013. Which section would you refer to if the PQ identified Claims of:

1   xyz.com are told that A has posted comments online about B, and B has asked xyz.com if those comments can be removed.

2   Your client has been told of action against them for defamation, and they want to know if they are liable. Which section would be the most appropriate to outline counter-arguments?

3   A is a university professor, and has been told by his journal editor that another academic has been defamed in his latest publication.

4   In a crowded and noisy bar, two students, A and B, are talking loudly. A shares with B some gossip, but B doesn't hear properly. She repeats the gossip to A just as the music stops. The whole bar hears what she says just as the subject of the gossip walks past her.

5   Your client who goes by the name SpeedyLaw123 has found malicious comments about his intellect from other international trade lawyers on a blogging site, legalchatblog.vk.com. He would like to know what action he can take, and against whom.

Academic skills – Consider how you would structure a PQ that included the prompt for one of the five preceding statements.

Academic skills – How would your answer be structured if your client had written all four statements, and had to give advice on all four? Would you use party, issue or CLEO?

Identification sheet

Sub-Claim	Law	Evaluation	Outcome

Planning sheet

By party	By Issue	By CLEO

Researching sheet

Case	Variable 1	Variable 2	Variable 3	Outcome	Legally and/or factually similar?
Example *Adams v Lindsell*	Offer sent by post	Acceptance received by post	Purpose – to accept an offer	Acceptance letter is posted into a letterbox	

Flashcard ideas

Next are different ways you can create your flashcards to help your learning and revision. Paper and online versions (eg Quizlet) are available for free.

Front	Back
What's the difference between an offer and ITT?	An offeree is committing to be legally bound upon acceptance ITT isn't legally binding; an advert *(Partridge v Crittenden)*, a shop window display *(Fisher v Bell)*, communication can be for further information *(Stevenson v McLean)*
Brogden v Metropolitan Railway Company (1877) 2 App. Cas 666	A contract can be accepted according to the conduct of the parties
What constitutes a valid offer?	Clear, certain, unequivocal. *Treitel* "Expression of willingness to contract on specified terms with the intention that it is to become legally binding as soon as it is accepted by the person to whom it is addressed."
Examples of ITTs	Adverts are generally ITT Goods on display in a shop window Goods on a shop shelf (Offer occurs when taken to the till to pay)
Definition of 'offer'	*An expression of interest between the offeror (the person making the offer) and the offeree (to whom an offer is made) to be bound by terms*
What is a unilateral contract?	A contract where only one party has negotiated terms (eg missing pet reward, if you eat a whole chili pizza you don't pay for the meal)

Person A makes offer   Person A makes ITT
↓   ↓
    Person_____
↓   ↓
Person _____   A _____
↓   ↓
Contract formed   Contract formed
	Person A makes offer Person A makes ITT
	↓ ↓
	    Person B makes offer
	↓ ↓
	Person B accepts offer A agrees to terms
	↓ ↓
	Contract formed Contract formed

Vocabulary Flashcard **obligation (noun)** *Phonetic pronunciation –* ob-li-**gey**-shuhn *IPA -* ˌɒblɪˈɡeɪʃən	*Other word forms* to oblige (v) ob-**lige** to obligate (v) obligatory (adj) ob-**lig**-a-t(o)ry obligated (v) **ob**-lig-a-ted obligable (adj) obligational (adj) obligating (v/adj)

Template writing sheets

Use these blank sheets to help you answer your own university PQ.

Claims

Claim paragraph	What is the broad issue of the PQ?
	What are the general legal elements for that broad issue?
	Identify which element(s) will be focussed on
	Repeat for each Claim if there are multiple

Law

Law paragraphs	General claim or legal statement and/or definition
	Use a source with an outcome that is relevant to the PQ, and lead on to a point of legal/factual similarity/difference or contention/ argument
	Specific exceptions to the rule/cases with legal or factual conflicts
	Possible defences
	If discussing a line of cases to show similarities/differences, or how a legal principal has developed over the years, relate later cases to your general statement. Don't just write a list of legal principles/cases
	A summary of the significance of the point(s) of law raised

Evaluation

Evaluation paragraphs	Claim/topic	Briefly identify the specific element that you are discussing
	Legal principles	Summarise the key legal issues identified in the Law section/the gap/grey area that exists to make the Claim contentious
	Assumption	What evidence or case law is there to support your client's case?
	Counter-argument	What evidence or case law is there to weaken your client's case?
	Rebuttal	How can this be negated or minimised?
	Decisions	How have the decisions in previous cases progressed the understanding of this legal element?
	Connection to PQ	Having established previous cases, lines or argument and legal outcomes, detail how these have a bearing on your client's case

Outcome

Outcome paragraph	A legal statement on the primary Claim(s)
	Summary of main Claim(s) in relation to the discussed legal/factual similarity/difference or contention/argument
	Difficulties either party has in proving a point
	Possible remedies
	How a court would likely rule

Part A – about problem questions

■ **Self-check A1**

1 The four stages of CLEO are:

Claim _____

Law _____

Evaluation _____

Outcome _____

2 PQ means **problem question**

3 Put these stages of reading the PQ into the correct order

5 __ Identify the key facts

6 __ Identify the legal issues

4 __ Identify the party or parties, and the role your client in the PQ

3 __ Identify who you are advising and what you are advising them about

7 __ Make a timeline of events

2 __ Read the question

1 __ Read the scenario

4 Match the question prompt of the question to the description

D1, C2, B3, E4, A5, F6

■ **Self-check A2**

1 In which CLEO section would you most likely:

1 Discuss legal principles **Law**

2 Give advice to the person(s) in the situation **Evaluation**

DOI: 10.4324/9781003125747-5

3   Identify any problem areas from the text describing the situation **Claim**

4   State the course of action or liability of each party **Outcome**

2 Match the CLEO section with its general purpose

a) **Claim** This is what the question asks

b) **Law** These are the tools I need to answer

c) **Evaluation** This is how I worked out the answer

d) **Outcome** Here's my answer

3 In which CLEO section would you most likely find the following ten sentences:

a) "The question at issue is whether a contract has been formed." **Claim**

b) "In the case at hand, Bob telephones Amy at 10am to terminate the contract." **Claim**

c) "In *Carlill v Carbolic Smoke Ball Co Ltd*, an advert with clear terms and precise intentions was held to be an Invitation to Treat." **Claim**

d) "Thus the note could be reasonably held to be an advert." **Outcome**

e) "Silence cannot be imposed upon another party as acceptance." **EVAL**

f) "The defendant's actions don't appear to be consistent with someone who has accepted the offer." **EVAL**

g) "It is unclear in which order Bob read the acceptance letters." **Outcome**

h) "According to the principles of contract law, there are four elements to a legally binding agreement." **Claim**

i) "An offer is a promise from the offeror to enter into a contract with the intention of being bound by the offeree's terms." **Law**

j) "The notice states 'or nearest offer' suggesting that the price can be negotiated." **EVAL**

4 Put the following sources of law into order according to their strength of argument

Statutes

Case law (precedent)

Treatises, legal journals, textbooks

Legislative papers

Statutes/case law from other countries

5 Match the following sources to the type listed in item 4:

Department for Media, Culture and Sport, *Online Harms White Paper* (CP 57, 2019) **Legislative paper**

Fitch v Snedaker (1868) 38 NY 248 **Other jurisdictions**

Norrie, A., 'After Woollin' [1999] Crim LR 532 **Legal journal**

Copyright, Designs and Patents Act 1988 **Statutes**

Donoghue v Stevenson [1932] AC 562 **Case law**

6   Which of the following outlines is the most representative of PQ answers? **D**

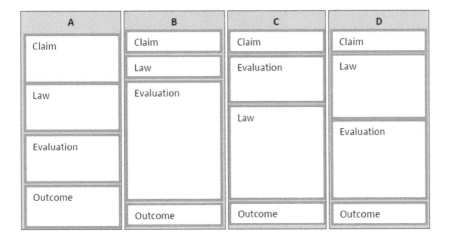

7   Look at the final sentences of two Claims sections from two different student answers and consider their neutrality.

a)   *Therefore, X will be under an obligation to pay Y the money owed under the contract signed*

b)   *The issue is whether X's termination of the contract is valid.*

Tick the relevant box(es) to identify the characteristics of each final Claim sentence

Which sentence (1, 2 or both) gives the following:	a	b
Gives the position (X's obligation)	√	
Suggests a discussion of both sides will follow (No position given, unlike preceding characteristic)		√
Identifies the Issue (Termination of the contract)		√
Suggests the focus will be on contract terms (The terms are *money owed* and *termination of contract* respectively)	√	√
Will be more persuasive than expository/explanatory (Will need to persuade reader that the position given is correct)	√	
Is neutral (No position given, unlike preceding characteristic)		√

8   Evaluate the given sentences from each section, and create an outline of what
     the answer could be. Note, this question (g) looks more at the structure/para-
     graph level, while the next question (h) looks more at the sentence level.

Claim		
i) Under English law there are four elements needed for a contract to be formed. . . . Therefore, X will be under an obligation to pay Y the money owed under the contract signed.		
Law		
h) The first question is whether the advert is an offer or an Invitation to Treat (ITT).		
Evaluation option A	*Evaluation option B*	*Evaluation option C*
a) If it's an offer	g) The advert	d) *Offeror v Offeree A*
b) If it's an ITT	c) Method of acceptance	e) *Offeror v Offeree B*
Outcome		
f) The acceptance is valid only when . . . It would follow that the contract is immediately effective, preventing a revocation of contract.		

9   Repeat the same exercise as in the previous question for another classmate's
     answer to the same PQ. Here the subheadings have been provided, and the
     topic sentences are mixed up. Think about which topic sentence best fits the
     purpose of the structure.

Claim		
g) The case is related to the provision of IT services . . . The issue is whether X's revocation of the contract is valid.		
Law		
h) The first question is whether the advert is an offer or an Invitation to Treat (ITT).		
Evaluation option A	Evaluation option B	Evaluation option C
If it's an ITT	The advert	Offeree v Offeror A
b) By introducing a new term, Y has . . . a contract had been concluded at that time.	f) The basic difference between and offer and ITT . . . the advert lacked the certainty to be an offer.	a) A bilateral contract has been entered into in this case as . . . had formed a binding contract.
If it's an offer	Method of revocation	Offeree v Offeror B
d) Should the advert be an offer and subsequent counter-offer . . . a contract exists due to a lack of retraction.	c) Revocation must be communicated, but needn't be directly received . . . the offer had not been withdrawn at the time it was accepted.	i) The general rule is that an offer cannot be accepted without knowledge of it . . . even if knowledge came from a third party.

> Outcome
>
> **e)** The acceptance is valid only when . . . It would follow that the contract is immediately effective, preventing a revocation of contract.

Understanding the CLEO process

Task A1 – Using the same judgment, identify the start of the Law, Evaluation and Outcome sections.

Claim	The crucial question is: was it a binding promise or only an innocent misrepresentation?
Law	In applying Lord Holt's test . . .
Evaluation	Turning now to the present case . . .
Outcome	One final word . . . I would allow this appeal accordingly.

A non-legal work through

Task A2 – Without distracting yourself with the answer, read the non-legal PQ only and see if you can identify what information is relevant, what is essential and what information is not necessary.

A NON-LEGAL PROBLEM

Jack is a pre-sessional law student at Sometown University ~~and wants to go on to study employment law~~. He was **set his assignment on the 2nd**, with the **deadline on the 16th at 5pm**. ~~He works really hard: planning, researching in the library and writing several drafts of his work until he is happy.~~

~~Eventually,~~ Jack submits his work at **5.10pm on the 16th** and **later** discovers he received a score of zero **due to his late submission**.

Advise Jack

Key

Irrelevant information has been ~~struck through~~ because it is not important

Important information has been written in standard font

Essential information has been written in **bold**

Understanding the CLEO process – end of chapter questions

■ **Self-check A3**

1 Look back at the provided non-legal answer. How has the author structured his or her answer?

CLEO headings are given, and the Law section is broken down into sub-headings. The Evaluation section contains the same subheadings and order as was in Law.

2 The author has used subheadings (lateness, mitigation, timeliness). Consider why the author has used this approach?

It is a simple case between two parties, with three topics (Lateness, Mitigation, Timeliness) which are dealt with each in turn. The issues in the answer aren't deep enough to warrant having sub-topics, but the use of subheadings gives the answer a structure that helps guide the reader. Note, in this PQ, there are not enough parties to suggest changing the structure to party-based, and the contentious issues aren't separate enough to change to CLEO-based.

3 What do you notice about the pattern of the subheadings?

The topics of *Lateness* , *Mitigation* and *Timeliness* in Law are repeated in the same order in the Evaluation section.

4 Have a look at some of the vocabulary used. Highlight any words that are either new to you, or are being used in a new (technical/legal) way.

Your own answers here

5 There may be words used together that you have noticed (eg personal computer or time passed, late submission, as well as legal terms such as liable to be awarded, mitigation claim). Look through the preceding answer to help identify these collocations (noun + noun/adjective/adverb combinations) and colligations (verb and noun).

   a) Set   an assignment

   b) Regulations   state

   c) Minor   illnesses

   d) Suffer   a headache

   e) Certificate   supports

   f) Support   a claim

   g) Financially   support

   h) Financial   difficulties

   i) Reject   a claim

j) Submit   coursework/work

k) University   rules

l) Rules   provide

m) Medical   proof

n) Submission   date

o) Register   a claim

6   Identify which words or phrases from the preceding answer are used to:

a) introduce a section, **In the case at hand (returning back to the PQ)**

b) introduce another point, **In *Donald v Sometown* (refer to a key case)**

c) state a stronger point, **Furthermore**

d) introduce an opposing point, ***Rather than* (signals a contrast)**

7   Which word in the *Mitigation* section suggests a lack of certainty and caution in its assertions?

Would

8   Which word in the *Timeliness* section is repeated several times in order to tell the reader that there is uncertainty in the conclusions drawn?

If

Part B – researching and writing

Identifying Claims in a PQ

Tasks B1–6 – Your own answers to get you thinking about potential crimes within your own jurisdiction.

Revisit the earlier task on the non-legal PQ for another attempt at identifying the breadth and depth of issues.

Task B7 – Try to group the Claims into similar points. Use the point numbers to help.

a   What is Jack's role as a seller? (Point 1)

b   The nature of the advert – is it an offer or ITT? (Points 2, 4, 5)

c   The item being sold (Point 3)

d   Does the nature of the correspondence matter? (4, 6, 8, 9, 10, 12, 14, 15)

e   Communication methods (6, 7, 8, 10, 11, 12, 13, 14, 16)

f   The timings of the communications (7, 13, 15)

Critical thinking – Could be subdivided further into purpose of correspondence (revoke, offer, accept)

Task B8–9 – Your own answers

Task B10 – Put the events into chronological order

Date	Event
10 May	Peter offers 2800 via email
11 May	Peter posts revocation letter
12 May	Jack reads and accepts Peter's emailed offer of 2800 Jack sends a reply accepting offer via email
13 May	Jack receives Peter's posted withdrawal

Performing searches

Task B11 – Some of these sources don't appear to be from courts. Which sources are they? What is the source of that information? How do you know?

Entries 3, 6 and 11 are from the *Independent* (newspaper), SCRIPT-ed (journal article), and N.L.J. (a law journal) respectively.

The formatting looks different, such as dates are in round brackets ( ) not square [ ], publication name follows date, article title follows case name, author's name is given, and there are no court names or abbreviations.

Task B12 – Which of the following court reports would be the most authoritative, and which would therefore be chosen to support your point?

Entry 9 (UKHL)

Task B13 – Put all the cases from Figure 2.4 in order of most authoritative to least authoritative

1	*Douglas & Ors v. Hello! Ltd & Ors* [2007] UKHL 21 (02 May 2007)	House of Lords
2	*Douglas & Ors v Hello Ltd. & Ors* [2005] EWCA Civ 595 (18 May 2005)	All Court of Appeal, ordered by date, newest first
3	*Douglas & Ors v Hello Ltd & Ors* [2003] EWCA Civ 332 (3 March 2003)	
4	*Douglas & Ors v Hello! Ltd.& Ors* [2003] EWCA Civ 139 (12 February 2003)	

5	*Douglas & Ors v Hello! Ltd. & Ors* [2004] EWHC 63 (Ch) (23 January 2004)	All High Court, ordered by date, newest first
6	*Douglas & Ors v Hello! Ltd. & Ors* [2003] EWHC 2629 (Ch) (07 November 2003)	
7	*Douglas & Ors v Hello! Ltd & Ors* [2003] EWHC 786 (Ch) (11 April 2003)	
8	*Douglas & Ors v Hello! Ltd.& Ors* [2003] EWHC 55 (Ch) (27 January 2003)	
9	*Douglas & Ors v Hello Ltd & Ors* – Show me the money! (A Caddick) (2007) N.L.J. 2007	Journal articles from two law journals. NLJ better known
10	*Douglas v Hello! – An OK! result* (G Black) (2007) 4:2 SCRIPT-ed	
11	*Douglas & Ors v Hello Ltd & Ors* – Hello! Claims victory over Zeta Jones photos (S Howard) (2005) *Independent*	Newspaper article

Task B14 – There are nine law reports cited in entry nine of the *Douglas v Hello* results. Order them from most authoritative to least

1	[2007] 2 WLR 920	Weekly Law Reports
2	[2008] 1 All ER (Comm) 1, [2007] 4 All ER 545	All England Law Reports
3	[2007] Bus LR 1600	The Business Law Reports (Specialist ICLR)
4	[2007] 19 EG 165, [2007] BPIR 746, [2007] EMLR 12, [2007] EMLR 325, [2007] IRLR 608,	(in any order) Non-ICLR Law Reports

Task B15 – How have the aforementioned cases been ordered? By descending date

Task B16 – Which court and law report would you choose and why? Number 5 because it's a judgment of the second highest court in the UK, and Law Report entry 7

Task B17 – Here are some definitions of positive, neutral and negative judgments. Decide which definition belongs to which category and place them accordingly in the boxes.

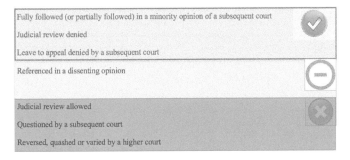

Turning research into Law

Task B18 – (Extension) Using your existing contract law knowledge, continue identifying corresponding case law. Review your own or given source of Law and consider the relevance and importance of each claim (as **Task B9**) by noting a tick (√) for key (major) Claims a plus sign (+) for minor issues and leave blank if the Claim is of no importance or relevance.

(Sub) Claims	Law
1 "A private watch collector." Not selling as a professional	Research establishes this point is not relevant
2 "Specialist . . . watches website." Check if this is still shown to 'the public'	✗
3 "Pre-owned." Not new, so less buyer protection for Peter?	✗
4 "Sees the post." Not stated if the advert is an offer. How can it therefore be accepted to form a contract?	*Carlill v Carbolic Smoke Ball Co* – an advert may be an offer if it is sufficiently certain and shows intent. *Partridge v Crittenden* – a magazine ad was ITT unless made by manufacturer (✓).
5 "Online." Is this different to seeing it in a shop, magazine?	Follows *Pharmaceutical Society v Boots* where selling online = ITT. When is contract made? At payment or when order is accepted?
6 "Immediately emails/Next day, Peter revokes." Timing – Is there a cooling off period?	Cooling off period not relevant
7 "Peter . . . emails Jack." Delivery of communication (email) versus letter	*Adams v Lindsell* – offer accepted once posted (✓)
8 A £200 reduction is requested by Peter. How does this impact if it's an offer and how it can be accepted?	*Stevenson v McLean* – enquiry or counter-offer *Routledge v Grant* – Offers can be withdrawn at any time before they are accepted (✓) *Hyde v Wrench* – counter-offer cancels original offer (✓)
9 "Revoke." Does the purpose impact any communication method?	✗

(Sub) Claims	Law
10　"Method of communication of withdrawal to home address"	See 12
11　Home v business address – which is the correct correspondence address?	✘
12　How should a withdrawal be communicated? Same as first communication or is any method acceptable? This isn't a price renegotiation.	*Henthorn v Fraser* – first method of communication should remain unless explicitly stated method in advert
13　Jack doesn't read the email the same day/time as it's sent.	*Brimnes* – communication is received once it reaches the technology of the recipient, not read.
14　"Jack . . . posts." Jack doesn't accept by the same method as the email.	*Yates v Pulleyn* – any communication method unless stated
15　Jack hasn't yet received Peter's letter of withdrawal.	*Byrne v Van Tienhoven* – withdrawal must be communicated to Jack (✓)
16　Withdrawal is sent by letter.	See 14
17　Advise only Jack (seller/ offeree) not Peter (buyer/ offeror)	

Task B19 (Extension Task) – Student's own answers

Task B20 (Beginner's Task) – Student's own answers

Task B21 – Make notes on the space on the right to summarise what each of these ten seminal cases is about

Adams v Lindsell [1818] 106 ER 250	Acceptance must usually be communicated to the offeror unless a letter of acceptance is posted, where it is received as soon as it is posted (postal rule).
Brogden v Metropolitan Railway Company (1877) 2 App. Cas 666	A contract can be accepted according to the conduct of the parties.

Carlill v Carbolic Smoke Ball Co Ltd [1893] 1 QB 256	An advert containing a unilateral offer can be accepted by anyone performing its terms.
Felthouse v Bindley [1862] 142 ER 1037	A person cannot impose an obligation on another to reject an offer.
Fisher v Bell (1961) 1 QB 394	Goods displayed in a shop window with a price are an Invitation to Treat, not an offer. The offer is made when the customer presents the item to the cashier together with payment. Acceptance occurs at the point the cashier takes payment.
Harvey v Facey [1893] AC 552	An indication of the lowest acceptable price does not constitute an offer to sell, but is considered the beginning of entering into negotiations.
Hyde v Wrench [1840] 3 Beav 334	A counter-offer cancels the original offer.
Partridge v Crittenden [1968] 1 WLR 1204	Adverts are usually Invitations to Treat.
Pharmaceutical Society of GB v Boots (1953) 1 QB 401	A product in a store with a price attached is an Invitation to Treat, not an offer.
The Brimnes [1975] QB 929	Withdrawal of an offer is when communication could be read, rather than when it is read.

Task B22 – See answers to **B18**

Claim answers

Task B23 – Consider which structure would be most suitable for these PQ summaries

a   A shopkeeper displayed a flick knife with a price label in his shop window. **Issue**

b   A company director sends letters to shareholders asking for money to grow the business. In truth, the money is to pay off company debt. **Any, dependent on the complexity of the answer**

c   A second-hand car dealer was asked if there was a history of outstanding finance on a car, to which he replied he was not aware of any. While it was true the dealer wasn't aware of any, this was due to his lack of reading the car's history. **Issue or CLEO**

d   A fashion brand contracted all five members of a famous K-pop group to adver-
    tise their product. However, one suddenly left the group. **Issue or CLEO**

e   The Cargo Receivers brought a claim against the Carriers for the loss of two
    containers' worth of deer meat due to raised temperature caused by a sup-
    posed electrical malfunction. The Carrier argues that because Waybills were
    issued, Hague Rules apply rather than Hague-Visby by referring to Article
    1(b), thereby significantly limiting their responsibility to 100GBP per con-
    tainer. The Cargo Receivers argue that each deer steak was a 'unit' for the
    purpose of the Hague or Hague-Visby Rules. **Any**

f   A shipment of soya was destroyed due to condensation. The cargo claimants
    argue that the loss and damage was caused by the negligence of the Carrier
    under Article III of the Hague Rules. The Carriers in turn are relying on
    exemption from Article IV Rule 2(m) of the Hague Rues, and pleading that
    condensation damage was inevitable. **Issue**

g   George, a famous pop star and style-icon, entered into an agreement for a fash-
    ion store to use his image to publicise his new album. Shortly after, the store
    used a similar image on the next season's clothes. George is unhappy about his
    image being used without his consent. **Issue**

h   Ahern (manufacturer) sold goods to Carling (wholesaler) with a binding
    agreement that Carling would not sell the items below the price given by
    Ahern. Carling also agreed to pass on the same pricing terms to their custom-
    ers. Carling sold items to Frederiksen who sold the items at discounted prices.
    Party or Issue

End of Claim chapter questions

1   What is the purpose of each of the sentences in the Claim paragraph?

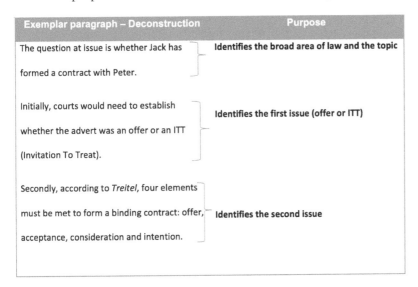

Exemplar paragraph – Deconstruction	Purpose
The question at issue is whether Jack has formed a contract with Peter.	Identifies the broad area of law and the topic
Initially, courts would need to establish whether the advert was an offer or an ITT (Invitation To Treat).	Identifies the first issue (offer or ITT)
Secondly, according to *Treitel*, four elements must be met to form a binding contract: offer, acceptance, consideration and intention.	Identifies the second issue

2   What is the broad area of law, and the topic? **Contract law is the broad area. Contract formation is the topic. Both can be identified by the phrase "formed a contract". Anything more explicit than this is unnecessary (eg under contract law).**

3   What do you notice about the first use of specialist terms (ITT)? **The abbreviation has been written in full. Herein, just writing ITT is wholly acceptable.**

4   What do you think *Treitel* is and why is it written in italics? **It is the name of something being cited or referenced, in this case, a famous professor's book on contract law.**

5   Will all four elements of contract formation be discussed? **They have all been identified for completeness, but only those relevant to this PQ need to be discussed in depth. In this case, the elements of consideration would be omitted (as it is likely that money would exchange hands for the watch) and intention (as there is no mention in the PQ of any reason to suspect lack of intention by either party).**

6   Has Issues been written in order of importance, process or strength of argument? **By process. Without establishing if it's an ITT or offer, the discussion of the other elements would be in an unusual and illogical order. If it was written in order of importance, the four elements would be first. This PQ requires the type of advert to be established first before analysing whether a contract is formed as this is a key issue with differences that follow.**

7   What writing structure do you think will be used, By Party, Issue or CLEO? **Two Claims have been identified (offer or ITT; the four elements), and with only two parties (Jack and Peter), By Issue would be the most appropriate organisation.**

8   Why do you think that revocation of offer is not mentioned at this stage? **Despite Peter having clearly tried to withdraw from the contract, discussion of revocation will be of no relevance if a contract has not been lawfully formed yet, as you can only withdraw from a contract, you cannot withdraw from a contract you haven't yet entered into.**

9   Factual or legal issue?

    a) Can a child enter into a contract? **L**

    b) Under what circumstances are contracts with children voidable and unenforceable? **L**

    c) An academically gifted 10-year-old asks a professor for private tutoring **F**

    d) Two parties dispute a contract that was agreed verbally **F**

    e) When can an employee be fired? **L**

f)   What's the difference between an employee and a contractor? **L**

g)   Who brought the hazardous material onto the land? **F and L as 1 element of nuisance**

h)   Why did the employer fire the employee? **F**

i)   Did the company violate the national minimum wage? **F**

j)   Is a flick knife in a window of a shop next to a price tag offering the item for sale? **L**

k)   A car driver has a sudden medical emergency while driving. **F**

l)   Professionals must act within the rules of their governing body. **L**

Law answers

Task B24 – The main types of legal authorities are listed. Rank them in order of most to least persuasive.

Statutes **1**

Case law **2**

Legal commentaries **3**

Journal articles **4**

Legislative papers **5**

Public policy arguments **6**

Case law from other jurisdictions **7**

Task B25 – Rank which of these imaginary sources would be the most authoritative for Jack's PQ.

Sales of Goods Act 2015 **1st**

Jones v SneakersReseller247 [2019] QB 7942 **2nd**

Davies, J., 'Contract Termination' [2019] Journal of Contracts 4864 **3rd**

Department for Trade and Business, *Doing Good Business Online* (AB 57, 2019) **4th**

JP Smith, *The Australian Law of Contracts*, 3rd edn, Any Publisher 2020 **5th**

Contractlaw.co.uk **6th**

Note that the website, even though it would seem a perfect fit for the PQ, is not an authoritative source, and would be seen as a very weak source of argument.

Task B27 – Which search terms are the most suitable for Jack's PQ?

offer   consideration   ~~implied terms~~   ~~termination~~

~~mistake~~   acceptance   revocation   ~~warranty~~

~~damages~~   ~~intent~~   ~~unilateral offer~~   ~~compensation~~

~~repudiation~~ offeror   ~~breach of contract~~ ~~good faith~~

Task B27 – Which search terms would you use for Jack's PQ?

Student's own answers

Task B28 – The four sentences of this Law paragraph have been jumbled up. Look back at the box on page 51 for help to correct the order.

1   One definition of acceptance is that an offeree finally and unconditionally accepts the terms and conditions offered by the offeror. CITATION

2   If the offeree claims acceptance but attempts to alter the terms of the original offer or add new terms, he shall be deemed to have rejected the original offer and made a counter-offer.

3   In *Hyde v Wrench* CITATION the court held that there was no contract. The claimant rejected the defendant's offer when he gave a new offer.

4   Cancelling and invalidating an original offer means it cannot be accepted again.

Task B29 – Where can the three linking words that follow be placed to improve the flow and connection of the paragraph?

. . . there was no contract because the claimant rejected . . . For example, in *Hyde v Wrench* . . . Therefore cancelling . . .

Task B30 – Identify the purpose of each of the sentences from **Task B28**, and match them to the descriptions that follow.

1   Make a legal statement

2   Introduce the point of contention/argument

3   Reference an authority

4   Explain the source's significance to the PQ

Task B31 – The Law paragraph from **Task B28** has been further developed. Rearrange the sentences into the correct logical and fluent order, referring to the box of page 51 if needed. Consider the topic of each sentence if you need help ordering.

1   One definition of acceptance is that an offeree finally and unconditionally accepts the terms and conditions offered by the offeror. CITATION

2   If the offeree claims acceptance but attempts to alter the terms of the original offer or add new terms, he shall be deemed to have rejected the original offer and made a counter-offer.

3   For example, in *Hyde v Wrench* CITATION the court held that there was no contract because the claimant rejected the defendant's offer when he gave a new offer.

4   However if an offeree accepts and then asks about final terms or possibility of negotiation, it is not a counter-offer and the contract is deemed to be valid at this point. CITATION

5   In addition, an offer cannot normally be withdrawn once it is accepted CITATION although there are exceptions, such as withdrawal by post CITATION

6   Although there is no precedent, some commentators CITATION argue that it is possible for the offeree to withdraw the acceptance through a quicker form of communication, possibly resulting in a situation where the offeror knows about the withdrawal before the acceptance.

7   Therefore cancelling and invalidating an original offer means it cannot be accepted again.

Task B32 – Can you identify any additional discourse markers in the more developed Law paragraph? Where are they situated within each sentence? What is their purpose?

Beginning of line 4 (However) to introduce a conflicting point to the *Hyde* ruling

Beginning of line 5 (In addition) to add another separate conflicting point to the first argument.

Middle of line 5 (although) to introduce the opposing argument

Start of the final clause of line 5 (such as) to introduce an example

Beginning of line (Although) to concede a point, in this instance, that there is no strong authority to support the argument that follows

Task B33 – [Advanced task] Are there any signposts in **Task B31** that could be removed to improve the flow?

For example – the words "In *Hyde* . . ." make it clear that the case is being exemplified

Therefore – it being the final sentence of the paragraph would suggest its purpose is to conclude the point and bring the discussion to some kind of close.

Task B34 – Identify the purpose of each of these Law sentences in **Task B31**

1   Make a legal statement

2   How is the source's outcome relevant to the PQ? Follow on to the point of contention/argument

3   Reference an authority to support the preceding point

4   Develop a point of law/fact from another source

5   Add further (point of law/fact) arguments from an additional source

6   Develop the point from the additional source

7   Summarise all the sources' facts and outcomes

Task B35 – Look back at your answers to **Task B21**. Which of these seminal cases do you think are the most relevant to *Jack v Peter*?

Adams v Lindsell [1818] 106 ER 250 **Relevant and important**	Acceptance must usually be communicated to the offeror unless a letter of acceptance is posted, where it is received as soon as it is posted (postal rule).
Brogden v Metropolitan Railway Company (1877) 2 App. Cas 666 **Neither relevant nor important**	A contract can be accepted according to the conduct of the parties.
Carlill v Carbolic Smoke Ball Co Ltd [1893] 1 QB 256 **Relevant but not important**	An advert containing a unilateral offer can be accepted by anyone performing its terms.
Felthouse v Bindley [1862] 142 ER 1037 **Neither relevant nor important**	A person cannot impose an obligation on another to reject an offer.
Fisher v Bell (1961) 1 QB 394 **Relevant but not important**	Goods displayed in a shop window with a price are an Invitation to Treat, not an offer. The offer is made when the customer presents the item to the cashier together with payment. Acceptance occurs at the point the cashier takes payment.
Harvey v Facey [1893] AC 552 **Neither relevant nor important**	An indication of the lowest acceptable price does not constitute an offer to sell, but is considered the beginning of entering into negotiations.
Hyde v Wrench [1840] 3 Beav 334 **Relevant and important**	A counter-offer cancels the original offer.

Partridge v Crittenden [1968] 1 WLR 1204 **Relevant and important**	Adverts are usually Invitations to Treat.
Pharmaceutical Society of GB v Boots (1953) 1 QB 401 **Neither relevant nor important**	A product in a store with a price attached is an Invitation to Treat, not an offer.
The Brimnes [1975] QB 929 **Relevant and important**	Withdrawal of an offer is when communication could be read, rather than when it is read.

Task B36 – Regarding the *Jack v Peter* case, which of these sources (a–h) would you consider as being the best suitable for discussing ITT or offer?

- The first precedent or decisions from the highest court [imaginary cases]

  a) *Colin Watchseller v Ronald Watchbuyer* [2016] EWCA Civ 999 – *England & Wales Court of Appeal* – **important as the most recent and from the highest court**

  b) *David Watchseller v James Watchbuyer* (1840) 2 Beav 777 – *Beavan's Chancery Reports* – **oldest and therefore could be the first case to set the precedent**

  c) *David Watchseller v James Watchbuyer* [1960] 1 WLR 111 – *Weekly Law Reports* – **a valid case but not as strong as the other two**

- The *obiter dictum* (judge's verbal decision) fits your PQ's gaps

  d) "If I advertise to the world that my dog is lost, and that anybody who brings the dog to a particular place will be paid some money, are all the police or other persons whose business it is to find lost dogs to be expected to sit down and write me a note saying that they have accepted my proposal? Why, of course, they at once look [for] the dog, and as soon as they find the dog they have performed the condition." *Carlill v Carbolic Smoke Ball Ltd* [1892] EWCA Civ 1 (Bowen LJ) – **read this carefully and consider which type of contract this relates to, or what the findings of the Carlill case refers to. Both are about unilateral contracts (such as the return of a dog for a reward) not bilateral (where action is needed by both parties in return for something, eg cash for a service). Therefore, Bowen LJ is not suitable for our PQ.**

- The most factually similar to *Jack v Peter*

  e) *Fisher v Bell* – flick knife for sale in the window. Offer made when presented to cashier – **not factually matching but could be used as a supporting case for offer/ITT discussion**

  f) *Hyde v Wrench* – a counter-offer cancels the original offer – **only relevant if you're pursuing the argument that there was a counter-offer made, otherwise irrelevant**

g) *Partridge v Crittenden* – adverts are ITTs due to a limited number of items available for sale – **best fit as Jack's advert on the website was for a single watch, so an ITT**

h) *R v Nedrick* – *mens rea* in murder – **wholly irrelevant**

Task B37 – Match the brief statement in a student's answer (1–5) with the organisational structure (a-e) for a murder PQ with a Claim of self-defence

A5, B2, C3, D1, E4

a   General claim or legal statement and/or definition = **Common law definition of murder. Elements of self-defence**

b   Use a source with an outcome that is relevant to the PQ, and lead on to a point of legal/factual similarity/difference or contention/argument = **3x cases**

c   Specific exceptions to the rule/cases with legal or factual conflicts = **Self-defence allowances**

[If discussing a line of cases to show similarities/differences, or how a legal principal has developed over the years, relate later cases to your general statement]

d   Possible defences = **Arguments of what is "proportionate"**

e   A summary of the significance of the point(s) of law raised = **What is needed to be shown to fulfil self-defence requirements**

Alternative note-making styles – end of chapter questions

Task B38 – The research notes that follow have been organised By Issue. Write the most appropriate subheading in the spaces preceding the cases by reading the short commentary to guide you.

RESEARCH NOTES FOR OFFER AND ACCEPTANCE PROBLEM QUESTION

Law

Consumer Rights Act 2015 [no obligation to disclose faults]

11(2) of Electronic Commerce Regs – internet contracting (not email exchanges) take place 'once recipients are able to access them'.

Cases

a   Is the advert an ITT or Offer?

Partridge v Crittenden – advert in magazine is ITT

Carlill v Carbolic Smoke Ball – evidence to be bound = offer

---

cont.   **b Communication method**

Brinkibon v Stahag – telexed acceptance

Entores v Miles Far East – instantaneous comms – contract complete when received by offeror

c Communication timings

Adams v Lindsell – acceptance of offer – accepted immediately upon posting

Yates v Pulleyn; Tinn v Hoffman – offeree can choose speediest method of acceptance if not stated/unclear in advert acceptance

Thomas v BPE Solicitors – business email – sent in evening, received in working hours

d Revocation

Byrne & Co v Van Tienhoven – offers can't be revoked after acceptance (BUT commentators disagree and state exceptions)

Mondial Shipping v Astarte – message left on answering machine, offer revoked depending on when machine states the message will be listened to [in commercial contracts]

Treatise

Treitel on the Law of Contract

Task B39 – Some of the planned legal sources seem irrelevant to the given PQ. Which do you consider to be poor selections by the student?

The following are either irrelevant or weak cases in light of the arguments in the PQ:

- Consumer Rights Act 2015 [no obligation to disclose faults]

- 11(2) of Electronic Commerce Regs – internet contracting (not email exchanges) take place 'once recipients are able to access them'

- *Byrne & Co v Van Tienhoven/Mondial Shipping v Astarte* – There was no revocation or attempted revocation in our PQ. It could be mentioned to show depth of reading, but spend minimal time on this case, almost including it as a point of interest more than a point of discussion.

Task B40 – Next are the sentence types that are normally seen in the Law section of a PQ answer. Reorder them so that they are presented in the most persuasive and logical order. Not all may be needed for every answer dependent on the nature of your PQ.

ORGANISATION OF LAW SECTION

General rule

Identification of, and general rule regarding sub-issue

Clarify relevance on source giving specifics eg cases with conflict (categorised by similarity of fact or law), exceptions or ruling detailing and development

Possible defences

If discussing a line of cases to show similarities/differences, relate later cases to your more general rule. Avoid writing a list of legal principles/cases

A sentence or two to summarise the point of law raised

Repeat for next sub-issue

Task B41 – Read the example Law paragraph that follows, and identify the different stages mentioned in the preceding box. The answer key follows.

A BASIC PROBLEM QUESTION ON CONTRACT – EXAMPLE LAW PARAGRAPH – BY ISSUE

Is the advert an ITT or offer?

To establish the nature of the advert, courts would need to evaluate whether the advert was meant to induce parties into negotiation, or whether the offeror by signing is stating they are willing to be bound by the terms of the contract. There is no legal definition of what is an advert or an ITT, though key cases are helpful in distinguishing between the two. In *Carlill v Carbolic Smoke Ball*, a unilateral contract was held to be capable of acceptance without communication to that effect as the advert was to the world at large. Advertisements are normally considered ITTs (*Partridge v Crittenden*) for two main reasons: the wording of the advert lacks the required details needed by the offeror to make an informed decision, and secondly, the offeree normally has a limited supply of stock. It would therefore follow that the advert would be seen as an ITT by the courts.

ORGANISATION OF LAW SECTION

Subheading to identify the claim/topic from the PQ

A summary of the significance of the point(s) of law raised

General claim or legal statement and/or definition if not clear in the subheading.

If discussing a line of cases to show similarities/differences, or how a legal principal has developed over the years, relate later cases to your general statement. Don't just write a list of legal principles/cases

Possible defences

Specific exceptions to the rule/cases with legal or factual conflicts

Use a source with an outcome that is relevant to the PQ, and lead on to a point of legal/factual similarity/difference or contention/argument

Short summarising sentence which will lead into the Evaluation section in Issue or Party/be the Evaluation in the CLEO structure

---

Task B42 – Now identify the organisational stages in the Law section that follows (use the same key).

A BASIC PROBLEM QUESTION ON CONTRACT – EXAMPLE LAW PARAGRAPH – BY CLEO

Method of acceptance

Peter sends Jack an email offering £2800 for the watch, which Jack is free to accept or reject. To be effective, any acceptance must be communicated to the offeror, which Jack does, by post, on the 12th.

In bilateral contracts, acceptance can be in any form as long as it is communicated to the offeree (*Taylor v Laird* citation). Here, a ship's captain voluntarily gave up his position and worked as a crew member on the return journey without telling or asking his employer. Upon return, he tried to claim wages, but it was held that he had not entered into a contractual agreement with the defendant and thus was unable to claim wages. Where the offer states a specific method must be used which is not adhered to, there is no contract (*Eliason v Henshaw* citation). Here, it was a term of the offer that an acceptance was to be sent to a specific company branch, but the plaintiff sent it to another branch. The plaintiffs received the acceptance and replied stating the same, but

---

cont.   as they had not been correctly informed of their intention, had bought
goods elsewhere. When the plaintiffs' delivery was not accepted, they
unsuccessfully sued.

However, this American case seems at odds with English law where an alternative
but equally speedy method of acceptance is used (*Tinn v Hoffman* citation) and
that the offeror's objective remains (*Manchester Diocesan Council for Education
v Commercial & General Investments Ltd* citation). It would seem that Jack's sole
objective is to receive offers, so any specific reasons of limiting risk or for proof of
tracking appear weak arguments.

Where no method of acceptance is given, but is implied, such as an online
advert as in the instant case, it would seem logical that an email sent within
the platform's forum or an address is copied and pasted into Peter's own email
provider, is replied to in the same media. Additionally, *Quenerduaine v Cole*
citation found that the speed of acceptance can be deduced from the medium
of the offer, therefore an offer made by email should be replied to by equally
expeditious means. This could be due to the nature of the goods being sold
(ie it is a perishable good), or subject to price fluctuations or available for only
a short time (*Chitty on Contracts* citation) none of which are relevant to Jack's
watch.

In the given case, it would be difficult for Jack to justify his use of the postal rule
having received an offer via email, and it is therefore likely that a court would find
that at this point he had accepted the offer and intended the offer to be accepted
at that time. Whether or not he had communicated that acceptance to Peter (as
per *Taylor v Laird*) would be difficult to adjudicate as Peter would no doubt argue
that his offer should have been emailed back, whereupon he would be unable to
revoke his earlier offer.

**Note – there is no General Claim as the subheading makes the content clear. Also,
as this is structured in a CLEO organisation, the Evaluation is the final paragraph
in green text.**

Evaluation answers

Task B43 – Student's own answers

Task B44 – Filling in the gaps where necessary, decide on the suitability of each
case to support the *Jack v Peter* PQ, and consider how each case can help your
evaluation by fact or legal principle.

	Method of offer	Method of acceptance	Communi-cation purpose	Contract formed when	Legally and/or factually similar to *Jack v Peter*?
Jack v Peter	Email	Post	Accept an offer		
Adams v Lindsell	Post	**Post**	Accept an offer	**Acceptance letter is posted into a letterbox**	**Legal and factual**
Dunlop v Higgins	**Post**	Post	Accept an offer	**Acceptance letter is posted into a letterbox**	**Legal and factual (simply reconfirms** *Adams*)
Holwell Securities v Hughes	**Not applicable**	**Post**	**Accept an offer**	Upon receipt of letter when it's a contractual term	**Irrelevant – no terms given in PQ**
Entores	**Not applicable**	Telex/Fax	**Accept an offer**	Acceptance was received	**Legal principle –** when received not read by recipient
Stevenson v McLean	Post	Post	**Revoke an** offer	When letter is delivered	**Legal and factual**
The Brimnes	**Not applicable**	**Instanta-neous communi-cation (eg Fax/Email)**	Accept an offer	Received by offeror at that time and place	**Legal –** Principle only but Jack isn't a business
Thomas v BPE Solicitors	**Not applicable**	Email	**Accept an offer**	**When read during business hours (if a business)**	**Legal –** Principle only

End of Evaluation chapter questions

Task **B45** – Student's own answers

Task **B46** – Your PQ client has a contentious case or element. In which way or ways can it be argued against?

- The opposing argument fails to reach the legal standard. – **True**
- Facts can be argued against. – **False**
- The law is unclear on a legal element. – **True**
- Facts can be disputed. – **False**
- The judge needs correcting. – **False**
- Citing a legally similar case – **True**
- Citing a factually similar case – **True**

Task **B47** – Name the three types of arguments you can make, and order them from strongest to weakest

1 Refuting the accuracy (strongest)
2 Counter-arguing
3 Partially conceding (weakest)

Task **B48** – Which is the most appropriate structure of writing each topic or element within an Evaluation section? **A**

Task **B49** – Match the pro-gun statements (1–8) with the relevant anti-gun view (a-h)

1d, 2c, 3a, 4e, 5b, 6g, 7f, 8h

Task **B50** – Identify the topic that connects the argument and the counter-argument. What argument style is being used by the eight counter-arguments (a-h) to rebut the original statement? Refutation, rebuttal, counter-argument, concession, or is the counter-argument unsound? One example has been done for you with the topic underlined.

Pairs	Argument style	Topic	Justification
1d	Unsound	There is no link between mass shootings and gun ownership.	There is too big a step to link the number of shootings (yes with a gun) in the whole of a country by <u>mass shootings</u>. Only a weak conclusion or correlation can be drawn

Pairs	Argument style	Topic	Justification
2c	Counter-argue by rebuttal and refutation	Guns have legitimate uses and violent/sick people only use for malicious reasons.	**Rebuts** blaming the <u>user</u> not the gun, and further **rebuts** by stating who lawfully uses guns. Then **refutes** any widespread ban on guns as violent/ill people will continue to gain access to a gun
3a	Counter-argue by rebuttal	Homeowners can and should bear arms.	**Rebuts** with the idea that guns in houses protect the <u>homeowner</u> if a burglar even thinks there may be a gun in the <u>house</u>
4e	Counter-argue by rebuttal	Guns are mostly used on the holder not on others.	**Rebuts** with any harm by guns is used most often to <u>harm the user</u>, not to harm other people
5b	Counter-argue by rebuttal	The steps needed to legally obtain a firearm licence	**Rebuts** that a <u>test</u> is needed to obtain a gun with the view of his own <u>legal rights</u>
6g	Counter-argue by refuting and rebuttal	The gun safety record of Norway	**Refutes** the <u>truthfulness</u>, then **rebuts** stating gun-murder still happens
7f	Concession and rebuttal	Armed police are needed to reduce gun crime.	Acknowledges and **concedes** guns are needed, and **rebuts** with a <u>self-defence</u> argument
8h	Counter-argue by rebuttal	Are cars more dangerous than guns?	**Rebuts** that <u>cars</u> kill many more people than guns

Task B51 – Can you think of how you can counter the preceding anti-gun views? What research do you think you'd need? **Student's own answers**

Task B52 – Think of ways you could rebut (argue against) the following positions, the central Claim, which of the three styles you use (see **Task 36**) and your argument against each of my points. **Student's own answers**

Task B53 – Read the following counter-offer answer written By Issue. Identify the organisational patterns from **Task B48** and include the heading and subheading (eg assumption, position, case and rebuttal). Answer key follows.

Counter-offer

Counter-offer

Alex decided to accept Bob's offer at 3pm, but wanted the consideration to be paid in cash. The issue here is whether Bob changed the original offer if he paid in cash, or if this created a new offer which needed to be accepted. Under contract law, when the offeror makes an offer to the offeree, the offeror may generally choose to accept or reject it. Once the offer is accepted, it will be subject to contract law. However, the offeree also has the right to bargain where any implied or express terms can be negotiated. Any acceptance of an offer at any stage of negotiation must be consistent with the terms of the offer, and any material alteration or alteration to the terms of the offer by the offeree does not constitute acceptance. *Hyde v Wrench* illustrated that if the offeree is unwilling to accept the offeror's offer, or the offeror changes the conditions of the offer, the offeree can reject or propose a new condition to become a counter-offer. Alex's initial offer to Bob did not specify the terms of payment. When Alex decided to accept Bob's offer, she wanted Bob to pay in cash. *If Bob agrees to being paid in cash, then there is no objection and there is no counter-offer.* On the other hand, if Bob does not agree to be paid in cash and discusses this with Alex, the key question is whether Alex has added a new term or merely requested clarification. The exact words used by Bob and Alex are not given, but there needs to be a counter proposal ie a specific offer or rejection rather than an answerable question, for example a delivery schedule. In *Stevenson, Jacques & Co v McLean* a telegram requiring clarification of a term was held not to be a counter-offer, so an original agreement remained valid. *Without the exact wording, one cannot be certain, although it would likely be held by a court that an enquiry on the method of payment rather than a term on contract would be seen as a request for information.* So Bob can choose to accept or reject Alex's offer of payment in cash. Anything other than acceptance will produce a counter-offer which would need to be accepted in turn by Alex in order to be legally binding.

Brief outline of specific claim
Legal principles relating to claim
Assumption /Point + position + *case to clarify* + *rebuttal, refutation or concession of Assumption in PQ*
Transition
Assumption/ Point + position + *case to clarify* + *rebuttal, refutation or concession of Assumption*
How this relates to PQ

Task B54 – Notice the change in tense in each element and sub-element. When is past and present tense used?

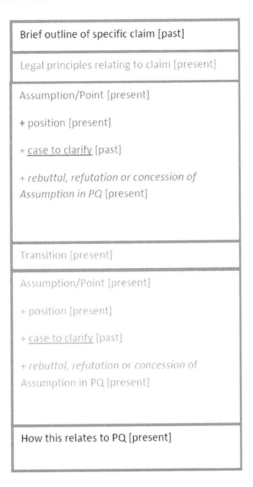

Brief outline of specific claim [past]
Legal principles relating to claim [present]
Assumption/Point [present] + position [present] + <u>case to clarify</u> [past] + *rebuttal, refutation or concession of Assumption in PQ* [present]
Transition [present]
Assumption/Point [present] + position [present] + <u>case to clarify</u> [past] + *rebuttal, refutation* or *concession* of Assumption in PQ [present]
How this relates to PQ [present]

Task B55 – The sentences used to explain the cases in Assumption 1 (**Task B53**) are poorly written. One word is repeated and overused. Paraphrase this sentence

An acceptance must completely mirror the terms being offered, and any changes to those terms must be accepted or there has been no contract formed. As per *Hyde v* Wrench, if an offeree makes changes to an offer or makes alterations to the original offer, then the offeree can choose to accept or reject the new terms, or propose a counter-offer. In the case at hand, as the payment terms weren't explicitly stated Alex's initial offer to Bob did not specify the terms of payment, so Bob is within his rights to assert his preferred payment method. Following *Hyde v Wrench*, only if Alex does not object, then there is no counter-offer from her.

Task B56 (Extension Task) – Student's own answers.

Outcome answers

Task B57 – Complete the following table changing the nouns into verbs and vice versa. See flashcards for ideas on how to present this and expand to include pronunciation, adjective and adverb forms too.

Noun	Verb	Noun	Verb
acceptance	accept	offer	offer
contract	contract	repudiation	repudiate
failure	fail	supply	supply
implication	intrepret	termination	terminate

Task B58 – Rewrite the following *if*-clause sentences so the result/condition changes order in the sentence. Some words and/or word forms may need to be changed or omitted for the sentence to be logical and retain the same meaning. There may be several alternative answers and structures.

We would be grateful if you could send the documents to us at your earliest convenience.	If you could send the documents to us at your earliest convenience, we would be grateful.
I am confident that if the goalkeeper had had a bonus clause in his contract, he would have stayed with the team.	I am confident the goalkeeper would have stayed with the team if he had had a bonus clause in his contract.
Had the company secretary not neglected the security of the documents for which he is responsible, we wouldn't have been named in the court summons.	We wouldn't have been named in the court summons had the company secretary not neglected the security of the documents for which he is responsible.
Legislation introduced in 2000 allows shareholders to be contacted electronically if they give their express permission.	If shareholders give their express permission, they can be contacted electronically following legislation in 2000. If shareholders give their express permission, following legislation in 2000 they can be contacted electronically.
If one partner goes bankrupt, creditors can pursue the remaining partners for the whole debt.	Creditors can pursue the remaining partners for the whole debt if one partner goes bankrupt.

Unless directors have given personal guaranteees, they are not liable for the company's debts if they run the company lawfully.	If directors have given personal guaranteees, they are not liable for the company's debts if the company has been run lawfully.
I'll be able to argue the contract is invalid if you show me the claimant continued under his existing contractual duties. However this claim will hold only if it can be objectively demonstrated to have been the offeree's intention.	If you show me the claimant continued under his existing contractual duties, I'll be able to argue the contract is invalid. Only if it can be objectively demonstrated to have been the offeree's intention, the claim will hold.

Task B59 – Identify the key elements of an Outcome in the following sections (not all elements are always present).

- A legal statement on the primary Claim(s)

- Summary of main Claim(s) in relation to the discussed legal/factual similarity/difference or contention/argument

- Difficulties either party has in proving a point

- Possible remedies

- How a court would likely rule

A BASIC PROBLEM QUESTION ON CONTRACT – EXAMPLE OUTCOME PARAGRAPH

As Jack placed an ITT, selling in a personal not a corporate or professional capacity, he should not be expected to reply to emails within office hours (*The Brimnes*). Therefore, the email offering £2800 for the watch, duly accepted upon posting, would strongly suggest the conclusion of a valid contract, and Jack will be able to have a claim of breach of contract if Peter refuses his consideration of £2800.

Tasks B61-B65 – Identify the key elements of the following Outcome sections and colour-code as earlier

---

TASK B60

In conclusion, it is in A's best interest to honour the initial contract with B, and he should be liable for the costs provided for by the agreement. However, A should be able to pursue a claim against C because A had continued to conduct his side of the contract by performance.

TASK B61

There appears to be two possible outcomes. A could sue B, but it would seem unlikely that B has enough money or insurance cover. Therefore, A could sue S who could be liable for B's actions under vicarious liability. This would likely be the best remedy as B is unlikely to be seen as an employee due to the degree of control of the employer, the nature of the payment and the employment contract.

TASK B62

In pursuing a claim of damages by misrepresentation, Z would be wise to use s. 2(1) of the Act. He would be able to claim for direct losses, and possibly for subsequent losses. An alternative available to him is suing for breach of contract, having relied upon M's expert status and relying upon his specialist advice to make a decision. The courts would balance these claims against M's argument that it was outside the contract, and that Z's previous experience made him less reliant on M's expert claims. While marginal, it would appear that the certainty of numbers and costs in the negotiations shows intention for the contract to proceed.

TASK B63

Sarah is highly likely to be found guilty of murder, and depending on her age at the time of the murder, could expect a sentence starting at 12 years if she was a minor at the time of the attack, or a minimum of 15 years if she was over 18 years of age.

TASK B64

It would seem that W's contract with O would more likely be voidable for misrepresentation than for mistake. The difference in *Shogun* and the instant case is that the contract of immediate vicinity was not formed face to face, and therefore W would have to bear his losses. That said, there has been criticism of the 3–2 majority decision in its fairness and the seller's position to better protect himself against risks, so W could be advised to take a risk as O would have been in a better position to uncover his client's dishonesty.

Task B65 – Identify the key claim(s) purely from the Outcome section

1   Has A formed a legally binding contract with B? What action can A take to claim for his losses?

2   What options are available to A? Which strategy would you advise and why?

3   Which offence has been committed and how could this best be remedied? What actions are available to Z?

4   What offence(s) have been committed? What penalty could Sarah expect for each crime identified?

5   Are there any ways W can revoke his contract with O? Under which reason would you advise? Are there any risks to taking this course of action?

Task B66 – Identify all the different types of hedging language used in the Outcomes of **Tasks B60-B64**

B60 – should be liable, should be able

B61 – appears to be, could sue, seem unlikely, could sue, could be liable, would likely

B62 – would be wise, would be able, possibly for, An alternative, would balance, While marginal, would appear

B63 – highly likely, depending on, could expect, if

B64 – It would seem, more likely, would have to bear, could be advised to

Part C – academic skills

Task C1: Consider which of the following 12 sources in the box need to be cited and which do not, and place them into the appropriate column:

Reference needed	Reference not needed
The exact words of a judge	Your own opinion
The maximum sentence of a particular offence	A commonly known fact
Paraphrasing of a dissenting judge's *obiter*	
A case name	
Your own opinion which develops another author's work	
Your own opinion from a previous essay	
Summarising a case (eg a case brief)	
A statute	
Combine two authors' points by paraphrase and summary	
Memorising and reproducing the exact words of a judge	

Task C2 – Should the following statements be accepted as factually true, contentious or common knowledge, and which would need to be referenced?

a   There is gold on the moon. It is factually true, and probably not a well-known fact, so would need a citation.

b   Jesus Christ was born on 25th December. Despite Jesus Christ representing only the Christian faith, it is probably well known around the world that his birthday is celebrated on Christmas Day, so no citation is needed.

c   There are four elements needed to create a binding contract in English law. Depending on the audience – for non-lawyers definitely needed, but for contract lawyers, probably not but worth including for good practice.

d   A little-known fifth element needed to create a binding contract is *capacity*. Contentious as it goes against the established rule of four elements, so must be cited.

e   The legal system in Turkey is civil law. Depending on the audience – for non-lawyers and maybe non-Turkish people definitely needed, but for Turks and lawyers, not strictly needed. A statement that English law is common law would not be needed.

f   Around 70% of the earth's surface is covered by water. Factually true, but an exact measurement isn't strictly needed unless the focus of the statement is, say, the ice caps melting and rising sea levels.

g   The death penalty still exists in America. Factually true and widely accepted.

h   The death penalty still exists in 30 American states. Most people would know it existed, but not the number nor which states, so a citation is needed.

i   The death penalty hasn't been used in over a decade in 11 states. The detail in this statement would need a citation. Note that the statement is fluid and could become incorrect or out of date quickly if an execution occurred.

j   *Death Row* is the name of the special jail cells where prisoners facing the death penalty in America are held. A commonly used phrase, not attributed to a particular person.

k   Another word for the death penalty is capital punishment. A common alternative name ie no reference to a dictionary or thesaurus needed.

l   Some people oppose the death penalty. A common and logical statement not needing support.

m   The Northern Irish Assembly, Scottish Parliament and Welsh Senedd enjoy different levels of legislative autonomy. True, but could reasonably be assumed that a knowledgeable UK reader and lecturer would know this. Detail such as Wales can raise taxes through the sale of land and property would need citing, although not necessarily for Land Law students.

n   The Northern Irish Assembly, Scottish Parliament and Welsh Senedd's funding is worked out by the UK government using the Barnett formula. True, but less likely to be known by the average reader. Again, detail beyond this surface statement would need citing.

o   The Scottish Parliament makes best use of its funding. Contentious as it is an opinion. Would definitely need to be attributed.

p   A *unicorn* is the name given to a privately started company which is now valued at over $1bn. As this is a new (it can be traced to a blog post from 2013 by Aileen Lee) and a relatively niche term, so it could well need to be cited. However, as words become more used and recognised in everyday speech, the term loses its uniqueness and therefore may in the future not need to be cited. Think about how the term *selfie* has now become commonplace.

q   Deliveroo, Revolut and Just Eat are examples of unicorn companies. Not necessarily needed but good practice to cite. These famous companies match the definition and can reasonably be assumed to be valued at over a million US dollars, and the word is in common usage now especially in the world of trade, business and finance.

Task C3 – Identify the following eight parts of this student writing

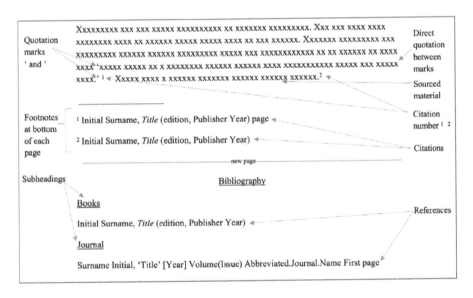

Task C4 – Complete the following statements in your own words.

1   Source types (eg books, journals, cases) are placed under their own **subtitle/ subheading** in a bibliography.

2   Authors' names are different in footnotes and bibliographies because <u>**bibli-ographies have surname + first name initial, footnotes are first name + surname.**</u>

3   <u>**Full stops**</u> are the final characters in footnotes and are omitted in bibliographies.

4   Whether the source was used as a a) _____, b)_____, or c) _____ it will appear in the bibliography **direct quotation, paraphrase or summary**.

5   The sources appear alphabetically by surname in <u>**bibliographies.**</u>

6   In footnotes, the sources appear <u>**in the order in which they appear in the text.**</u>

7   The name order of multiple-authored texts appears <u>**as per the source.**</u>

8   What effect does del Guayo's surname of two names have on the order of the bibliography? <u>**His surname begins with a "D" despite it not being capital-ised, so appear after Gaeta in the bibliography. Other similar surnames begin with O', D', Le, van der.**</u>

Task C5 – What two structural differences are there between the Davies and Bar-rett articles? **The Month (January) in Barrett is the equivalent of Davies' issue (1), and Barrett will have been directly quoted on p69.**

Task C6 – which words within the article title are written in inverted commas and why is this? **'Lack of capacity' because they appear this way in the J title.**

What do you think 's' means, and what does it refer to? **Section, s44 of MCA 2005**

Look at the case name within the citation. How is it different when it is part of a journal article title compared to if it were a case name you were presenting to sup-port your point? **Not in italics here but be *R v Kurtz* in my written answer/footnotes**

Has source 3 been directly quoted from? How do you know? **Yes, page no (75) after first page (74)**

Task C7 – Where on the preceding figure can you find the following information?

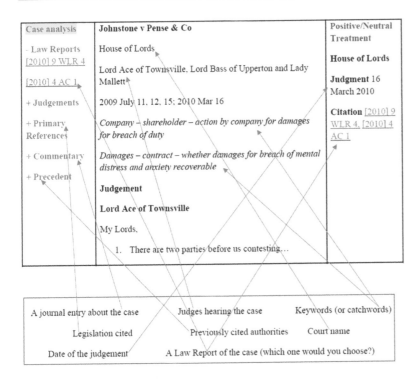

Task C8 – *The Wagon Mound* case was reported in [1961] UKPC 2, [1961] AC 388; [1961] 1 All ER 404. Which of the three given reports is the 'best'? **AC 388**

Task C9 – Why is the word *Harrow* in brackets in the Karsales case? The party name is written in full. Companies sometimes have their location as their full company name and should be written in full when cited.

Task C10 – Can you identify the jurisdictions of the preceding cases? Note that US cases should give the shortened state name unless it is from that state's highest court, in which case give the abbreviation of the state.

Antons Trawling Co Ltd v Smith [2003] 2 NZLR 23 **NZ**

Johnson v Capital City Ford Co. 85 So. 2d 75 (La. Ct. App. 1955) **USA**

Lefkowitz v Great Minneapolis Surplus Store, Inc. 86 NW 2d 689 (Minn, 1957) **USA**

Masters v Cameron [1954] HCA 72 **Australia**

Siemens Industry Software v Lion Global Offshore Pte Ltd [2014] SGHC 251 **Singapore**

Tercon Contractors Ltd v British Columbia (Transportation and Highways) [2010] 1 S.C.R. 69 **Canada**

Task C11 – Some case citations cite a law report, others the traditional citation, and others a neutral citation which may include both. Identify the following parts of each citation in the box and place into the table in order.

Full citation	*Nisshin Shipping Co v Cleaves & Co Ltd* [2003] EWHC 2602, [2004] 1 All ER (Comm) 481	*HIH Casualty and General Insurance v Chase Manhattan Bank* [2003] UKHL 6, [2003] 2 Lloyd's Rep 61
Party names	*Nisshin Shipping Co v Cleaves & Co Ltd*	*HIH Casualty and General Insurance v Chase Manhattan Bank*
Claimant	*Nisshin Shipping Co*	*HIH Casualty and General Insurance*
Defendant	*Cleaves & Co Ltd*	*Chase Manhattan Bank*
Year + court	[2003] EWHC	[2003] UKHL
Case number	2602	6
Year + volume	[2004] 1	[2003] 2
Report name	All ER (Comm)	Lloyd's Rep
First page	481	61

Tasks C12 – Which part(s) of the preceding table can create i) the case name, ii) the neutral citation and iii) the law report?

Case name	*Nisshing Shipping*	*HIH Casualty*
Neutral citation	[2003] EWHC 2602	[2003] UKHL 6
Law report	[2004] 1 All ER (Comm) 481	[2003] 2 Lloyd's Rep 61

Task C13 – Look up a case or law report that interests you. Identify the elements within it

Student's own answers

Task C14 – Under which bibliographic subheading would you place citation number 5 and 7? **Websites**

Task C15 – Match the abbreviation to the type of division

para/paras pt/pts s/ss sch/schs subpara/subparas sub-s/sub-ss

Acts are divided into	part(s)	**para/paras**
	section(s)	**pt/pts**
	subsection(s)	**s/ss**
Schedules are divided into	schedule(s)	**sch/schs**
	paragraph(s)	**subpara/subparas**
	subparagraphs	**sub-s/sub-ss**

Task C16 – Find two ways that a section of an Act in the Stop and Search text was presented

> . . . section 1 of the Police and Criminal Evidence Act 1984 which provides

> 6 Police and Criminal Evidence Act 1984, s 1.

Task C17 – Which Act has cited two sections and how is this presented in the footnotes?

> Terrorism Act 2000. Two sections are written as ss

Task C18 – Why is s 60(3) of CJPO not cited in the footnotes?

> CJPO is previously cited, and the section is named in full.

Task C19 – Is citation number 6 necessary?

> No, as the statute is given in full in the body text

Task C20 – Should citation number 6 appear in the bibliography under the Statutes subheading?

> It absolutely should

Task C21 – Look at the website legislation.gov.uk for assistance with the following questions

a   To what does Employment Rights Act 1996, s 1(4)(c)(ii) refer? Statement of initial employment particulars must contain the days of the week the worker is required to work.

b   According to the Companies Act 1985, sch 1a what is 'significant control'? 25%

c   Cite the statute that modified dates provided by the Stamp Duty Land Tax (Temporary Relief Act) 2020. pt 4 Finance Act 2003

d   Cite the statute that modified amount of tax paid under the Stamp Duty Land Tax (Temporary Relief Act) 2020 for residential homes. s 55(1b) Finance Act 2003

e   Cite the statute that modified amount of tax paid under the Stamp Duty Land Tax (Temporary Relief Act) 2020 for additional properties. sch 47A Finance Act 2003

f   How do you cite subsection (1a) of section 6 of the Unfair Contract Terms Act 1977? Unfair Contract Terms Act 1977, s 6(1a)

g   How do you cite the words "except in so far as the term satisfies the requirement of reasonableness" from the aforementioned statute? Unfair Contract Terms Act 1977, s 6(1a)(b)

h   Does this section apply to consumer contracts? If not, cite the source of that legislation. No – Consumer Rights Act 2015, s 31 OR section 31 of the Consumer Rights Act 2015

i   Which schedule should be researched if looking for guidelines on the test of reasonableness in UCTA 1977, and how should it be cited? Unfair Contract Terms Act 1977, sch 2.

j   To what does Consumer Protection from Unfair Trading Regulations 2008, SI 2008/127, reg 6 (4)(d)(i) refer? Prices must include tax

Task C22 – How are the in-text citations for both Ministry of Justice sources different? Same "top level" URL but first is "by ethnicity and legislation over time", and second is "by ethnicity and area"

Task C23 – Would the Ministry of Justice source be cited once or twice in the bibliography under the Websites subheading? Once, because the information comes from one webpage titled Stop and Search

Task C24 – Does the date in the Pavis source refer to the date the programme was first broadcast on radio, the date the programmes were uploaded to the BBC website as a podcast, the date I first listened to the audio, or the date I last listened to the audio? The date it was uploaded to the BBC website. The date it was first aired on radio preceded this, but I did not listen to this version. I only listened to the podcast; hence I must cite this source as some editing or changes may have happened.

Task C25 – Is Pavis the host of the show, or an expert or guest on the show? It doesn't matter. The point is that Pavis is the person who said the material of interest.

Task C26 – Why is the EUR-Lex source URL (web address) different to the other websites? It begins with https:// and only web addresses that begin www can have the http:// or https:// omitted. https://eur-lex.europa.eu therefore needs to be given in full.

Task C27 – Why is the Ministry of Justice source not given as Ethnicity-facts-figures.service.gov.uk, gov.uk or anything in between? The Ministry of Justice is the government department which published the document, and therefore departments within governments are cited.

Task C28 – Identify the number of judges, the court, any titles of the judge(s) and their role within the court if applicable

a   One judge, High Court (Mr Justice), he is a QC (Queen's Counsel)

b   Two judges, Court of Appeal, no titles nor roles

c   One judge, most likely SC but could be any, Lord, Master of the Rolls

d   One judge, most likely SC but could be any, Lord, President of the SC

e   Two judges, High Court (JJ), no titles nor roles

f   One judge, Supreme Court, no title nor role

g   Two judges, (note too that *obiter dictum* (singular) has become *obiter dicta* (plural)), most likely Court of Appeal, John Smith is a *Sir*

h   One judge, Supreme Court, (a Baroness but *Lady* is a higher), President of the Supreme Court

i   **How else could Mr Justice Southey be written?** This is the only option as he's a barrister

j   **Why are only three citation numbers given?** A and B follow the case name. H follows a direct quote. C-G <u>would</u> have citation numbers at the end of that sentence if the case had not been previously cited

k   **What does dissenting mean?** Disagrees with the majority of the other judges

Task C29 – One of the most famous judges was Tom Denning who served in the High Court, Court of Appeal, House of Lords and as Master of the Rolls. Look through each of these cases and work out how his *obiter* should be cited.

Anglo Continental Holidays – [Lord] Denning MR

Central London Property Trust – Denning J

Entores – Denning LJ

J Spurling – Denning LJ

Lewis – [Lord] Denning MR

Mandla – [Lord] Denning MR

Miller – [Lord] Denning MR

Nettleship – [Lord] Denning MR

Scottish Co-operative Wholesale Society – Denning LJ

Task C30

a   **Long** – introduced by a colon : at the end of the previous sentence, no speech
    marks, indented on left and right side, justified text (straight edges down left
    and right margin), and there is a gap above and below the quoted passage.
    Punctuation follows the closing speech mark unless it is a question mark or
    exclamation. **Short** – single speech marks to identify judge's words, formatting
    remains as the rest of the text.

Tip: The length at which a short direct quote should be formatted as a long pinpoint is when
it exceeds three lines of text.

---

b   In the first reference, the case name is given as full party names. Subsequent
    citations are the first party name only. Both are italicised.

c

   i)   Judge's title + name + "quotation" + citation number // full case citation
        + [paragraph/page number]

   ii) Surname +Judge's abbreviation + "quotation" + citation number // full
        case citation

   iii) Judge's title + [at para/page + number] + "quotation" + citation number
        // full case citation + [paragraph/page number]

   iv) "quotation" + citation number // full case citation + [paragraph/page
        number] (judge's surname + abbreviation)

d   Earlier judgments needn't be cited in the footnotes nor bibliography.

e   An *n* number has replaced the full case name. The *n* number means look back
    at that citation number which saves repetition, so *n 4* would mean refer back
    to source number four for the first and full citation. *n 9* is acceptable but would
    mean to refer back to Lord Hodge's pinpoint at paragraph 95.

    n 4 refers back to a pinpoint, so any further reference to *n 4* cites this exact
        paragraph.

    n 5 can cite *n 4* as only the paragraph number has changed.

    n 8 is a general case citation (think of it as a base) so general and pinpoint cita-
        tions can refer back to the base.

Note: It is usual for the first citation to be the case only, on to which pinpoints can
be attached

Note: Extra information can appear after the *n* such as the page/paragraph number
and the judge's name in brackets.

f   Lord Millett in *Johnston* was the original source, cited by Flaux LJ who devel-
    oped it, and finally cited by Lord Reed in the instant case.

g   The student has selected two main parts of information from the same sentence of paragraph number of the judgment which are most important. The missing words in the middle would have added nothing to the argument.

h   The first three citations have the attributed the judge's name to the pinpointed text, so repetition isn't necessary. Lord Hodge's words have not yet been attributed to a particular judge in the text, which it is therefore necessary to do in the footnotes.

i   The page or paragraph number of the pinpoint.

j   i) per Chadwick, LJ ii) at para 89 and iii) based on Lord . . .

k   The paragraph number is given in the main text "[at para 89]"

l   Words should be written exactly as it is in the source text which includes any emphasis written by the judge/author, Latin terms and the first party name in a case.

Note: If you want to emphasise a word to clarify your point, write (emphasis added) at the end of the footnote.

m   Cases

n   n 8

o   n 8

p   The student has italicised the words "the same" to describe losses by the company and the shareholder. It would logically follow that this distinction would be addressed very soon after, for example a case where company losses were not the same as a shareholder's for a particular reason. In the instant case, the difference was that shareholders were also employees or creditors.

q   The pinpoint would have the start and end page/paragraph in square brackets separated by a dash, for example:

---

¹ *Sevilleja v Marex Financial Ltd* [2020] UKSC 31 [79–80].

² n 1 [197–8].

³ *Johnson v Gore Wood & Co* [2001] 2 AC 1 [62D-F] (Millett LJ).

⁴ n 1 [95–96] (Hodge SCJ).

Task C31 – Connect the subsequent footnotes to the original.

1   Original

2   Original

3   Footnote 1

4   Original

5   Original

6   Footnote 5

7   Original

8   Footnote 7 paragraph 856

9   Footnote 4 paragraph 14

Task C32 – Answer the questions about the preceding footnotes

a   Why is the use of ibid not permissible for citation number 8 referring back to n7? Because 8 contains different information about the source (page 856 not first page – p851 – as is needed for first mention)

b   When could ibid be used for citation number 8? When referring to the same page number (856)

c   How would the 1998 Act be cited at citation number 10? CDPA 1988. or n1.

d   How would section 51 of the 1998 be cited at citation number 11? CDPA 1988, s 51.

e   Could citation number 10 be "n1, s52"? No, it is not permissible to use n numbers with Acts with additional information.

f   Add paragraph 22 to the judgment of *Lucasfilm* from the UKSC. *Lucasfilm Ltd v Ainsworth* [2011] UKSC 39 [22].

g   Add paragraph 28 to 29 to the previous footnote. *Lucasfilm Ltd v Ainsworth* [2011] UKSC 39 [28]-[29] *note* n2/ibid [28]-[29] cannot be used as n2 refers to multiple law reports, and ibid to paragraph 22. The root source needs to be cited.

Task C33 – Put the following names into the correct columns. Not all of the details in the author's name are needed.

Author's name according to book/website title	Family name/Surname	First name/Given name
Geraint Brown	*Brown*	*Geraint*
Jon D. Reason	Reason	Jon
Marcia Passmore-Evans	Passmore-Evans	Marcia
Diamond, John-Lee	John-Lee	Diamond
Montel RUSH	Rush	Montel
Professor Simon Ace	Ace	Simon

Author's name according to book/website title	Family name/Surname	First name/Given name
MOORMAN, George	Moorman	George
BBC	BBC	-
Montell, Brook & Day LLP (Barristers at law)	Montell, Brook & Day LLP	-
Dr. Francis del Pierro	del Pierro	Francis
Ronald van der Westhuizen	van der Westhuizen	Ronald
E. Alfred McCormick	McCormick	E
Larry Orsinger II Jr	Orsinger II Jr	L
Pan Linwei	Pan	Linwei
John Shaftle MA	Shaftle	John

Task C34 – Put the names into the correct order for a bibliography

Ace, S.

BBC

Brown, G.

del Pierro, F.

Diamond, J.

McCormick, E.

Montell, Brook & Day LLP

Moorman, G.

Orsinger II Jr, L.

Pan, L.

Passmore-Evans, M.

Reason, J.

Rush, M.

Shaftle, J.

van der Westhuizen, R.

Task C35 – Identify what is wrong, if anything, with the following citations and correct them

a   (*The Achilleas*) *Transfield Shipping Inc v Mercador Shipping Inc* [2008] UKHL 48 – **The ship's name should follow the parties' names**.

b   Bhanawat A 'Rotterdam Rules – Redefining and Introducing the Electronic Bill of Lading' (2019) <www.marineinsight.com/maritime-law/rotterdam-rules-redefining-and-introducing-the-electronic-bill-of-lading/> accessed 19 August 2018 – **The accessed date is before the published date (possibly entered the wrong way round), and https:// isn't needed.**

c   Di Lieto G and Treisman D, *International Trade Law* (1st edn, Federation Press, 2018) – **First editions don't require the edition number**.

d   Electronic Commerce (EC Directive) Regulations 2002 (SI 2002/2013) – **correct**

e   *Hadley v Baxendale* (1854) 9 Exch 341 – **correct**

f   Limitation Act (1980) – **year shouldn't be in brackets**

g   Mahafzah Q and Naser M, 'The Inadequacy of the Existing International Maritime Transport Regimes for Modern Container Transport' [2019] 13(4) Modern Applied Science < www.researchgate.net/publication/330933467_The_Inadequacy_of_the_Existing_International_Maritime_Transport_Regimes_for_Modern_Container_Transport> accessed 29 July 2020 – **correct**

h   Misrepresentations Act 1967 s 2(2) – **only the main Act is needed**

i   Murray C, Holloway D, Timson-Hunt D, Dixon G *Schmitthoff: The Law and Practice of International Trade* (12th edn, Sweet & Maxwell, 2014) – **Names should state "Murray C and others" for 4+ authors.**

j   Nikaki T and Soyer B, 'A New International Regime for Carriage of Goods by Sea: Contemporary, Certain, Inclusive AND Efficient, or Just Another One for the Shelves?' [2012] 30(2) Berkeley J Intl L 303, 305 – **The page number (305) isn't required in a bibliography, only the footnotes.**

k   van Haersolte-van Hof J & Holland R '*What makes for Effective Arbitration? A Case Study of the London Court of International Arbitration Rules*' in Peter Quayle and Xuan Gao (eds), 'International Organizations and the Promotion of Effective Dispute Resolution' (Brill Nojhoff, 2019) – **The & between the authors' names should be "and". Also, the formatting of the chapter name and book title should be swapped around.**

Task C36 – Place those 11 sources into bibliography page giving suitable subheadings

Books

Di Lieto G and Treisman D, *International Trade Law* (Federation Press, 2018)

Murray C and others, *Schmitthoff: The Law and Practice of International Trade* (12th edn, Sweet & Maxwell, 2014)

van Haersolte-van Hof J and Holland R 'What makes for Effective Arbitration? A Case Study of the London Court of International Arbitration Rules' in Peter Quayle and Xuan Gao (eds), '*International Organizations and the Promotion of Effective Dispute Resolution*' (Brill Nojhoff, 2019)

Journals

Mahafzah Q and Naser M, 'The Inadequacy of the Existing International Maritime Transport Regimes for Modern Container Transport' [2019] 13(4) Modern Applied Science < www.researchgate.net/publication/330933467_The_Inadequacy_of_the_Existing_International_Maritime_Transport_Regimes_for_Modern_Container_Transport> accessed 29 July 2020

Nikaki T and Soyer B, 'A New International Regime for Carriage of Goods by Sea: Contemporary, Certain, Inclusive AND Efficient, or Just Another One for the Shelves?' [2012] 30(2) Berkeley J Intl L 303

Case Law

Hadley v Baxendale (1854) 9 Exch 341

Transfield Shipping Inc v Mercador Shipping Inc (The Achilleas) [2008] UKHL 48

Statutes

Limitation Act 1980

Misrepresentations Act 1967

Statutory instruments

Electronic Commerce (EC Directive) Regulations 2002 (SI 2002/2013)

Websites

Bhanawat A 'Rotterdam Rules – Redefining and Introducing the Electronic Bill of Lading' (2019) <www.marineinsight.com/maritime-law/rotterdam-rules-redefining-and-introducing-the-electronic-bill-of-lading/> accessed 20 July 2020

Task C37 – Match the letter to the following question pattern types:

a   What was the basis for the conflicting judgments in dismissing protecting GlaxoSmithKline's colour purple (Pantone 2587C) and allowing the Mars Petcare's purple (Pantone 248C)? **compare/contrast**

b   How can companies convince the ECJ that their shade of purple has protectable and distinctive character? **Problem/solution**

c   What are the advantages and drawbacks of preventing the monopoly of certain shades associated with industries or products? **Advantage/disadvantage**

d   Evaluate the arguments used in GlaxoSmithKline and Mars Petcare in protecting their respective shades of purple. **For/against (or Argumentative)**

e   Organic Petfood Products Ltd wants to know if they can use a similar colour packaging of their pet food to Mars Petcare's products. **PQ**

Task D1 – What was the purpose of the changes in Section 1(1)?

To add to s 1(1) Any person who manufactures, sells or hires or offers for sale or hire, or exposes or has in his possession for the purpose of sale or hire or lends or gives to any other person

To add to s 1(1)(b) . . . fifty pounds level 4 on the standard scale

To add to s 1(1)(b) . . . a fine not exceeding two hundred pounds level 4 on the standard scale or to both such imprisonment and fine.

Task D2 – How has this altered the advice you would give A in the PQ, compared to the advice given to the defendant in *Fisher v Bell*?

The amended 1961 Act would put the defendant in a much weaker position as the flick knife was in a shop window with a price tag, so while still being an ITT, it is likely that a court would find that the knife was exposed for the purposes of sale.